Harvard Historical Studies / Volume LXXXIII

Published under the direction of
the Department of History from the income
of the Henry Warren Torrey Fund.

COLLEGES IN CONTROVERSY

The Jesuit Schools in France from

Revival to Suppression, 1815–1880

John W. Padberg, S.J.

Harvard University Press

Cambridge, Massachusetts, 1969

Distributed in Great Britain by Oxford University Press, London

Library of Congress Catalog Card Number 75-78523
SBN 674-14160-1

Printed in the United States of America

To my mother and to the

memory of my father

PREFACE

The Jesuit colleges of the sixteenth, seventeenth, and eighteenth centuries have been studied extensively, both in general and in many of the particulars of their existence. This is especially true of the schools in France, where the educational system of the Society of Jesus attained its most widespread development and its greatest renown. Learned works have treated of everything in these schools from their teaching of geography to their influence on the French drama through the medium of the Jesuit theater.

When one turns to the nineteenth century, however, the difference is striking. There are more than enough polemical writings both for and against the Jesuit colleges; there are some school histories, more often than not written for a commemorative occasion and as a result abounding in too many of the pieties appropriate to the celebration; but no scholarly monographs exist either of individual schools or of particular institutions (such as the theater or the philosophical curriculum) within the system as a whole. Perhaps this should not be surprising, since there is not even an extended general treatment of the whole group of colleges as such, and it is often only after such an over-all view that detailed accounts of particular institutions within the context of the system can be undertaken.

Yet this group of nineteenth-century colleges was important. They were not, to be sure, on the same level as their predecessors before the suppression of the Society of Jesus in 1773. Neither in geographic spread, nor in numbers of students, nor in influence then and later did they equal, much less surpass, the colleges of the era when the Jesuits were the "schoolmasters of Europe." But they were important for their own time and for the totally different situation in which they were revived and carried on in the face of previously nonexistent obstacles.

Both friends and enemies paid these schools the compliment of taking them seriously, and the latter did so perhaps even more than the former. The Jesuits themselves expended on them the largest number of men, and quite often the best men, in a Society rising out of almost total destruction. More than any other of their works, the colleges were usually the first apostolic enterprise which bishops requested of the Society, and in no city in which a college was founded was there lacking a group of laymen intensely devoted to it. The Jesuit schools were almost always the prime target of opposition to the Society and an importance was attributed to them that might have been flattering if it had not also been so dangerous. Finally, year after year, if one is to believe both the opposition and the families which sent their children as students, these colleges turned out graduates with a particular cast of mind, a definite attitude, and a distinctive outlook on life and on the society in which they were to live. Whether the Jesuits did indeed accomplish this is an important but still unsolved question. That a good number of people believed they did is certain.

Nowhere were all these statements about the nineteenth-century colleges more applicable than in France. There the Jesuit schools developed more fully than anywhere else in Europe. France was the country of the Revolution itself, and the reactions to it, both favorable and unfavorable, came across clear and strong, confronting these colleges with completely new experiences. It was clear who their devoted friends were, and just as clear whom their enemies included. Eight Jesuit schools arose after 1814 only to be swept away by determined opposition in 1828. Exile colleges attempted to continue a tradition on the borders of France, and in so doing strongly shaped the practices of the schools which arose in France after the Falloux Law of 1850—seventeen of them in the first four years, another dozen after 1870, until in 1880, by the terms of the Ferry Decrees, the Society was forbidden as a corporate body to teach in the French college classroom. Little by little in the following years the Jesuits returned to their schools but never in an atmosphere of open and secure possession until, after a decade and a half of uneasy peace, in 1901 the French government again expelled them from their classrooms and expropriated their buildings.

It is with the period from revival to suppression of the Jesuit colleges, between 1815 and 1880, that this study will deal. Enough has been written of a polemical nature about the schools; not enough has been done to describe their foundation and internal functioning in the Second Empire and in the early years of the Third Republic, and always in the context of the restored Society of Jesus. What did the Jesuit colleges set out to do? Upon what resources did they draw? How did they go about achieving their purpose?

The circumstances in which the Society found itself after the Restoration and how it reacted to that situation are essential to an understanding of the first attempts at schools in the minor seminaries and in the exile colleges. The patterns of existence and the formation of traditions in these early schools helped provide answers to old problems and engendered new ones in the new colleges which sprang up so rapidly in France after 1850.

What were the general intellectual ideals proposed to the

students? How was the curriculum structured? What specifically did these schools teach? What subjects received the greatest emphasis and why? Who were the teachers and students and where did they come from? What was the emotional climate of the place, what were the religious ideals and motives set forth by the teachers and hopefully practiced by the students in turn? What extracurricular activities, although the term would not have been recognized at the time, varied the daily round of existence in the rather closed world of a boarding school? All of this needs telling.

Variety certainly existed among the Jesuit colleges. The original archives of a good number of them as well as descriptive writings about all of them are part of the background of this study. But a remarkable uniformity of method and purpose and outlook among all these schools was also one of their special characteristics, and that uniformity makes possible a study that applies to all of them.

The changes which also existed within this variety and uniformity were brought about in part by changes within the French school system, in part by changes in political and social circumstances, and in part by the internal development of the schools themselves. Just as the years of "peace with restrictions" under the empire had conditioned those schools now in existence for twenty years, so too the republican government influenced the form and style of the new schools founded after 1870. An Indian summer of prosperity trailed off into the bleak days of 1880. With the last distribution of prizes in August of that year, an era, neatly defined between revival, legality, and suppression, came to a close for the French Jesuit colleges.

What was the internal life of those colleges during that era? What influences helped to shape that life and what influence in turn did the colleges hope to exert on their students and on their milieu? This study will attempt in some detail to answer those questions.

I have turned to many people in the preparation of this

work, and they have been uniformly kind in their responses. All of them are present in grateful memory as these lines are written, but I would like to mention explicitly the assistance of the archivists of the Jesuit collections at Toulouse, Lille, and Rome, and especially the unfailingly generous and intelligent help of the archivist and the librarians at Les Fontaines, the Jesuit house at Chantilly near Paris. Professor Thomas P. Neill of Saint Louis University first introduced me to the delights and the complexities of nineteenth-century history. The late Professor Crane Brinton and Professor H. Stuart Hughes of Harvard University continued a work well begun and, in addition, from the very first they encouraged and furthered the plans for the present study. To each of them my gratitude. Finally, the Reverend John F. Bannon, S.J. of the department of history at Saint Louis University began twenty years ago to encourage with counsel and friendship a neophyte history student; he continues to do so today as a colleague. To him personally and as one representing all of my fellow Jesuits and all that they have done for me in companionship I offer my simplest and deepest thanks.

John W. Padberg, S.J.

Saint Louis, Missouri
January 2, 1969

The archives of the four provinces of the Society of Jesus in France, the provinces of Paris, Lyons, Toulouse, and Champagne, as well as the general Jesuit archives in Rome, furnish the larger part of the primary sources from which this study has been fashioned. These sources are in great part in manuscript, often in the form of letters received or fair copies of letters sent, chronologically bound in "Registers." The archives also contain much useful printed material, such as the annual province catalogs which list the residence, status, and occupation of each member of each province. Though each of these archives is systematically ordered, still there is no absolute uniformity among the Jesuit provinces nor of the provinces with Rome in their cataloging, and as a result all material is cited here as it is cataloged in its own archive. In the notes, each Jesuit archive is identified as follows:

ARSJ. Archivum Romanum Societatis Jesu (general archives of the Society of Jesus, Rome).

PSJ. Archivum Provinciae Parisiensis Societatis Jesu (Paris province archives, Chantilly [Oise]).

LSJ. Archivum Provinciae Lugdunensis Societatis Jesu (Lyons province archives, Paray-le-Monial [Saone-et-Loire]).

TSJ. Archivum Provinciae Tolosanae Societatis Jesu (Toulouse province archives, Toulouse [Haute-Garonne]).

CSJ. Archivum Provinciae Campaniae Societatis Jesu (Champagne province archives, Lille [Nord]).

The French national archives, AN, are identified by traditional letter and number designation. Section F^{19} of these archives is the most useful for material on religious questions and on education under religious auspices.

CONTENTS

COLLEGES IN CONTROVERSY

I

THE RESTORED SOCIETY
OF JESUS IN FRANCE

When the Society of Jesus was restored throughout the universal Roman Catholic church on August 7, 1814, there was only one fully trained Jesuit in France. Thirty-six years later, within six months of the passage of the Falloux Law on March 15, 1850, Jesuits in two provinces of the Society were preparing to open, direct and staff eleven colleges.[1] These years fall into two periods: from the Restoration to the 1830 Revolution; and from the July Monarchy to the passage of the Falloux Law in the Second Republic. In both periods problems within the Society itself and the opposition from without helped shape the attitudes which the French Jesuits brought to the task of teaching the several thousand students who were to attend their schools for the next generation. The restoration of the Society in the aftermath of the revolutionary upheavals of a

1. PSJ and LSJ, *Catalogi Provinciae Franciae et Lugdunensis Societatis Jesu* (Paris and Lyons, 1850).

generation, its own bitterly contested existence in France, its internal difficulties, two political revolutions, and the "school question" in all its complications were still vividly real in 1850.

The Society of Jesus was in a far different position in 1814 than it had been when Clement XIV suppressed it on August 13, 1773. In 1749, the last year for which we have access to complete statistics, it directed and staffed six hundred and sixty-nine schools or colleges, spread over every country of Europe and over many lands on the other continents. In France in 1814, Pierre de Clorivière, born in 1735, was the only Jesuit left to recall the former glory of the French Assistancy with its ninety-one colleges and twenty seminaries, its forty thousand students, and more than three thousand members.[2]

Clorivière had entered the Society in 1756 and had become a parish priest in France after the suppression. He had been a nonjuring priest during the Revolution, carried on his priestly work in hiding, and he even managed to found two religious congregations in those troubled years. Members of his family were guillotined; he was arrested in 1801 and again in 1805. From prison he requested and received of the General of the Jesuits in White Russia readmission to the Society. These brief background remarks about a most extraordinary man can serve as a first indication of what to expect of the early years of the restored Society in France, of its mentality, its reactions, its perhaps unquestioned convictions.[3]

2. Statistics in Alfred Hamy, S.J., *Documents pour servir à l'histoire des domiciles de la Compagnie de Jésus dans le monde entier de 1540 à 1773* (Paris, 1892), 1; and Alexandre Vivier, S.J., *Status Assistentiae Galliae Societatis Jesu, 1762–1768* (Paris, 1899), XIII. Vivier's book is an attempt to reconstruct the situation of the Jesuits in the years immediately following their governmental suppression in France. The figures given in the text are those of the official Jesuit catalogs of the five provinces of the French Assistancy for 1761, the year before that suppression.

3. The papal brief of suppression of 1773, *Dominus ac Redemptor*, took effect in a particular locality, in accord with its own terms, only when officially promulgated in a house of the Society by the bishop of that place. As a somewhat ironic result, the Society lived on legally and canonically in Prussia and in Russia where the non-Catholic sovereigns, Frederick the Great and Catherine the Great, refused permission for promulgation. This state of affairs lasted in Prussia until 1786, in Russia until 1820. The Holy See was aware of this from the

Equally important is the background of his first recruits. They were already priests who belonged to the Fathers of the Faith or to the Society of the Sacred Heart, groups founded in 1791 and 1797 for the express purpose of joining the Society of Jesus if and when it should ever be restored. They, too, had often paid a heavy price, sometimes in imprisonment and more often in exile during the revolutionary years. Even when Napoleon allowed the Church to return to a semblance of normality, he was quite adamant that the name of the Jesuits not even be pronounced, and that "everything which could lead to talk about that Society should be avoided in the journals. I shall never permit its re-establishment in France . . ."[4] Despite the protection of Cardinal Fesch, Napoleon's uncle, the small group of Fathers of the Faith had to disperse more than once and hope for better days.

Those days seemed possible with the downfall of the empire. Within a month after Napoleon's abdication, Thaddeus Brzozowski, the Jesuit Superior General, commissioned Clorivière to undertake the restoration of the Society in France.

May 7/18, 1814.

Reverend Father: The Peace of our Lord!

I do not know if your reverence is in good health, but I wish and hope so, and so I am writing to you. We have learned from the public press the happy events which have just taken place in your land with the help of God and the care and efforts of the Allied Sovereigns. Good men rejoice

---

beginning, at first simply voiced no disapproval, then tacitly tolerated and even encouraged and finally formally approved of it. Until the restoration, a vicar-general was regularly elected in Russia. In the later years before the restoration he could receive individuals and even groups as Jesuits. See Stanislas Zalenski, S.J., *Les Jésuites de la Russie Blanche,* trans. by Alexandre Vivier, S.J. (2 vols.; Paris, 1886). Also see the biography by Jacques Terrien, S.J., *Histoire du R. P. de Clorivière, S.J.* (Paris, 1891). On his connection with the Fathers of the Faith before the restoration of the Society, see André Rayez, S.J., "Clorivière et les Pères de la Foi," *Archivum Historicum Societatis Jesu,* 21 (1952), 300–328.

4. *Correspondance de Napoléon I, publiée par ordre de l'Empereur Napoléon III* (Paris, 1858–1869), X, 29.

to see rulers given back to you, and the vicar of Jesus Christ restored to his See . . . What consequences so happy an event can have for Holy Church, for religion, and for the piety of old it is easy to see; and to wish and hope for them is pleasant and sweet. Whether, and how quickly, the same salutary results will come to the Society of Jesus, suppressed by the coterie of the *philosophes,* whether your most pious King will vindicate its innocence and good name, you yourself will be able to know that more quickly than I. Therefore, since by reason of my office I must look to the interests of the Society, and since I am so far away and besides do not know which of our former members are still alive, would your Reverence let me know their names and their dispositions with regard to the Society, which had been their Mother? . . .

Perhaps it is not yet time, now at the beginning, to treat with your very pious King about the education of youth, about catechism, about sodalities, about the recall of the Society of Jesus to France. If anything is able to be done, at least by preparing the disposition of princes and other important and well disposed personages, I delegate that to your Reverence, acting prudently and cautiously with the advice of prudent men . . .

I ask God earnestly and daily that unto His greater glory he give you the spirit of wisdom which will enlighten you and guide you in beginning this work prudently and carrying it to a happy conclusion, so that with the respect we owe to the Institute of the Society, it will be not a new, but the old Society which lives again . . .

Your Reverence's Servant in Christ,
T. Brzozowski, S.J.[5]

Clorivière received the letter in June 1814. That same month Joseph Varin, the director of the Fathers of the Faith in France,

5. PSJ, Clorivière, Brzozowski to Clorivière, May 7/18, 1814.

asked to be received as a Jesuit. On June 19, 1814 he and three companions became the first novices in France since the 1760's. By the end of the month there were six other candidates. On August 7 Pius VII officially restored the Society throughout the world. A little more than a year later there were ninety-one French Jesuits, many of them already mature men, priests, and members of the Fathers of the Faith. They were all under the direction of Clorivière, who was Master of Novices and Superior for France. Of course it was impossible to settle into the ordinary routine of the two-year training of a Jesuit novice, not to mention the years of further training that usually followed that first period of testing for member and Society alike. The formal novitiate for most was cut down to the bare essential. Sometimes within a few months these early recruits, most with some philosophical and theological studies (often interrupted) and with pastoral experience of one kind or another, were sent out to work at the appeal of bishops all over France.

In those first years the Jesuits were engaged especially in four fields. First, there was the work of re-evangelization of the country itself by means of popular mission preaching, undertaken by the Société des Missions de France and by several religious orders, a work to which the Jesuits gave a large number of priests. Second, even though it took few men, the congregations, especially the Congrégation at Paris, was the work of the Jesuits. Third, there was the usual individual direction of souls, carried on from the residences of the Society. Finally, and increasingly important in terms of men involved and attention given to it, came the work of education. Not colleges strictly speaking, but eight *petits-séminaires,* or minor seminaries, were the vehicles of this work. These schools, because they are so important in determining the educational experience of the restored Society, will be treated at length in the next chapter.[6]

6. There is an excellent work on popular mission preaching by Ernest Sevrin, *Les Missions religieuses en France sous la Restauration* (2 vols.; Paris, 1948–1959).

All these works and the increase in numbers of the Society in France from 1815 to 1825, just before the storm of denunciation broke violently over their heads, were accomplished in the penumbra of illegality that surrounded all unauthorized orders and congregations, but especially the Jesuits. Brzozowski's idea of an appeal to the king for a formal restoration of the Society was hardly possible. Louis XVIII was a realist, and the report that went to Rome in 1820 of his response to an informal petition from Clorivière is certainly characteristic: "Let the Fathers take up again neither the name nor the dress of the Society, let them work without making a lot of noise about their affairs, and they have nothing to fear." Without official recognition and without legal corporate existence or rights, the Society also saw no official prohibition. Each member expected to appeal to the common law rights of individuals under the Charte "to profess his religion with an equal liberty and obtain for his worship identical protection." The same report to the General said that "the King is sympathetic to us, most of the members of the royal family are equally so, but the ministers are hostile, and in both Chambers our friends are rare." The hostility of the Chambers was disquieting; to authorize a religious congregation was a legislative act.[7]

If there was little hope of legislative authorization under Louis XVIII, there was even less under Charles X. He personally might have acquiesced, but in the minds of much of the political opposition behind the extravagances of the Ultras lay the secret power of the Jesuits.

There are two classic works on the Congrégation. The older one is by Geoffroy de Grandmaison, *La Congrégation, 1801–1830* (Paris, 1890), in which he maintains that the organization was strictly religious and by no means the secret political network that it was reputed to be by the liberals of the Restoration. The second is by G. de Bertier de Sauvigny, *Le Comte Ferdinand de Bertier (1782–1864) et l'enigme de la congrégation* (Paris, 1948). This latter work admirably untangles the threads of religion, politics, personal ambition, and misinformation which went to make up the legends that clustered around the Congrégation.

7. ARSJ, Franc., Grivel to Fortis, 1820; and Charte, 1814, art. 5.

Undoubtedly the Jesuits wholeheartedly supported the monarchy. Their priests who gave missions chanted just as loudly as others

> Vive la France
> Vive le Roi
> Toujours en France
> Les Bourbons et la Foi.[8]

The Society's members along with the rest of the clergy often "in the work of reconquest [of France to the faith] exhibited the fanatic ardor of the weak who have themselves experienced persecution and feel that their power is far from assured."[9] Yet this was not quite the same thing as "the story that they turned their novice-house at Montrouge into a fortress where 50,000 members of the order set themselves to small arms drill and artillery training." Supposedly Charles X was saying Mass there, after scuttling through a tunnel which connected the place with the Tuileries![10] One of Pierre-Jean de Béranger's most famous songs celebrated this subterranean passage:

> Hommes noirs, d'où sortez-vous?
> Nous sortons de dessous terre,
> Moitié renards, moitié loups,
> Notre règle est un mystère.[11]

8. "Long live France/Long live our king/ Always the Bourbons/And the faith we sing." The *Constitutionnel,* the *Journal des Débats* and the *Globe* of the time, to name only the relatively responsible journals, make instructive reading on the point of identification of Jesuits with the radically royalist groups.

9. G. de Bertier de Sauvigny, *La Restauration* (Paris, 1955), 439.

10. Adrien Dansette, *Histoire religieuse de la France contemporaine* (2 vols.; Paris, 1948–1951), I, 279. This was a rather long tunnel at that; Montrouge was a southwest suburb of Paris. The place was of particular concern to the anti-Jesuit publicists. Books and pamphlets of the time bore titles such as: *Halte-là! ou la terreur à Montrouge; Le Huron de Montrouge; Les Jésuites en goguette ou une Scène à Montrouge; Montrouge peint par lui-même ou les Trois derniers conseils de guerre tenus les 17, 18 et 26 Juin 1828 par les Révérends Pères Jésuites de la Province de France; Les Sept bêtes de Montrouge.*

11. "Men in black, whence issue you?/We crawl up from underground./Half-way foxes, half-way wolves/Our way of life is mystery-bound." See Bertier de Sauvigny, *La Restauration,* 279.

The heatedly romantic level of these attacks is well mirrored in one of the letters that was sent to Montrouge, and which was reproduced in a meticulously kept diary of the house:

> Tremble, satellites of Loyola; your last hour is going to sound. Vile rabble, filthy corrupters of youth, monsters of treachery, tremble; hypocrites, criminals, the colossus of your power is going to collapse and it will crush you under the ruins. Cursed race, enemies of your fatherland, you will perish. Burdened by your crimes, your name will be held in abhorrence by all future peoples . . . 40,000 defenders of our liberties have sworn your destruction . . . 40 more days and Montrouge will be no more!
>
> signed: Geoffroy—friend of the Constitution
> Jouvillier—friend of Liberty
> Métrouvel—friend of Equality
> Gordeau—friend of the Republic
> Tournilly—enemy of Traitors[12]

The chef-d'oeuvre of the attack came not from the political liberals, but from the Count de Montlosier, a convinced royalist, monarchist, and ardent Gallican. In his *Mémoire à consulter sur un système politique tendant à renverser la religion, la société et le trône,* published in 1826, he saw the Jesuits everywhere and in everything. "A vast system, or not to mince words, a vast conspiracy against religion, against the king and against society itself has arisen."[13] That system was made up of four plagues or calamities, the Congregation, the Jesuits, Ultramontanism, and the encroachments of the priests into everyday affairs. Montlosier's charges came at just the right time and were debated passionately in press and legislature.

---

12. PSJ, D^2 1: 2422, Montrouge. A "friend of Fraternity" is conspicuous by his absence.

13. Montlosier, *Mémoire à consulter,* as quoted by Joseph Burnichon, S.J., *La Compagnie de Jésus en France: Histoire d'un siècle, 1814–1914* (Paris, 1914–1922), I, 351.

As a matter of fact, the Society was by no means as powerful or as important as popular opinion would have it. It was enough of a problem simply to get the Jesuits reconstituted again in their own internal life. Far from having thousands of members in 1824, as was reputed, there were 108 priests, 131 scholastics and 81 brothers in the French province. They hardly merited the interminable flow of attacks against them in the next four years—attacks even by such responsible men as Cousin and Guizot who railed against the Society in their university courses.

The Jesuit schools were the focal point of the attack. If the majority of the nation was really not at all directly involved with the question of the Jesuits, the *pays légal,* the middle class, taxpaying, politically active part of the country (and it was this part of France that could educate its sons), was passionately divided on the subject. Burnichon sums up the Jesuit attitude in their schools:

> Along with religion, and piety, the principles of the monarchy were at the base of the education given by the Jesuits in their minor seminaries. There is nothing to hide here: they were ardently royalist . . . while the spirit of sedition raged in the royal colleges. Certainly the Jesuits themselves were attached by conviction to the legitimate royalty which appeared to them as the guarantee of the Christian traditions of France against Voltairian impiety and revolutionary atheism. But even if it had been otherwise, they would not have been able to restrain or conceal the fervor of the monarchical sentiments of the clientele which flocked to their establishments. It was, in effect, the families most devoted to the Restoration and especially the old nobility which confided their sons to them. Besides, one should not judge that epoch by the ideas of today. The words "empire" and "republic" had at that time a purely seditious sound; one would have greatly surprised the Jesuits in saying to

them that they were engaged in politics, because they testified to their loyalty toward the monarchy and the royal family. For them this was simply to act as good Frenchmen, something they considered it their duty to do.[14]

Most important and most true is the remark about the Jesuits being surprised at the accusation of "politics." For all of the Restoration period this seems certain. Only in the July Monarchy did many of them really become aware of and face up to the light in which they were presenting themselves. For some, this awareness never dawned, especially when the "other" monarchy of the "Napoleonic usurper" was re-established, or even more forcibly when, after 1870, "republic" became increasingly synonymous in their minds with anti-Catholic and anticlerical.

After the victory of the moderate monarchists in the 1827 elections and the easing of the press restrictions by the Vicomte de Martignac, the relatively liberal minister of Charles X, the attacks on the educational work of the Jesuits grew ever more violent. Finally, after much pressure, the king signed the two Ordonnances of June 16, 1828. The second of them was only intended to emphasize the *seminary* character of the minor seminaries and to put a limit to the extension of this type of secondary education which, supervised by the Church hierarchy, escaped direct state control. But the first order was directed precisely against the Jesuits:

> As of October 1 . . . the eight establishments directed by persons belonging to a non-authorized Congregation and presently existing at Aix, Billom, Bordeaux, Dôle, Fourcalquier, Montmorillon, Sainte-Anne d'Auray and Saint-Acheul are subject to the regulations of the Université.
>
> From the same date no one can be or remain charged either with the direction or with the teaching in an educa-

14. Burnichon, *La Compagnie*, I, 289.

tional establishment subject to the Université or in an ecclesiastical secondary school if he does not affirm in writing that he does not belong to any religious congregation not legally established in France.[15]

These eight schools were the minor seminaries confided by the bishops to the Society. Much of the episcopate, led by the archbishop of Paris, refused to accept these regulations, and only the persuasion of Leo XII finally brought compliance. As a matter of fact, both sides gave ground, for the government was not always exigent in the details of the second ordinance. But there was no relenting on the Jesuit schools. They were closed, but not, however, before protests had come from enough municipal and departmental councils and especially from jurists eminent enough to make the Jesuits feel, rightly or wrongly, that there was a strong case for the illegality of the enactments in the light of the Charte.

The signing of the Ordonnances somewhat calmed the anti-Jesuit agitation in the legislature. Petitions for total expulsion were regularly presented and received, but nothing actually came of them. The Society tried to avoid the limelight in its work, and the members who had been teaching took up other positions in France (where five new residences were founded in this year) or in the missions, or in the exile colleges, especially at Brugelette after 1834.

If 1828 was a difficult year for the French Jesuits, 1830 appeared to them almost catastrophic. The July Revolution of that year had a violently antireligious character. Throne and altar had been too closely linked by friends and enemies of the Bourbon monarchy to allow the one to be overthrown without touching the other. In the first days, the Jesuit residences were among the most prominent objects of these attacks. A Hunga-

15. Ordonnances du 16 Juin, 1828, art. 1. See Dansette, *Histoire religieuse,* I, 201.

rian diplomat in France wrote of the Society at the time: "The roles of schemers, knaves, scoundrels in the comedies or melo-dramas are always represented by Jesuits. Also, the worst insult that you can offer to anyone is to call him a Jesuit."[16]

A month after the July days, the provincial of France wrote to the General to describe the situation as he saw it:

> The streets are hung with inflammatory posters against the Jesuits . . .
>
> I am very worried. It has been a good month now that everything here has been aflame . . . I have very good reason to believe that letters abroad are intercepted and opened. Yours probably will have suffered the same fate, leaving me without counsel and guidance in the most critical state of affairs, I think, that the Society has under-gone in France . . .
>
> Our priests, most of them, are disguised, hidden, or dispersed. The good Christians beg us not to leave the country. We will not do so, so long as the danger does not become clear and open. If that should happen, I do not think it would be your wish that I expose [our members] to certain ruin in keeping them in a land that devours its own inhabitants. Already Montrouge has been sacked and ruined, all our Jesuits chased out and hunted; five of them ran the risk of losing their lives. St. Acheul had it the same day . . . They came to our residence in Paris three times; the Fathers are no longer there. Vitry was ransacked the day before yesterday . . . The populace sacked, stole, ate, and drank for almost twenty-four hours . . . I have urged everyone to be extremely prudent. I can assure you that all of our Jesuits are in an excellent frame of mind. Priests, scholastics, novices, brothers, all would seem happy to suffer for our Lord. They are really reliving the great early days of the Society.[17]

16. Comte Rodolphe Apponyi, "Autour de la Révolution de 1830," *Revue des Deux Mondes* 71 (October 15, 1912), 798.

17. ARSJ, Franc., Druilhet to Roothaan, Aug. 31, 1830.

As the July Monarchy began, the future of the Society in France seemed most inauspicious. Close to fifty priests were dispersed all over the country. Most of the younger members were in exile. Although the closing of the eight minor seminaries had been a blessing in that they no longer drained off a large proportion of the young Jesuits long before their spiritual or intellectual formation was completed, at the same time it cut off a fertile source of recruits to the Society.

Contrary to the first expectations, the storm passed quickly enough, and within a year of the 1830 Revolution, one of the Jesuit witnesses of the period was writing: "Since the month of September 1831, especially, the public spirit grew better day by day in France; religion again was taking its place in men's hearts; priests were respected; the prejudices against our Society almost completely vanished. People knew who we were and where we were, and they did not disturb us. A large number even of those who had been against us, gave evidence to us of their esteem and friendship."[18]

Many new residences were offered to the Society. After the expulsion from the minor seminaries, and up to 1835, there were enough men to open and staff houses at Toulouse, Paris, Metz, Lyons, and Lalouvesc. From these houses the Jesuits occupied themselves again in pastoral and catechetical work throughout the country—not only in churches, but also in municipal institutions, in prisons, and even in some of the government colleges. For the first time since its restoration, members of the Society from France undertook missionary work outside the country. French Jesuits went to Algeria, Canada, China, Syria, Madagascar, and Ceylon, and to Louisiana and Kentucky.[19] The Society had so prospered in France

18. *Les Etablissements des Jésuites en France depuis quatre siècles: Répertoire topo-bibliographique,* ed. Pierre Delattre, S.J. (5 vols.; Enghien, Bel. 1949–1957), II, 604, "Relation manuscrite sur les événements de 1830." This work will be referred to henceforth as *EJF.*

19. The group in Kentucky moved after some years to New York, where it was the nucleus of the founding community of Fordham University. The New York schoolboy was a source of immense puzzlement to the French Jesuit.

that in 1836 the country was divided into the two Jesuit provinces of Paris and Lyons.

If in these years the Society had its share of external trouble, internal problems also were not wanting. Two crises in particular arose over philosophical and theological doctrines held and taught by some of the Jesuits themselves. The names usually given to the ensemble of positions are "Mennaisienism" and "Ontologism." The former was already a problem well before 1830, and the latter continued to be so well after 1850. Both also help to illustrate the conditions in which the Jesuits pursued their studies, and the problems which were to be present in their college teaching in later years.

In 1820 Félicité de Lamennais, still the great ultramontane champion and not yet disillusioned by an increasingly conservative papacy, had elaborated in the second volume of the *Essai sur l'indifférence* his theory of a certitude which rested essentially on faith, and of a system in which the content of faith was finally ascertained and guaranteed not so much by individual reason, as by the "general reason" expressed by everyone in those propositions of universal consent to which no exception is or can be taken. Thus, its popular name of the "philosophy of common consent." "To avoid the scepticism to which philosophy leads the isolated, individual man, in place of looking in himself for the certitude of a first truth, he must start from a fact; the fact is the insurmountable faith inherent in our nature; and he must admit as true that which all men believe invincibly. Authority, or the general reason, or common consent is the rule of judgment for the individual man."[20]

Of course, to reduce here to the bare bones of one statement is to impoverish a system elaborated with grace and style and passion and subtlety by a man of undeniable gifts and great prestige. It also does not explain the attraction of these or

20. Félicité de Lamennais, *Défense de l'Essai sur l'indifférence en matière de religion* (Paris, 1821), 179–180.

similar doctrines to men such as Louis de Bonald, Joseph de Maistre, Jean-Baptiste Lacordaire, Philippe Gerbet, or Dom Prosper Guéranger. But attractive it was, and among the reasons for its influence was the triumphant revenge it seemed to take on the reputed "pure reason" of the eighteenth-century *philosophe,* ultimately responsible in the eyes of the Restoration for the atheist impieties of the Revolution.

Unfortunately an inevitable simplification of positions produced a clear contest between reason and faith, between a "pure" Cartesianism and the philosophy of *sens commun.* To much of the French clergy the choice could not but be obvious, and the teachings of Lamennais made triumphant progress in religious circles. The French Jesuits of the Restoration were no exception, and while there were determined opponents of the system, it is probably not too much to say that some of the most prominent men of this first generation, men such as Nicolas Loriquet, Philippe Delvaux and the two provincials, François Renault and Didier Richardot, were at least at one time ardent partisans of "Mennaisienism."[21]

A serious division resulted "in a manner more or less pronounced in every house. Here the superior was for Lamennais, there he said nothing, elsewhere he was against him. Nowhere was there any check on overexcited opinions."[22] Finally in 1823 the divisions broke out into the open, and for the sake of peace, Aloysius Fortis, the General, published on October 4, 1823, an *Ordinatio* or directive on the problem. The Mennaisien doctrine (as explained by Jean Rozaven, the assistant for France, who was an ardent opponent and who prepared much of the memorandum) was summarized in the following points:

21. Burnichon, *La Compagnie,* II, 18. Even some of the Jesuit writings of presuppression days were called into the fray, and the famous treatise of Claude Buffier, S.J., *Traité des premières vérités et de la source de nos jugements . . .* (Paris, 1724), was re-edited (and changed to fit current needs) with the additional title: . . . *Ouvrage qui contient le développement primitif de l'autorité générale adopté par M. de Lamennais comme l'unique fondement de la certitude: Pour servir d'Appendice au t.II de l'Essai* (Avignon, 1822).

22. PSJ, D² 1: 2422, Montrouge, "Memoires sur l'histoire de Montrouge."

1. There is no other criterion of truth than *le sens commun.*

2. Only faith engenders certitude.

3. The existence of God is the first truth which we know.

4. From the existence of a contingent being one cannot deduce the existence of a necessary being. In other words, it is reasoning in a vicious circle to say: I exist, therefore God exists.

5. Finite intelligence, by the very fact that it is finite, is always and in everything subject to error.

6. In catholic schools, false systems have prevailed which lead to atheism and the overthrow of religion.

7. Man would not be able to be certain, unless by *sens commun,* either of his existence or of his thinking.[23]

Without attaching any qualification of true or false to the doctrine, and without even naming Lamennais, the General prohibited the teaching of these propositions within the order itself. Rozaven remarked rather drily in a letter, "You will receive, I think, in a little while a directive from Father General, prohibiting the teaching of the principles of M. de Lamennais. I hope that the defenders of authority will have no trouble in submitting their individual reasons."[24]

This did not prevent partisans of the doctrine from examining, discussing, even from adopting the doctrine, as long as they did not teach it formally, and the difference continued even after the directive. Rozaven and Lamennais themselves met in Rome in 1824 without any satisfaction. Some Jesuits asked to be relieved of their vows because of the Society's stand, and the quarrel within the Society reached even into the General's headquarters.

The dispute eventually reached the public domain in the

23. PSJ, Ordinationes Patrum Generalium, Fortis, Oct. 4, 1823.
24. PSJ, D² 1: 2422, Montrouge, Rozaven to Gury, Oct. 1, 1823.

late 1820's, and it was used by partisans of Lamennais such as the *Mémorial Catholique* and by opponents such as *L'Ami de la Religion*. Lamennais was incensed by this Jesuit opposition but when he inquired about the General's directive, he was told by the provincial, Nicolas Godinot, that it was considered a matter purely internal to the Society, especially since Lamennais was not censured nor even mentioned in the document. Lamennais vigorously complained that the Society had secrets which it could not divulge to him but which everyone seemed to know about anyway. Godinot may well have been within his strict rights and duties, but surely this was to give to Lamennais real and justifiable complaint that, despite the Society's careful distinctions, the matter was public knowledge and distorted knowledge to boot.

In all this controversy, too, another element was involved. The political and social theories of Lamennais became inextricably mixed in the problem. This aspect came to a head in October 1830 when, within three months of the Revolution of 1830, the first number of *L'Avenir* appeared, bringing with it the heady and, to many, scandalous program of Catholic liberalism. Deeply committed to progressive doctrines that were espoused by the younger French clergy, feared by the French monarchy, and totally incomprehensible to the papacy of Gregory XVI, the three "pilgrims of God and liberty," Lamennais, Lacordaire, and Montalembert, went to Rome in December 1831 with their program, only to see it rejected coldly by Pope Gregory XVI.

Somewhat earlier in 1831 Rozaven had published a detailed and careful critique of the philosophy and theology of Lamennais. Even so, a good number of Jesuits still saw in the Mennaisien theory of the authority of common sense a doctrine "so conformed to, or better, almost identical with catholic doctrine, resting on the same base, having the same rule, that it would not know how to be a false or harmful doctrine." As such it had the sympathy of all Catholics, while all the unbelievers were hostile to it.[25] On August 15, 1832 appeared the encyclical *Mirari Vos* in which, although Lamennais was not mentioned by name, his doctrines were condemned. By the time of the condemnation of his *Paroles d'un Croyant* in the encyclical *Singulari Vos* July 15, 1834, Lamennais regarded freedom and the Church as mutually incompatible, and he was to go his increasingly lonely, bitter, and violent way to the end, a clairvoyant genius whose loss to the Church was a tragedy.

With the second encyclical and its reprobation of "that fallacious philosophical system" there was an end to open controversy in the Society. The provincial, François Renault, wrote a circular letter to all the superiors in which he said that since "the last Encyclical has quite evidently condemned the system of Philosophy which was at the base of all these doctrines," the General had asked "that those who had more or less adopted these systems, say today what they think in a clear and precise manner."[26] But "liberalism" and, especially, accusations of it were to continue to be a problem within the Society, while these condemnations of the 1830's played their part in the very conservative attitudes which lasted so long.

Ontologism, the second internal dispute of the Society, seemed in some respects a reprise of the earlier dispute. It did not have the external repercussions for the Jesuits that had been involved in the case of Lamennais, but it was even more troubling within the Society itself. The accusation of "teaching ontologism" was to agitate several of the colleges; in reaction, a particular type of rigid and arid "scholasticism" too often prevailed.

Basically, ontologism was in philosophy a theory concerning the origin of ideas, and in theology a theory of the nature of God's relations with the world external to Him, and of the way in which man knows God. According to one of its proponents, a one-time Jesuit, we can "sum up ontologism in this proposi-

25. ARSJ, Germ., Genet to Roothaan, Jan. 3, 1831.
26. PSJ, Litterae Encyclicae Patrum Provincialium, Renault, 1834.

tion: The human intellect attains essentially and immediately the infinite Being himself (not such as he is in himself), but as it sees in him the *metaphysical* essences, or the universal, eternal and immutable ideas of created things."[27]

Ontologism claimed for its distant ancestors and proponents Plato, St. Augustine, and St. Bonaventure among others, and more immediately the archbishop of Cambrai, François de la Mothe-Fénelon and, especially, Nicolas de Malebranche, whom all, opponents and proponents, recognized as the most authentic of ontologists. The system was, in one form or another, widely taught in Catholic schools in the middle of the nineteenth century, and vigorously combatted at the same time by philosophers and theologians who saw grave problems in it. It raised serious questions about the meaning of the intuitive vision of God, which, the Church taught, comes only at supernatural beatitude. It also seemed to involve a possibly pantheistic emanation of creatures from the divine essence. In its favor, according to its proponents, the system firmly grounded the certitude of man's knowledge in the very essence of the unchangeable, absolutely certain, supreme Being.

Many of the Jesuits who were to be teachers in the colleges after 1850 had been students of Father Jean-Pierre Martin, professor of theology at Vals who was supposedly propagating a type of ontologism. A teacher since the 1820's, and since 1837 director of studies for the French Jesuit scholastics, self-taught himself, a tireless worker, and a compelling personality, Martin was one of the dominant influences on the training of almost a generation of Jesuits.[28] By the late 1830's some doubts were al-

27. Jules Fabre, *Réponse aux lettres d'un sensualiste contre l'ontologisme* (Paris, 1864), 52. Fabre had been a Jesuit for many years and, before he left the Society, a teacher of philosophy at the minor seminary of Montauban and the Jesuit college at Toulouse. Later he taught in the theological faculty at Paris, and after retracting his theories in the light of the ecclesiastical decrees from the Holy Office in 1861 he became bishop of Bayeux.

28. Martin was an illustration of the hurried improvisation in training forced on the Society in the years after its restoration. He became a Jesuit in 1814, at 22 years of age. That very year he began teaching philosophy, and continued

ready being expressed about his positions; by 1840 controversy had begun, and Jesuits on both sides were expressing their apprehensions to Roothaan, the General of the Society. Despite a long examination of the problem, no decision had yet been reached when he visited Vals in 1848. Then the controversy became acute because scholastics in exile from Germany, Piedmont, and Rome came there to study and expressed astonishment at the novelties being taught. To the quite adverse observations of a board of Roman examiners in 1849, the rector responded very frankly to Roothaan: "Do you realize that this position becomes by the very fact of that letter extraordinarily difficult and hardly tenable? . . . It is the whole teaching of Vals which is attacked and pursued . . . I am suffering, Reverend Father, and cruelly; all our professors are in the same condition; all the Frenchmen even."[29] The professors also wrote strong letters of justification to Roothaan, and correspondence went on continually.

Despite a change of professors, and despite a formula of clarification drawn up by one of them, the controversy did not end until a directive came from the General in 1850.[30] Again without calling into question the orthodoxy of the proponents of the "system of Vals" or condemning the opinions as such, for which he had no authority, Roothaan simply forbade, for the sake of security, the teaching of some seventeen propositions in philosophy and theology. To give but one example from each, one was not to teach:

> God in His most simple unity contains really, though without form, all distinct and diverse beings. Therefore:

---

until 1821 when he was ordained and became professor of theology to his own Jesuit brethren. This position he held until the appointment as prefect of studies in 1837 gave him the opportunity to write while directing the education of the young Jesuits at Vals for ten more years.

29. ARSJ, Franc., Boulanger to Roothaan, Feb. 1, 1848.

30. Among the newcomers were three, Franzelin, Passaglia, and Schröder, who were to figure very prominently in the coming decades of the reign of Pius IX. Franzelin, later a cardinal, and Schröder were much involved in the Vatican Council. Passaglia wrote the papal document in which Pius IX proclaimed the dogmatic definition of the Immaculate Conception.

(a) God, as simply being, is every existent being.
(b) Also, outside of and besides God, nothing is.
(c) God is totality, in such a way that there is no medium between God and nothing.
(d) Being, as being, exists in such a way that it could never not be.

Supernatural being consists in the intimate, physical, and substantial communication of God as God to the soul and in the union that this brings about. From this there comes to the soul a new power of acting by the very act of God, which is in such a way proper to the soul that the act of God and the act of the soul are numerically one, and are substantially united to the faculties of the soul.[31]

In reality, the problem did not end with the directive. However sincere the adhesion to it, it was hardly possible simply to shed a generation of teaching and influence. On the other hand, one had also to guard against an indiscreet zeal which saw everywhere platonism or "Martinism." Through the 1850's there were still complaints from both sides; in 1858 another directive came from the General on philosophical studies, including the problem of ontologism. In 1861 the Holy Office issued a decree against the "Errors of the Ontologists" and even on into the 1870's it was a subject of concern.[32] All of this was to help make the teaching of philosophy in the colleges somewhat incoherent for a number of years.

By 1833 when Renault became provincial, the July Monarchy was firmly in power, the antireligious passions of the first year had abated, and Louis-Philippe saw with an ironic but practical eye the respect which the Church was again gaining. Such respect could be put to use, for the bourgeois government

31. ARSJ, Lugd., "Ordinatio pro studiis superioribus ad R. P. Ludovicum Maillard, Praepositum Provinciae Lugdunensis," Jan. 6, 1850.

32. *Acta Sanctae Sedis*, 3 (1867–1868), 204 ss., in Henricus Denzinger, S.J., and Adolphus Schönmetzer, S.J., *Enchiridion Symbolorum*, 32nd ed. (Freiburg, Breisgau, 1963), nn. 2841–2847.

wanted order and peace above all. That always perceptive observer, Alexis de Tocqueville, commented on how the faith found proper place in this order: "Most of the liberals whose antireligious passions had previously pushed them to the front of the opposition, now spoke a different language than they had before. They all recognized the political usefulness of a religion."[33]

The French Jesuits, too, benefited from such a policy, even though they were still in the eyes of the government an illegal and dangerous association, only to be quietly tolerated. The Chamber regularly indulged in what might be called a Jesuit day.[34] Renault, the provincial, realized the position of the Jesuits, and he decided to speak about it directly to Thiers, then the Minister of the Interior. His account to Roothaan followed: "I asked for a meeting, and it was arranged. I told him [Thiers] who I was; I explained our principles . . . These principles, my frankness and my air of liberty pleased him. He told me what you yourself have so often said, that we should keep ourselves outside of any parties, that in acting thus we could count on the protection of the government which wanted religion. He himself spoke to me also with frankness; he was even open about certain difficulties in his position; you would have said almost as friend to friend. In fine, Father, I left satisfied with him, and without flattering myself too much, I believe he is satisfied with me." In the same letter, Renault mentioned

33. Alexis de Tocqueville, *Correspondance inédite*, II, 48, as quoted by Henri Guillemin, *Histoire des catholiques français au XIXe siècle* (Paris, 1947), 93.

34. One can hardly blame the government for being concerned at the time. At the request of Charles X and by order of the General, two of the Jesuits, among them the former Provincial, Druilhet, lived for a short time (June to October 1835) in the Bourbon court-in-exile at Prague as tutors of the young Duc de Bordeaux. Three names that figure prominently in the royal entourage, the Duc de Blacas, the Baron de Damas, the Marquis de Foresta, are the family names of three prominent French Jesuits of the mid-nineteenth century. No wonder the widespread conviction that the Society was legitimist at heart. The journals were in a frenzy about the matter when the news got out, and even the legitimist organs feared for the spirit of the young prince, raised by such mentors, and warned that the unpopularity of the Jesuits would inevitably involve the royal family and close off forever any hope of a restoration.

an interview that Father Laponce had about Jesuit colleges with his relative, Guizot, Minister of Education: "Here is the tenor of some of the Minister's answers: Just so there's no interference . . . , when the moment comes, when we discuss the law on freedom to teach, there will be no fear of being involved in exceptions; there will be none of those for anyone. *You would be there, included under common law then.* Basically to sum up everything in one word, I believe that the king and his ministers wish to do us as much good as they can or perhaps as they dare to do."[35]

It was, in fact, this question of freedom of teaching which was the neuralgic point for Catholics and for the government during all of Louis-Philippe's reign. Perhaps in the long run it was providentially so; at least it kept the Church from a compromising cooperation with the government which the latter quite obviously desired for the sake of its own stability. When revolution came in 1848, the Church, after previous years of bitter fighting, clearly was not identified with the regime. As a result it emerged with the respect of the leaders and in many cases with the affection of the people.

The Charter of 1830, subscribed to by Louis-Philippe and by the men who put him on the throne, stated quite clearly: "It [the government] will make provision, by individual laws and with the shortest possible delay, for . . . public education and the freedom of teaching." Through eighteen years of delay and equivocation, that provision was never fully put into effect. The story of the battle for freedom of teaching is well known,

---

35. ARSJ, Franc., Renault to Roothaan, Aug. 20, 1835. Roothaan used to tell Renault that his letters were not explicit enough. This is surely an example. There were humorous incidents too. Returning from Switzerland in May 1835, the Provincial had his baggage searched quite thoroughly at the frontier; the officials kept the forms "Informatio ad gubernandum" and sent them on to Paris, perhaps thinking that they had stumbled on part of a Jesuit plot. The papers were returned to Renault from one of the ministries without comment. They were forms for those to be proposed as rectors or superiors in the Society, and to the government the questionnaire must have seemed strange enough: "Is he master of his passions? Is he humble, modest? Does he seem united to God in prayer?" (Burnichon, *La Compagnie*, II, 205).

and there is no need to retell it except insofar as it concerned the Jesuits and the schools.

The conquest of primary education was relatively easy and brief. Montalembert, Lacordaire, and de Caux deliberately opened a private primary school in March 1831, after informing the police of their intention. In two days it was closed and the men put on trial. They lost their case but won their cause through Montalembert's brilliant plea in the Chamber of Peers. By 1833 Guizot proposed a bill establishing freedom of primary education. Indeed, as he said, it provided everywhere "that the general atmosphere of the school should be moral and religious." It had little trouble in being enacted; it was good for the lower classes that they be under the influence of "the clergy, sublime preserver of public order."[36]

When it came to secondary schools, the men of the *monarchie censitaire* who were in power were hardly going to give a share in the education of their children to an obscurantist Church. For the members of this class, most of them at least mildly Voltairian skeptics, and some of them violently anticlerical, the lycée or college was the most powerful influence and the terminal point in that education. For them, the formation of an enlightened citizenry and of a progressive united France depended on a state monopoly of such education, no matter what the Charte said.[37]

Both sides talked of liberty. The Université and its parliamentary adherents could mean anything from the most hostile antireligious spirit of the Revolution to a genuine desire to give

36. Molé, in his entrance discourse into the Académie Française in 1840, as quoted by Guillemin, *Catholiques français au XIXe siècle*, 94.

37. A typical statement of this latter position: "Thus it is to the state that the grand direction of education belongs, the responsibility of founding schools for every career, of forming masters for all the professions; for just as the clergy, with reason, is considered the exclusive guardian of the faith, so to the state, in the same way, is confided the sacred custody of the way of life, the intelligence, the education and the patriotism of its children called one day to further its grandeur" (Charles Saint-Nexant, *Examen du projet de loi sur la liberté de l'enseignement secondaire* [Paris, 1848], 8).

the Church the freedom it wanted, even if they were convinced it would be abused. The Church and its partisans ranged from those who honestly and successfully wanted only free competition with the state schools to those who meant by "liberty" a Church monopoly in place of that of the state. From 1840 the battle was joined, especially after the bishops became convinced that the Université was a peril not only to the morals but also to the faith of the students. Their conviction about the danger was probably basically correct, despite the exaggerated terms in which it was often expressed. Sainte-Beuve is a witness, calm and moderate, but definite, about the schools in the 1840's: "As a whole, the professors of the Université without being hostile to religion, are not religious. The students are affected by this, and from this whole atmosphere they leave the Université, not nourished by irreligion, but indifferent . . . Whatever one might be able to say for or against this, praising or blaming it, one leaves the schools of the Université hardly a Christian."[38]

There were, of course, excellent teachers and convinced Christians, such as Charles Lenormant and Frederic Ozanam, in the Université. Even so, Montalembert could say of a period a few years earlier, when supposedly the atmosphere had even been better: "For myself, who was brought up in its [the Université's] midst and only there, I know what it is—I know, and if I had a son, I would rather send him out as a cabin boy on a fishing boat than have him be exposed to the dangers which I myself ran in the colleges of the Université."[39] Most particularly, the Catholics objected to the philosophy being taught. "The philosophical teaching of the Université through which all those aspiring to the baccalaureate had to pass was emancipated from religion, to which up to then it had been

---

38. Charles Sainte-Beuve, *Chroniques parisiennes* (Paris, 1843), 100, 122, as quoted by Burnichon, *La Compagnie*, II, 469.

39. Montalembert to Villain, Oct. 21, 1839, as quoted by André Trannoy, *Le Romantisme politique de Montalembert avant 1843* (Paris, 1942), 64.

more or less subordinated, and had passed under the control of a school, or to put it better, of a man; that man was M. Cousin."[40]

A campaign waged for liberty or against an official philosophy would have raised enough opposition; the actual campaign, as waged by too many, simply poured insults and calumnies on the whole educational system of the state. For example, the Abbé Combalot's work bore on the frontispiece the verse from Scripture, *"Herodes occidit omnes pueros"* ("Herod slew all the children"), referring to the massacre of the Innocents in the second chapter of St. Matthew's Gospel. The tone of the book was set right at the beginning. "The persecution of the Czar Nicholas against the Catholics is infinitely less deadly than the persecution of the monopoly." Further on, one learned that the state system formed "prostituted intelligences who go to search at the bottom of hell for the glorification of incest, adultery, and revolt." The state education "doubles a man's ability to do evil," and "hands over the students to the instincts of a beast." "Vicious habits, unnatural practices and loathsome morals become the dominant characteristic of the generation brought up in these colleges."[41]

There were enough other works of this kind, but the book which caused the greatest outcry and excited the most bitter opposition was the contribution to the fight by the only Jesuit to get directly involved literarily. *Le Monopole Universitaire* was first published at Lyons in 1841 with Abbé Desgarets, a canon of that city, listed as responsible for the work. In reality, Father Nicholas Deschamps, an inexhaustible, outspoken, and rather extremist Jesuit, was the author, and this soon became known.[42] Only the last one fifth of the book was concerned

40. Paul Thureau-Dangin, *Histoire de la Monarchie de Juillet* (3rd ed., Paris, 1884–1892), V, 469.

41. Théodore Combalot, *Mémoire aux évêques de France et aux pères de famille sur la guerre faite à l'Église et à la Société par le Monopole Universitaire* (Paris, 1843), as quoted by Guillemin, *Catholiques français au XIXe siècle*, 98.

42. N. Desgarets [Nicholas Deschamps, S.J.], *Le Monopole Universitaire*

with the monopoly from the point of view of the Charte. The first four fifths, more than five hundred pages, dealt with what was taught in the state schools. There the book sought to establish that this teaching did the following: (1) It insulted religion and all that religion respected; (2) it praised and exalted the enemies of religion and the errors contrary to religion; (3) it questioned and denied the particular dogmas of the Catholic religion; (4) it did not even spare those held in common with Protestant sects; (5) it unsettled the fundamental truths of all religion and of all society; (6) it entailed, as a consequence, immorality and crime in the colleges and in the nation.

To support particular assertions it was not too hard to gather citations, and long and complete and contextually correct ones at that, from some of the books used and some of the lectures given in the state schools. That process could even be defended as legitimate; such or such was what particular people and particular books did teach. But Deschamps went far beyond that. He imputed those teachings to the state school system as such; he broke in on the citations, argued, refuted, and insulted, fiercely and harshly. The royal colleges were a "sinkhole of every vice." "The infamous works of the Marquis de Sade were only eclogues compared to what went on in these colleges." "An unconstitutional monopoly enriches these impure blasphemers in wealthy sinecures, paid for by the very substance of our poor."[43]

The General of the Jesuits, angry at the tone of the book, described it well in writing to the provincial when there was question of a second edition: "Use all the authority which you can summon with the publishers of this book to cut out of it absolutely the personalities, the insulting epithets, everything which savors of acrimony. Such weapons are appropriate only

---

destructeur de la religion et des lois ou la Charte et la liberté d'enseignement (Lyon, 1841).

43. *Ibid.*, 527, 440.

for those who fight against the truth; its defenders ought to forbid themselves the use of them."[44]

Not everyone agreed about the unsuitability of the arms used and the opinions expressed. The liberal press returned in kind; the author was, for instance, an "epileptic" and a "drunken ruffian." Catholics, beginning with the bishops, were sharply divided on the book. The archbishop of Paris, for instance, disapproved publicly and was publicly contradicted by the bishop of Chartres. Some were convinced that the book said only the truth and said it well, and they used it as a storehouse of weapons for their attacks on the monopoly.

Among the Jesuits, too, the division was sharp. The provincial of Lyons thought that it was a service rendered to religion. Often, the greater the distance from Paris the more there was agreement with Deschamps' methods. In Paris, the provincial was distressed: "The recrudescence of anger against us is terrible at the present. It is the inopportune Monopole universitaire . . . which is principally the cause. The name of him to whom it is attributed is now circulating everywhere, and a minister who had a copy on his table within a few days after it appeared, said: 'It is those scoundrels the Jesuits who have done this.' "[45] Father Xavier de Ravignan, who was in a position to know well the government reaction, was dismayed at the book. Ravignan was probably the most prominent Jesuit in France at the time; preacher at Notre-Dame, where he attracted the most influential part of all shades of Parisian opinion, he was an intelligent man, well aware of what could and could not be done, on good terms both with governmental circles and their opponents. His reaction was a scandal to some of his brethren, who let the General know that they thought him almost disloyal to the Catholic cause. Replying to the complaints, he wrote to Roothaan: "When *Le Monopole* appeared, I do not know if I called the situation created by the

44. ARSJ, Lugd., Reg., Roothaan to Maillard, July 25, 1843.
45. PSJ, Reg., Boulanger to (?), May 13, 1843.

book an 'immeasurable disaster,' but I, along with the most sober men, men most devoted to the Society, saw in it an obstacle to the results which the obvious religious movement seemed to be bringing about more peacefully. As to the existence of the Society in France, I know all the irritation of the government against us on this point."[46]

Deschamps could not leave bad enough alone; after *Le Monopole* he fired such salvos as *L'Université jugée par elle-même,* and *La Grande moquerie ou Le Projet de M. Villemain sur la liberté d'enseignement.* While the provincial at Lyons was giving permission, however hesitatingly, for these compromising works, the one at Paris was sending a circular letter to all the Jesuit houses, urging "as a strict duty the avoidance in their discourses of everything which could relate, near or far, to politics . . . In particular, our Fathers must never speak of freedom of teaching, neither in their sermons or conferences, nor in the addresses which they would have occasion to give to any meetings of men or women."[47]

Meanwhile, two laymen and two journals, not yet mutually opposed, Montalembert with *Le Correspondant* and Louis Veuillot with *L'Univers,* together with Catholics carefully organized and solidly behind them, battled most effectively for freedom of education. A serious and needed discussion should have taken place on the rights of parental choice in education, on the rights of the state to surveillance of standards, on the place of liberty and the place of order. But this was made impossible by the heated atmosphere on both sides. It was especially frustrated through the diversionary tactics of a concentrated assault on the Society of Jesus by the convinced anticlericals and by those out of power who saw in this an easy way to embarrass the government.

Thus, from 1843 on, the side issue of what to do about the

46. Armand de Ponlevoy, *Vie du R.P. Xavier de Ravignan* (10th ed.; Paris, 1876), I, 272.

47. PSJ, "Litt. Encyc. PP. Provincialium," Boulanger, April 14, 1843.

Jesuits diverted attention in large part from the substantial question of what to do about education.

Students at the royal colleges were given composition subjects such as Arnault demanding of Parlement the expulsion of the Society. The productions of the battle of 1826–1828 were brought out again and improved upon. The *Journal des Débats* and other publications took up the cry with more or less literary grace. The usual books came out, and the most fantastic stories circulated.[48] Edgar Quinet and Jules Michelet at the Collège de France did little honor to themselves or to their profession with courses "transformed into a sort of malevolent diatribe against the Jesuits, in which for the former at least there was some appearance of order, plan and seriousness, while in Michelet's lectures there reigned a violent hatred, a furious anger, a sort of grotesque fear . . ."[49] Of course, people were incited to public manifestations and, urged on by Veuillot, there were counterdemonstrations at the lectures.

A rather moribund *Constitutionnel* came to life again, and reached what was then an enormous circulation in the tens of thousands with the publication of one of the first serialized works, Eugène Sue's *Le Juif Errant*. In ten volumes the poor Jew figured slightly enough; it was a story of the Jesuits, in-

48. For instance *Les Jésuites démasqués. Conseils de Satan aux Jésuites, Histoire dramatique et pittoresque des Jésuites, illustrée,* and the inevitable *Monita Secreta.* Among the numerous stories, the following is a restrained example. The Duc de Bordeaux visited Oscott College near Birmingham in England at the end of 1843. The *Journal des Débats* told its readers of the event: On January 1, 1844, the Duke stayed overnight at this college run by the Jesuits; the next day he was present at a part of *Athalie* in which, at the lines that spoke of God bringing a king back to his throne by the hands of priests, the students cheered and Jesuits waved their hats. He then took dinner with Father Wiseman, who was the Jesuit Superior and Provincial. Not a single one of the above "facts" is true, except that the Duke did pay a visit. Father Wiseman sent a letter on Jan. 8, 1844 to the *Journal,* demanding retraction. Of course he did not receive it. Wiseman will be recognized as the eminent diocesan priest, rector at Oscott, future restorer of the English hierarchy, first cardinal of Westminster, and never a Jesuit. See Burnichon, *La Compagnie,* II, 519–520.

49. Thureau-Dangin, *La Monarchie de Juillet,* V, 503–510. There are here many instructive examples of the level at which the polemic was carried on.

carnated by the villain, Father Rodin, in a life of theft, deceit, regicide, lust, and betrayal, that led to his being elected General, with hopes of becoming Pope. Virtue triumphed however; the princess who had been his companion in treachery went mad; he was despoiled of the two hundred million francs he had amassed, was poisoned, and died in spasms of agony. Possibly nothing did so much as this work to fix the popular image of the Jesuit and to inflame the popular mind against it, and when Thiers, whose mouthpiece was the *Constitutionnel,* called in 1845 for the expulsion of the Society, he had a willing audience.

To the defense of the Jesuits came, of course, such journals as *Le Correspondant* and *L'Ami de la Religion et du Roi,* but above all *L'Univers,* thus forming a lasting friendship and trust between the Jesuits and Louis Veuillot, its devoted, brilliant, and extremist editor.

From within the Society itself, the best reply was the simple, direct work of Ravignan, *De l'Existence et de l'Institut des Jésuites,* which appeared in January 1843. It was only Ravignan's personal eminence that allowed him to say openly and in print "I am a Jesuit," and to be the author of the first work in France in eighty years, since the suppression there in 1764, which bore proudly on the title page after the author's name, the words, "of the Society of Jesus." The book was not and did not pretend to be a point-by-point response to the accusations and objections a thousand times repeated against the Jesuits. Ravignan described the Society as he knew it, simply said "Here is just what we are," and concluded: "Either I am mistaken, or after this account, the reader in good faith has become aware of how a magistrate, a Frenchman, and a man of this nineteenth century was able freely and conscientiously to become a Jesuit, without, for all that, abdicating his reason and renouncing his age and his country."[50]

50. Xavier de Ravignan, S.J., *De l'Existence et de l'Institut des Jésuites* (7th ed.; Paris, 1855), 194.

How precarious the Society thought its position in the eyes of the public is obvious in the hesitation of superiors to publish the book. The records of the consultations at Paris testify to the recurring doubts and anxieties of the provincial and his advisers for months. There was no need to have hesitated; the work was an immediate success. But nothing better shows how exacerbated was the question of Jesuits and the schools than the absence from the book of any direct mention of the educational work of the Society. It would surely have raised a storm out of all proportions, but the omission was resented by some of Ravignan's confreres who would have put on a bolder face or who would have preferred the attitude of attack of *Le Monopole Universitaire.*

In 1843–1844 Jesuitophobia found further stimulation in the proposed educational law of François Villemain, Minister of Public Instruction. It provided hesitatingly and grudgingly for a slight advance toward liberty of teaching. But this time the bishops put the government in a difficult position. By March 1844 both sides were at the point of exasperation, and in the Chamber of Peers for a full month, from April 22 to May 24, there raged a remarkable debate on education. On the subject of Jesuits alone there were between thirty and forty speakers, most of them simply retelling the stories and the objections that had been told so often. They made a rather wearying collection in the *Moniteur,* enlivened only once in a while by such an original idea as that the Society was responsible for the excesses of the French Revolution: "It is to the spirit of revolt, the germs of which were placed in their students by the Jesuits who treated the truth as an enemy, that we owe that philosophy which . . . spread out to all enlightened classes, and mixed with the events of our great Revolution, . . . so much of the excess which defiled what was just and noble in it and brought on so many disastrous and bloody convulsions."[51]

51. *Moniteur,* Chambre des Pairs, April 29, 1844.

The bill was finally stillborn, but popular feelings did not die along with the proposed law. The *Litterae Annuae* of the Society itself described well the popular portrait: "We, the Jesuits, teach today, as we always have, all sort of evil; we are on the watch for inheritances, spy on family intimacies, worm our way into them and cause trouble. Among Catholics we fan the flames of hatred against the government, the Université and the Gallican articles; we dictate to the bishops everything they publish. We are, in a word, a sinister power, unable to be caught, irresistible, the enemy of the public welfare, and so we should be regarded as a plague never sufficiently to be detested and repelled."[52]

Early in 1845 the provincial of Paris was convinced that "it is hardly possible to escape this time a measure which will disperse us . . ."[53] Provisions were made to take care of the Paris scholastics at Brugelette, and those of Lyons at Turin. Guizot's government was in an embarrassing situation. It did not want to engage in such a persecutory measure as expulsion. Yet the tempest was not abating; the journals were constantly baying at official complacency before the Jesuit menace; the parliamentary opposition found it a most effective weapon with which to badger the government. There was a simple solution, and the Jesuits thought it was what the government wanted: "Our enemies wish, in frightening us, to bring us to dissolve ourselves of our own accord. They will not succeed."[54]

To extricate himself from the situation, Guizot had sent a mission to Rome to ask the Pope that he himself dissolve the Jesuits as an organized body in France, somewhat as had happened under the Restoration in 1828.[55] While Rossi, the envoy,

---

52. PSJ, "Litterae Annuae Provinciae Franciae," 1845.
53. ARSJ, Franc., Boulanger to Roothaan, Jan. 9, 1845.
54. ARSJ, Lugd., Maillard to Roothaan, Jan. 17, 1845.
55. Guizot's account of this whole maneuver is in his *Mémoires* (Paris, 1865), VII, 392. See Burnichon, *La Compagnie,* II, 615. It is not, however, a complete account; it contains much of the correspondence between the Ministry of Foreign Affairs and the envoy, but omits some important material.

cooled his heels at the Quirinal Palace and sent back rather colorful dispatches on the Jesuits, the spring of 1845 brought on another parliamentary attack. Thiers led the charge in the Chamber and demanded execution of the laws already on the books to dissolve the Society in France.

In June 1845, Antoine Vatismesnil, a former minister of Charles X and the very man who had been charged with putting into effect the 1828 Ordonnances, published his *Consultation sur les mesures annoncées contre les Associations religieuses.* The book dealt with all congregations, but the Jesuits were obviously in special view. Vatismesnil attempted to prove that there was no law which prohibited simple life in common, whether a person belonged to any *legally* recognized congregation or not, and that, even if such laws were to be passed, execution of them had to take place in accord with judiciary procedure and not by administrative decrees. It was the work of an eminent jurist, had the signed agreement of others of like stature such as the great lawyer Antoine Berryer, and helped to fix Jesuit opinion on the actions of government then and later.

In that same month Rossi finally was able to present to the Holy See his formal memorandum on the Jesuits. If the French government was in a difficult situation, the Curia was in one equally difficult. It was true, as the memorandum shrewdly stated, that religion had prospered remarkably in France in the last years, and Gregory XVI was hardly desirous of putting a check to the good relations that he enjoyed with Louis Philippe. On the other hand, he was in no mood to sacrifice the Jesuits. Finally, a way out was found. It was diplomatically suggested that Rossi might want to deal not with the Holy See, but directly with the Society itself, which in turn was informed of the delicate situation in which the Roman Curia found itself.

After much uncertainty, Roothaan agreed to diminish the size of several of the larger communities in the "interest of prudence." He remarked in one of his letters to the provincials: "We should do our best to keep in the background, and thus to atone for the excessive confidence which we have had in the freedom promised in the Charte but not found there." He also tried to make it clear that it was *not* a question of abandoning the houses. "If I received from above neither an *order* nor an express *recommendation* still it was remarked: *Vide et considera. Sapienti pauca.* Look and consider. A few words to the wise."[56]

For political purposes the government claimed publicly that "the congregation of the Jesuits will cease to exist in France and will disperse itself on its own; its houses will be closed and the novitiates dissolved."[57] This diplomatic exaggeration, to call it no more, raised a storm. The government and the liberal journals, of course, were happy. The king was relieved. "The Pope," he said, "has pulled a thorn from my foot."[58] Ardent Catholics were dumbfounded, and the French Jesuits themselves were utterly bewildered. They had no idea just where they stood if this was to be, as it seemed at first, a new "Brief of Suppression." Reacting strongly against the government's interpretation, Roothaan at first withdrew the concessions and then finally reinstated them: "The *ne plus ultra* . . . is contained in the letters of June 14 and June 21. I will make no others, without an express order, in writing, from the Holy Father."[59] The General left to the provincials the determination of details. At Paris and Lyons the communities of the main residences were dispersed into smaller groups; the novitiates and scholasticates, houses of training for young Jesuits at Avignon and Toulouse, Saint-Acheul and Laval, were changed or reduced in personnel. For some time Rossi complained and intrigued in Rome for further measures, but Roothaan had become intransigent. He told Maillard to let the journals "retail their

---

56. ARSJ, Franc., Reg., Roothaan to Rubillon, June 21, 1845, and ARSJ, Lugd., Reg., Roothaan to Rubillon and Maillard, June 27, 1845.

57. *Moniteur*, July 6, 1845.

58. Dansette, *Histoire religieuse*, I, 239.

59. ARSJ, Lugd., Reg., Roothaan to Maillard, Aug. 18, 1845.

official lies" and, without bothering to contradict them, to go on with the work of the Society.

The government got no further with the Holy See either, and it let the matter drop there, always officially maintaining that it had gained the complete victory which it had sought. During the next two years from time to time there were rumblings more or less serious in the Chamber, and the French Jesuits lived in continual anxiety all the way up to the Revolution of 1848. It would be a long time, too, before they ever again really trusted in legal guarantees. The Society was sure in 1845 that it could present a good legal case. It felt even more that way when, in 1880, after the Senate had rejected Article 7, Jules Ferry undertook to remove the Jesuits from their schools by purely administrative decrees. Rightly or wrongly, but very deeply, they felt that the use of *arrêts* of ancient *parlements,* personal edicts of bygone kings, and contested laws was arbitrary in the extreme. If this was liberalism in 1840 and republicanism in 1880, then in their minds liberal and republican unfortunately often became synonymous with hypocrite. This scorn and mistrust were misfortunes, for when a strong man came along, he seemed, in the light of experience, more of a security than a strong law, even when it was part and parcel of a constitution.

Before the strong man came along in the person of Louis Napoleon, there was disorder. Accustomed to being among the prime targets of a disturbance, the Jesuits in 1848 were even more surprised than the rest of the French clergy at the respect with which the revolution as a whole treated religion. But the movement of 1848 showed its incoherence here too. Most of the houses of the Society were at least menaced, and in a few places a temporary expulsion also took place. Yet the Jesuits were willing to accept with hope the new regime, even if they were hardly as enthusiastic as some of the higher clergy such as Cardinal Bonald who proclaimed, for instance, that the "flag of the Republic will always be for religion a flag of protection," or as Louis Veuillot, who said of the revolution that "God is speaking through the voice of events."[60]

By early March the provincial was noting danger signals. Several times he explicitly commented on the sight of people without jobs and, in discouraging the hope of a college in the near future in Paris, he thought "It would be of greater use to occupy ourselves with the workers." Unfortunately, the idea of calling into question the whole or, indeed, any important part of the social structure that brought on the misery of the workers seems never to have occurred. Charitable the Jesuits were, and the records of material help dispensed during all this time are impressive. No one, however, saw that this was not enough, and even if it had been recognized, there would hardly have been an audience.

In addition, the men who had defended and supported the Jesuits all through the latter years of the July Monarchy, men such as Montalembert, Dupanloup, Falloux, even Louis Veuillot, were basically satisfied with the established social structure of their times or at least they would have had difficulty in envisioning any other. The "Christian socialism" of *L'Ere Nouvelle* was tragically not for them. When the June uprising came, the provincial could say sadly that "the ones most guilty of it are not the ones in the streets." Yet it is doubtful that he or the rest of the Society would have disagreed with Montalembert's dictum that there was no middle course, that the choice lay between Catholicism and Socialism.[61]

A guest from Italy surely reinforced this fear of catastrophe. The Jesuit Superior General, Roothaan, after consulting Pius IX, had left Rome as the wave of revolution broke over the Jesuit residences in Italy. From the spring of 1848 until 1850, he made Marseilles his headquarters. From there he visited almost all the Jesuit houses in France and a very great number

60. Cardinal de Bonald, *Lettre pastorale,* March 2, 1848, and Louis Veuillot, *L'Univers,* February 27, 1848.

61. See Dansette, *Histoire religieuse,* I, 356.

in Holland, Belgium, England, and Ireland. Though it is almost incredible, his presence seems to have been unknown to the contemporary journals, which, given the state of opinion on the Jesuits, would hardly have lost the opportunity to publish such a piece of news.

As Roothaan prepared to leave France in 1850, the *"Loi Falloux"* was finally to make possible Jesuit colleges there. Through 1846 and 1847 the Comité pour la défense de la liberté had been able to gain no new legal ground in the school battle, despite the election of more than one hundred and forty of their deputy-candidates pledged to the suppression of the state monopoly. But the revolution changed everything, and article nine of the new Constitution of 1848 was clear and concise: "Teaching is freely exercised. Freedom of teaching takes place in accord with conditions of capability and morality set down by law and under the supervision of the state. This supervision extends to all educational establishments without exception." To the hopes raised by the constitution, Louis Napoleon, in search of Catholic electoral support, added yet others when he declared that to assure freedom of worship and freedom of teaching was to protect religion and the family. The Prince-President's new minister of education, Comte Falloux, made good his word.

That compromise was going to be necessary was obvious from the deeply held convictions of all parties in the educational battle and from the membership of the committee set up in 1849 to examine the conditions of a new law. Among the partisans of the Université were Thiers and Victor Cousin; on the opposite side were Montalembert and Felix Dupanloup, bishop of Orleans. The decisive factor in fashioning the new law, however, was the already existent change of will, if not of mind, in Thiers, which Dupanloup especially was able to bring around to the point of practical action. Without Thiers' support, any break in the state educational monopoly would have been impossible, but the events of 1848 had shaken his firm support of that monopoly. "With regard to liberty of teaching," Thiers wrote, "I have changed . . . not by a revolution in my convictions, but by a revolution in social conditions . . . The teaching of the clergy, which I have not liked at all for enough reasons, seems to me better than that which is being brewed for us. The Université, fallen into the hands of *phalanstériens,* aspires to teach our children a little mathematics, physics, and natural sciences, and plenty of demagogy. I see no salvation . . . except in freedom of teaching. I do not direct my hate nor the ardor of my resistance except toward where the enemy is today. That enemy is demagogy, and I will not hand over to it the last remnants of the social order, which is, today, the catholic establishment."[62]

Agreement came quickly on the fundamental working principle of the compromise and alliance between two rivals, Church and educational establishment. The Church would recognize the right of the state to supervise the primary and secondary schools to be developed by the Church; the state would accept the participation of the Church in the direction of public education. The specific details for primary education were quickly settled. Thiers was more than anxious to preserve from the "extremists" and the "agitators" the social classes that would attend such schools; in fact he would have turned over all primary education to the Church.

For secondary education, however, the agreement came with agonizing difficulty, and the stumbling block was again, above all, the Jesuits. The long exchanges in the commission meetings brought this out clearly.[63] Only with the greatest reluctance did Thiers finally agree that the Society of Jesus was also to be included when the Constitution declared, "Teaching is freely exercised."

62. Letter of Thiers to Madier de Montjau, May 2, 1848, in *L'Ami de la Religion,* June 18, 1848.
63. See especially H. de Lacombe, *Les débats de la Commission de 1849* (5th ed.; Paris, 1899). The earlier editions had inaccurately used the title "Procès-verbaux . . ."; the book actually was composed from the notes of Dupanloup.

The position of the Society, in turn, was made clear to its supporters, as the records of the consultors' meetings at Paris bear witness:

> . . . some of the [governmental] commission members wish to know the desires of the Society on the educational background and academic degree which would be required to start a college. Hence, what should we answer them?
>
> To all it seems that: (1) Neither preparation nor degree approved by [state] examination should be required, except perhaps of him who as Superior wishes to start a college; (2) This examination or bachelor's degree, for example, should not necessarily be sought from the Université, as was previously done, but from judges designated for this purpose in each department . . .
>
> As for inspection of colleges, it also seems that no other inspectors ought to be admitted than those mentioned above [i.e. not exclusively *universitaires*], who would visit at the same time the colleges of the Université in the same department.[64]

As in the extraparliamentary commission, so too in the Assembly, when the law was introduced, the opposition stuck especially on the admission of Jesuits to teaching rights, even though the committee of the Assembly, again headed by Thiers, reported favorably on the project. Outside the Assembly, during all the time of preliminary work the debate had raged no less passionately. Often Thiers' liberals were as outraged as Montalembert's Catholics to see the two of them coming to an agreement.

Among Catholics themselves, a deep split opened. If the Abbé Combalot was the most violent, with a letter in which he predicted to Dupanloup that "the law [would] leave on your memory a stain which torrents of tears will have difficulty in

---

64. PSJ, "Lib. Cons.," Jan. 8, 1849. The consultors of the province present at the meeting were Ravignan, Guidée, and Fournier, in addition to the Provincial, Rubillon.

removing,"[65] *L'Univers* was not far behind in ferocity; better no law at all, with some hope for the future, than this compromise that denied principles. *L'Ami de la Religion,* on the other hand, defended the law just as vigorously. From this time dated the bitter disagreements of Veuillot and Dupanloup.

The Jesuits, too, were in disagreement with each other. Certainly, not one of them was satisfied with the project, and even Ravignan, who was a good friend of Dupanloup and had worked with the Catholic members of the commissions to frame an acceptable law, expressed his reservations and convictions to them quite clearly. "But I criticized as a friend and certain friendly channels answered me with conviction that what [I] ask is impossible."[66]

Dissatisfaction, however, is a mild word to use for some of the reaction. Combalot maintained that most of his Jesuit friends were against the law,[67] and in regard to Ravignan he wrote that the sons of Voltaire could applaud at having for a helper a son of Loyola. Deschamps fiercely opposed the new legislation even after it had passed, especially the power of inspection that the state would have, supposedly contrary to the laws of God and the rights of the Church. This was the "deal with hell" that Christ spurned in the temptations in the desert.[68] It could only lead to indifferentism. It was anathema that the moral philosophy of Cousin, Michelet, and Guizot would be taught in Catholic schools, and that books harmful to the faith, such as Voltaire, the *Idylls* of Theocritus, and the philosophy of Reid and Fergusson, would be required. After publication of one of Deschamps' brochures, Roothaan was greatly displeased and asked Ravignan to express his regrets to Montalembert, Falloux, and others who had been attacked in it.[69]

Delvaux, rector at Brugelette in Belgium, thought as Des-

65. Théodore Combalot, *Lettre à Mgr. Dupanloup, évêque d'Orléans,* Bibliothèque Nationale, L^{d}4, 5206.
66. ARSJ, Franc., Ravignan to Roothaan, Sept. 11, 1849.
67. See Eugène Veuillot, *Louis Veuillot* (4 vols.; Paris, 1899–1913), II, 384.
68. ARSJ, Franc., Deschamps to Roothaan, Sept. 20, 1850.
69. ARSJ, Franc., Reg., Roothaan to Ravignan, Sept. 13, 1849.

champs did, and suggested as an explanation of some Jesuit support for the Falloux Law that "the fascination of Paris, so close to the socialist volcano and so close also to the summit of power, is doubtless . . . inevitable, because the most remarkable men of the Society do not escape it." He even thought that *L'Univers* did not go far enough; it had not yet dared to ask for the suppression of the state system as such.[70]

In the face of such recriminations against "a very great mistake which will be expiated by bitter regrets that come too late," Roothaan asked the advice of Rozaven, the French assistant, who summed up the moderate position: "Is the project good or bad? I answer: The project is not good, but it has good in it; it is less bad than what we have; it remedies some evil, and to remedy an evil is a good. It can be accepted and approved for the good which it includes. If we cannot obtain all that we ask and have a right to, is that a reason for refusing what is offered to us? The principle, *all or nothing*, can be applied in certain cases, but generally speaking, such an application does more harm than good."[71]

Finally the project came before the Assembly, and two months of debate ensued. When it treated of the Jesuits it was often just a dreary reprise of the debates of the 1820's and the 1840's. Victor Hugo with all the oratorical flourishes of which he was capable developed the theme that "Ignatius is the enemy of Jesus," and Arago, who as commissioner in Lyons had expelled the Society from its house there, was sure that the Jesuits were not and could not be true Frenchmen. Occasionally a light moment occurred, as when Thiers remarked: "I come now to the Jesuits," and from the left someone shouted, "That's already been done. You've already gone over to the Jesuits." Thiers replied, "Of course; I am a Jesuit," at which Montalembert broke in "Well then, I am not the only one of them in the Assembly."[72]

But the basic question with regard to the Society was, in a sense, not explicitly resolved. On the constitutional principle of liberty for every individual, Thiers defended ably and honestly, against the republican left especially, the right of the Jesuits to benefit from the new law. If an individual wished to teach, the law took no notice of what group, if any, he belonged to. Left unresolved by this maneuver was the whole question of "association" and the legal position, if any, of the Society. The law *implied* the Jesuits. Thus far the Assembly finally was willing to go, but it would go no further.[73] In 1880 the "implication" was swept aside by the Ferry decrees, and in 1901 the Law of Association completed the work against the congregations.

Apart from the implications for the Society of Jesus and for other unrecognized congregations, what did the law explicitly provide for? Any Frenchman 25 years of age or older with certain requirements of background training and personal character could open a school without previous authorization by the state. No "certificate of studies" attesting to the completion of a required course or to previous attendance at a state school was needed for presentation to a baccalaureate examination. The monopoly of the state system was destroyed. Private schools could be founded by individuals or groups; municipalities could determine the type of school they wanted; departments could help private schools financially. The state schools were transferred from the immediate authority of the Université or national educational establishment to the authority of departmental councils and to a superior council which contained

72. *Moniteur*, Jan. 18, 1850, quoted by Burnichon, *La Compagnie*, III, 362, 366–367.

73. It rejected decisively the "Bourzat amendment" of February 23, 1850, which proposed that "no one could maintain a school, public or not, primary or secondary, lay or ecclesiastic, nor be employed therein if he was part of a religious congregation not recognized by the State."

representatives not only of the central authority, but also of the clergy, the magistracy, and the locally elected officials. The state still maintained a right of inspection over all schools, and, most important, to it alone was still reserved the right to confer degrees.

The distinguished Greek scholar and *universitaire,* Barthélemy-Saint-Hilaire, started the long debate on the Falloux Law by spending five hours at a stretch in the tribune of the Assembly bewailing in it the triumph of religion over *laicité,* of faith over reason, of counterrevolution over the modern state, and Louis Veuillot put a period to it by writing bitterly: "No, this freedom which they pretend to give . . . is not freedom of teaching; it is not freedom of conscience; it is not freedom for the family; it is not freedom for the communes; it is not freedom for the Church; it is not freedom!"[74] But perhaps a more just judgment of the real situation, and of the difficulties which were faced at the enactment of the law was that "this [was] a compromise. Would a firm and bold call for freedom without restrictions be better? I do not dare decide. France is so little made for ideas of freedom such as exist in Belgium or New York, that perhaps there is need of a compromise. She shrinks at that giant's step which would so wonderfully advance her course."[75] That judgment was not unique to Adolphe Pillon, the Jesuit who made it. But in its pragmatic caution it was important, for in all of thirty years to come its author was, as a founder, a rector and a provincial superior, to be intimately involved in actually applying in the new Jesuit schools the Falloux Law passed by the Assembly on March 15, 1850.

74. Veuillot, *Veuillot,* II, 367.
75. R. P. Orhand, S.J., *Le Père Pillon et les Collèges de Brugelette, Vannes, Sainte-Geneviève, Versailles et Lille* (Lille, 1888), 96.

II

MINOR SEMINARIES
AND EXILE COLLEGES

The first educational experience of the renascent Society of Jesus in France took place in the minor or preparatory seminaries, and, after these schools were closed to the Jesuits, in the colleges-in-exile on the borders of France.

Two days after the accession of Louis XVIII a royal decree of April 8, 1814 recognized the right of fathers of families to choose the form and direction of the education of their children.[1] This was the first break in the state monopoly of education which Napoleon had created by the foundation of the imperial university in 1806 and by its further organization in 1808 and 1811.[2] Despite this one concession, however, and despite several internal, decentralizing changes, the monopoly was approved of and sustained by the Restoration governments.

1. *EJF*, III, 487.
2. In actual fact, even under Napoleon, many families had taken advantage of the minor seminaries created by the Concordat, and some of the authorities of the Université itself at least tacitly encouraged them.

But the minor seminaries did obtain a special position by request of the bishops and by a royal statute of October 5, 1814, which remained their charter until 1828. By its terms the bishops could establish in each civil department one ecclesiastical school for the education and instruction of young men destined to enter later the major seminaries, and they could also name its directors and teachers. If these schools were in a place where there was a lycée or communal college, their students had to wear ecclesiastical garb after two years. They were exempt from certain educational taxes, and were eligible for the state-administered baccalaureate examination and degree. Finally, no more than one minor seminary in each department could exist without special authorization. Four months later, the Restoration government added one last but very important stipulation: these were to be boarding schools only; no day student was to be admitted.[3] Under these conditions the Jesuits took up again in France the work of education from which they had been banished a half-century before. The minor seminaries, the exile colleges, and their programs, as described here in general, are the predecessors, the seeds, and the models of the colleges and of the programs to be discussed later at greater length.

The Society had hardly been restored when it was deluged with requests far beyond its means, and Clorivière, then and later, had to turn down one urgent appeal after another. Among the first to ask for Jesuits as directors and professors in their minor seminaries were the dioceses of Amiens, Bordeaux, and Poitiers, and these positions were accepted. Within three months of the restoration of the Society, it again took up direct educational work. The three minor seminaries of Saint-Acheul, Bordeaux, and Montmorillon opened in October and November 1814. In 1815 Sainte-Anne d'Auray opened in the diocese of Vannes, and in 1816 Forcalquier opened in the diocese of Digne. For five years the superiors in France and in Rome re-

<hr/>

3. Burnichon, *La Compagnie*, I, 226.

sisted other entreaties; there were simply no further men available; those already in the schools worked to the point of exhaustion. They often taught full time and studied philosophy or theology in addition. Worse yet, they were doing this as novices who, according to the prescriptions of the Jesuit constitution and rules, should have had two years of special training, time for prayer and reflection and study before there was even a thought of their taking on any external work at all. But in 1821 the Society accepted Aix-en-Provence, in 1823, Dôle, and in 1826, Billom, the last of their minor seminaries, in the city in which in 1558 the Jesuits had started their first college in France. There were also ephemeral foundations at Soissons in 1815 for both major and minor seminaries, and at Avignon in 1816.

For fourteen years these eight establishments absorbed the greater part of the attention and the men of the renascent Society. In 1828 of the 364 Jesuits of the French province, other than novices who by this time no longer went out into the schools, approximately 300 were directly employed in the minor seminaries.[4] There were several reasons for this concentration. First, the bishops pleaded repeatedly, troubled by the desperate lack of clergy in France after the generation of revolutionary upheavals and by the small prospect of vocations from the state schools.[5] Denis de Frayssinous, for a while Grand Master of the Université, expressed the sentiments clearly in 1817: "It is a fact of experience that from the thirty-six royal colleges [lycées], not a single student for the ecclesiastical state has come forth. It is a fact that the communal colleges furnish only a few of them. The conclusion is plain. If new hindrances are added to those of the Ordonnance of 1814, I say with the deepest sorrow and I shall prove with the utmost conviction: this is the end of the priesthood in France."[6]

4. Alexandre Vivier, S.J., *Catalogi Sociorum et Officiorum, 1819–1836* (Paris, 1894), *s.v.* 1828.
5. Eighty-seven seminaries alone were offered to the Jesuits in these early years.
6. Letter of Frayssinous to Eliçagaray (his successor on the Commission de

Second, the Superior General of the Jesuits wanted educational work to be again undertaken in accord with the traditions of the Society. The third reason for the concentration of Jesuits in education was that many lay Catholics were convinced, and in this the Jesuits joined them, that the royal colleges were not only utterly inimical to the altar and to the throne in general, but, of more immediate importance, to the intellectual and moral development of their own children. If France was to be saved as a Christian nation, and if children were not to be corrupted uttterly, they had to have a Christian education. Whether these sentiments corresponded to reality or not, they were vivid and unalterable, and they spurred on large groups to ask insistently for religious schools. Quicherat, in his history of Sainte-Barbe, says of the antigovernment spirit that "among . . . the royal colleges there were few that did not have their insurrection, and this was true throughout the whole length of the kingdom."[7] Thureau-Dangin, in turn, comments on "the spirit of impiety which reigned in the state schools, of which it is today difficult to form any idea . . . It was a hardened, corrupting atmosphere where under the twofold action of the example of the teachers . . . and of the tyranny of human respect among schoolboys, the student was almost assured of losing his faith and often also his purity."[8]

Then, too, there were memories. Archbishop d'Aviau of Bordeaux, for instance, when he successfully appealed for a seminary, recalled his Jesuit school days at La Flêche, and the notables of the department of the Jura asked that the great

l'Instruction Publique), October 16, 1817, as quoted in Burnichon, *La Compagnie*, I, 225n. See also Adrien Garnier, *Frayssinous* (Paris, 1925), especially chap. 14.

7. Jules Quicherat, *Histoire de Sainte-Barbe, collège, communauté, institution* (3 vols.; Paris, 1860–1864), III, 133.

8. Paul Thureau-Dangin, *Les libéraux et la liberté sous la Restauration* (2nd ed.; Paris, 1888), 232. See also A. Dansette, *Histoire religieuse de la France contemporaine* (Paris, 1948), I, 259–264, for further witnesses to the state of the schools and the society out of which they came, e.g. Veuillot, Flaubert, Chateaubriand ([The Université Imperiale] "teaches young Frenchmen debauchery and irreligion to the sound of the drum"), Gratry, Musset, Lacordaire, Lamennais.

Collège de l'Arc at Dôle be brought to life again. In a land where in almost every city of any size stood brick and stone reminders of two hundred years of the most completely developed educational system that the Jesuits had set up anywhere, the Society could hardly re-establish itself without dreaming, perhaps hoping, that such a system could flourish again.

Dreams or hopes did not, however, obscure the reality. Clorivière wrote to the Superior General in 1816: "Our boarding schools in France are in immediate dependence upon the bishops who entitle them officially "Minor Seminaries" and sometimes even give us the use of the buildings set aside for them by the Government. The houses which we have leased, as that of Amiens, have no legal existence except as seminaries and without this title we would be subject to the Université or be obliged to dissolve an establishment which did not wish to recognize it. So our colleges are quite precarious, since a bishop's successor can destroy what his predecessor has done, or the [present] bishop can himself change with regard to us."[9]

The bishops, on the other hand, were themselves realists, and as such were by no means likely to close these seminary-colleges. The word "seminary" was not simply a name; as seminaries, they fulfilled their functions very well. From Saint-Acheul, for example, every year thirty and sometimes up to fifty students entered the major seminary; from Sainte-Anne d'Auray came twenty or more. But above all they were colleges, and insofar as they received those not destined for the ecclesiastical state, they were, indeed, outside the strict letter of the law. In this they were like many other minor seminaries at the time, as everyone was well aware, including the government. The bishops only asked that a certain number of actual seminarians be taken care of gratuitously from part of the income accruing from the lay boarders. This often averaged out to approximately one fifth of the student body.

9. ARSJ, Franc., Reg., Clorivière to Brzozowski, Aug. 30, 1816, in *EJF*, I, 1481.

To legal instability was added that of finances. Ideally and according to the Institute of the Society (and in actual practice before the suppression), a college could be set up only when endowed with funds sufficient to provide for the buildings, the upkeep, and the living expenses of the teachers, so that thereafter instruction could be given freely. No benefactors were able and no cities were willing to establish such schools at the Restoration. The bishops had little or no money to give the Jesuits, and the buildings set aside officially for minor seminaries were usually in an appalling state of disrepair, as, at Sainte-Anne d'Auray, an almost empty house, or, as at Forcalquier, provided with "neither beds nor linen, nor furniture . . . in full winter."[10]

To get started the schools borrowed money and received some donations, both at times from the families of the Jesuits. For extraordinary expenses they contracted loans, sometimes from banks and sometimes again from the families of Jesuits or from former students. For running expenses they had to rely exclusively on current income. To a questionnaire from the government in 1828, the college at Bordeaux replied, "The establishment has no fixed revenue nor any contingent funds. The directors and assistants subsist only on the yield from the board and lodging fees."[11] These fees ranged from 450 francs per year at Sainte-Anne d'Auray to 525 francs at Montmorillon, and from 600 to 700 francs at Saint-Acheul, Bordeaux, and Aix, all quite considerable sums for the times.[12]

Although equally considerable reductions were often given and there were always students who paid nothing, these high fees could not help but restrict the already narrow base of recruitment among the convinced Christians who were usually, though not always, of the nobility or upper bourgeoisie. How-

10. *EJF*, II, 509.

11. L. Bertrand, *Histoire des Séminaires de Bordeaux et de Bazas* (Bordeaux, 1894), II, 282.

12. Burnichon, *La Compagnie*, I, 234.

ever, there seemed no other way to meet the problems posed by the state law forbidding simple day students and the Society's law forbidding direct tuition payment for the teaching itself.[13]

Despite the expenses, there was no lack of students. Sainte-Anne d'Auray, for instance, went from 60 in 1815 to more than 200 one year later; by 1824 there were 385. The enrollment in the other schools followed a similar pattern, except for Forcalquier, which lost students steadily because it was difficult to reach and yet too close to the school in Aix. The figures for 1824 are illustrative. Bordeaux had 318 students. Montmorillon, starting with 40 or 50, now had 305; Aix in only three years had gone from 200 to 360; Dôle, then one year old, had more than 250, and the next year there would be 400. Billom, founded when the horizon was already dark, would have in two years more than 300 students.

Of these eight schools, Saint-Acheul at Amiens was undoubtedly the most important. It started with 140 students; by 1824 it had more than 900, and not only did it never decline below this number, it had to turn away year by year more than 200 requests for admission. In prestige, in the opposition it aroused, and especially in its influence and in the documentation (still extant) of its life it had no rival.

Students came from many countries of Europe, and from all over France. The opposition in France clamored as strongly against it as against the novitiate at Montrouge: "Let us draw near and open those iron gates, bolted and reinforced, which

13. Bertrand, *Histoire des Séminaires de Bordeaux*, II, 282–284, gives the following figures from Bordeaux for Frayssinous' questionnaire: Only 120 students were paying the full pension of 600 francs, some 100 more seemed to be paying a considerable part. There were reductions of 26,000 francs for 80 students from "honorable and poor" families, an average of 325 francs apiece; 20 scholarship holders of the city and 11 others granted full exemption by the rector paid nothing at all personally. Only at Dôle and Billom, the two schools latest in foundation, were externs or day students allowed, and this by special permission of the Grand Master of the Université, sought by and given not to the Jesuits or to the bishop, but to the municipality itself, which asked to put its communal college at the disposition of the bishop.

keep us from entering these dismal regions. What are those cries which strike our ears? Is it some savage beast which is tearing apart a human victim and slaking its thirst in the blood? No! It is a man, a thousand times more cruel than tigers or leopards, who in a cold rage is torturing the hands of a helpless child of six years, a child whose limbs are already bloody from his furious blows."[14] Making due allowances for the romantic imagination, this is still rather incredible, and, more incredible yet, such productions were taken seriously.

Saint-Acheul was influential for more reasons than its numbers and the opposition it aroused. It was the first school of the restored Society in France; it existed indeed, even before that restoration. From it went rectors and prefects of studies to Aix, Montmorillon, Brugelette; many of the teachers for the later colleges first passed through this establishment. Finally, and most important, a plan of studies and the first set of rules for the educational work of the nineteenth-century French Jesuits were here first put into practice. All the minor seminaries used them, and the exile college of Brugelette adopted them as a starting point of its own work.

Both plan and rules were the work of Father Nicolas Loriquet. To him, too, is due the "Annales du Petit Séminaire de Saint-Acheul," a handwritten work of more than eight hundred pages detailing, at times day by day, the history of the house and school, and giving, task by task, the rules of procedure of every person and function in the establishment.[15] The regimen of each of the minor seminaries followed in great part that of Saint-Acheul, and so from the "Annales" we can gain an excellent idea of the internal life of these communities.

Peculiar to Saint-Acheul was its existence before the restoration of the Jesuits. In 1797 Louis Sellier, a layman who later became a Jesuit, founded a *pensionnat* at Amiens; in 1803 he

---

14. M. Hyacinthe, *Coup d'oeil dans l'intérieur de Saint-Acheul, ou de l'Education que donnent les Jésuites modernes à la jeunesse française* (Paris, 1826).
15. PSJ, 2220.

gave it to the Fathers of the Faith, among them the young Nicolas Loriquet. The creation of the Napoleonic Université made the existence of the *pensionnat* precarious, and it was finally suppressed in 1812. But with the fall of the empire, it rose again as the minor seminary of Saint-Acheul, staffed by its former masters, now Jesuits.

Loriquet's *Plan d'Etudes* was by no means something wholly new; he himself was explicit on this:

> Experience has too often made known that if it is some-times useful, it is more often pernicious to innovate, and that in education, as in everything else, nothing is more dangerous than to allow oneself to be dazzled by the ap-pearance of an imaginary perfection . . . There is nothing new, then, in this *Plan of Studies,* nothing which has not been advanced by the most famous man in the Republic of Letters and put into effect with success by those who have taken them for their guides. Fleury, Jouvency, Rollin, such are the men who are consulted and from whom are gathered our principles. It could even be said that in a good number of places one has done nothing but copy or abridge the immortal author of the *Treatise on Studies.*[16]

Surprisingly enough, the Jesuit *Ratio Studiorum* was not di-rectly used, though, of course, Jouvency's *Ratio Discendi et Docendi* was one of the great practical commentaries on it. Only some few years later did the old directives of the *Ratio* itself begin to be observed. In any case, there would have been little opportunity in these first hectic years to study or adopt it explicitly. Moreover, Loriquet's *Plan* was at hand, and he him-self was prefect of studies. The purpose of the school was quite clear. It was "to form the young men who dwell here in knowl-edge, in morals and in piety . . . not without order and method."[17]

16. PSJ, 2220, "Annales," Introduction.
17. *Ibid.,* 671.

The full course of studies lasted ten years, and so the youngest students would have been about 7 or 8 years old. This was a notable difference from the presuppression schools, brought about in part by the exigencies of the minor seminary system itself and in part by the royal ordinance of October 5, 1814, by which the minor seminaries were "to instruct from childhood the young men who might be able to enter [later] the major seminaries."[18]

The minimum entrance requirement was the ability to read and to write. The formal subjects taught were Latin, Greek and French grammar and literature, rhetoric, philosophy, history, geography, mathematics, "gentlemanly accomplishments" *(les arts d'agrément)*—drawing, fencing, music—and finally, and most important, religion. Religion was not only a subject taught but a spirit pervading the school; Latin was at the base of all the learning; rhetoric was the point at which all the studies converged, the end to be attained. Rhetoric implied not simply facility in speaking. Rather, in the classical tradition, it was to be the "art of convincing, of touching, of persuading, not only in public but also in private affairs, in a deliberation, in a discussion or business affair, in a simple letter, and even in a conversation," by the development and use of all one's imaginative and intellectual talents.[19] So strong, indeed, was that classical tradition that the precepts of rhetoric seem to have been taught not in French but in Latin.[20]

"Not without order and method," Loriquet had said, and on this he was explicit. He carefully divided the courses and subjects. He explained the method of teaching each subject. He set down the books peculiar to each stage. The constraint involved in this, so evident at first sight, was perhaps not unwarranted in the context of the utter disorder of so much of the French school system caused by the upheavals of a genera-

18. *Ibid.,* 95.
19. *Ibid.,* 815.
20. This problem of the vehicle of teaching, French or Latin, later became the subject of vigorous dispute, and it will be treated again in a subsequent chapter.

tion. The inexperienced Jesuit teachers, too, found it immensely helpful. Sent in large numbers into the schools without any specific preparation and out of touch with the old educational traditions of the Society, they greatly needed such a guide. Loriquet was also convinced that a student learned only when he learned by heart, rigorously by heart, and the teacher's task was to bring this about relentlessly. He should demand only a little at a time, but that little was to be done thoroughly.

The language classes, which started with the eighth form and continued up to the second, year by year, were concerned with two things. They incessantly inculcated the rules of grammar, and they tried to bring about the concomitant abilities to speak and write correctly and to appreciate literature as literature. By all accounts, the former was the easier. The place given to history and geography was unusual. Though it has been shown conclusively that these subjects were taught and extensively taught in the old Society, they had not entered into the *Ratio* explicitly, as they did with Loriquet's *Plan*.[21] He especially wanted "to give to history, previously too generally neglected, the rank which its importance seems to assign to it."[22] Of course, history was his chosen *métier* above all; he wrote some of the first elementary manuals of history for French schools, and so popular were they that even the state system used them for a time.[23] There was little or no trouble with his books on Latin and Greek history or on "sacred history," but his *Histoire de France*, fiercely antirevolutionary and anti-Napoleonic, though no more so than most Restoration writings, became famous in anti-Jesuit and anticlerical polemics all the way into the twentieth century.[24]

21. See, for example, François de Dainville, S.J., "L'Enseignement de l'histoire et de la géographie et le *Ratio Studiorum*," *Analecta Gregoriana*, 70 (1954), 123–156.

22. PSJ, 2220, "Annales," 819.

23. See Charles Sommervogel, S.J., and Augustin Backer, S.J., *Bibliothèque des écrivains de la Compagnie de Jésus* (Liège et Paris, 1869), II, cols. 809–817.

24. See Pierre Bliard, *Le Père Loriquet: La Légende et l'Histoire* (Paris, 1922), especially chap. 3 for a treatment of this point.

Besides the ordinary elementary arithmetic, a good course in higher mathematics found its place along with physics in a special second year of the "philosophy" course.[25] "Philosophy" in its first year treated especially logic, metaphysics, and ethics. It was taught, without any possible questioning of the fact, in Latin, the same language still used in the state schools. The approach seems to have been rigidly deductive, but the end supposedly to be attained by these purely rational means went far beyond them; all these subjects were to proceed "from consequence to consequence, from the first principle of reasoning and from certitude, all the way to the Christian religion, all the way to the Catholic Church, and [they were] properly to convince them [the students] that it is not possible to reason consistently without arriving at this last term of all the investigations of a man of good will."[26] Voltaire and the rationalist, along with Rousseau and the voluntarist, for this is the way they were conceived, were thus to be combatted in the philosophy course. In the light of such a radically rationalistic course, the charms of fideism or traditionalism as described in the previous chapter are not too difficult to understand.

Finally, at the periphery of the studies were the "gentlemanly accomplishments." In theory they were merely tolerated, mainly because they would be useful for the young man in later society. Drawing, fencing, and music were taught, but only in times of recreation; and music offered so many dangers that it might be better not even to have it on the program, and certainly "no soft, effeminate, or ardently emotional airs at all."[27]

There was nothing soft about the daily schedule of the school. Up at 5:00 A.M. (5:30 in winter), the students had an hour and a half of study before attending seven o'clock Mass,

25. When Loriquet arrived at Saint-Acheul, he immediately changed the classes from the old ways of reckoning and counting which were still being taught, saying that whatever the political future of France, the decimal system would stay! Burnichon, *La Compagnie*, I, 253.

26. PSJ, 2220, "Annales," 817.

27. Burnichon, *La Compagnie*, I, 254.

followed by breakfast at 7:30 and recreation until 8, when the morning class of two and one half hours began. After fifteen minutes of recreation, the rest of the morning was taken up with study until dinner at noon, followed by recreation, and then the rosary and study at 1:30. In the afternoon there was another class of the same length, a half-hour of recreation, ten minutes' reading of a religious book, study until 7:20, supper at 7:30, and at 8:15 night prayers and bed. On Wednesday and Saturday came a half-day free, time for long promenades and for games, which were much encouraged and invented with great ingenuity.[28]

Rivalry existed not only on the playing field. The *Plan d'Etudes* was faithful to the old *Ratio* in encouraging emulation among the students as a stimulus to work. Compositions, public examinations, contests in class, prizes, rank listings, and "academies" all came into play in ways to be described in further detail in connection with the later colleges.[29]

The surroundings in which the students lived were austere. All of the minor seminaries had to make do with inadequate quarters at the beginning, and the growth in the number of students always raced far ahead of the actual accommodations and the money available to build new ones. Even Saint-Acheul, certainly the most prosperous of the lot, crowded itself into the nooks and crannies of an ancient abbey, an equally old auxiliary building, a new three-story structure put up in three months in 1818 as a study hall and dormitory, and two houses near the main property. One of the study halls was the ancient stable on the farm next to the abbey. Into this conglomeration were jammed close to nine hundred boarding students, almost sixty

28. PSJ, 2220, "Annales," 672–673.
29. But a most unusual incitement should surely be mentioned here: One teacher of an elementary class at Saint-Acheul offered a pinch of snuff at the end of each day to the best student of the day. He who was first at the end of the week could not only regale himself, but could also offer, from the professor's snuff box, a pinch to his classmates who had good grades. The teacher was said to have obtained prodigies of effort!

Jesuits and probably as many lay domestic helpers. The other schools were proportionately less well off.

In any such situation, order and discipline would be a problem, and the problem was met here by an extremely strict surveillance.[30] A definite rigor of manner and outlook in these first Jesuits made it even stricter. Most of them, former Fathers of the Faith, had been accustomed to a very hard life during the previous years of upheaval, and they were determined that modern Christian youth was not going to turn soft in their hands. "Never are the students left to themselves; the vigilance of the masters extends to every place and to every instant of the day and night," affirmed the prospectus of the school. The teachers undertook some of this surveillance, but, usually under the direction of a single prefect of discipline, the Jesuit scholastics or seminarians who were at the same time pursuing their own studies of literature or philosophy or theology performed this office too. Diocesan seminarians assisted at times. In 1824 at Saint-Acheul, there were ten scholastics and fifteen "auxiliaries" as surveillants. Immaturity and inexperience obviously often showed up in such cases. Students, too, were sometimes appointed as a type of proctor and sub-subprefect for a month at a time, and although some apologists defended the practice as a type of student self-regulation, it was too easily open to the practice of students informing on each other.

Infractions of the rule led to a series of disciplinary measures; it was almost a penal code. Among the measures were confinement to one spot for a period of time, a special room where the law-breakers did extra school work, public reprimands, dining on one's knees, deprivation of the semiweekly promenades, "afflictive manual corrections," official warnings of great and imminent danger, "exile to the farm" (almost always a sign of

30. For instance the "Annales" mention an item that might not immediately be evident, but which was very real in a place so crowded and with such relatively meager facilities: "It was almost impossible to keep the children clean enough" (PSJ, 2220, "Annales," 702).

abandoned hope for a black sheep), and finally expulsion. "Of all faults," the prefects were told, "let them regard as least pardonable those which even from afar would touch on religion, or morals, or on obedience."[31] Such faults, and other misdemeanors too, brought decisive correctives.

But to be fair, we should also note that the main reliance of the prefects was constantly supposed to be placed on other means of discipline. It was stressed over and over that the weekly "conduct notes" were to be the regular indication of satisfaction or dissatisfaction at the student's demeanor, and that the really competent teacher or prefect should need no other control than simple praise or blame. Despite all the rules, the prefects of conduct were not supposed to be policemen (though, of course, too often they were). Rather, they were to show "kindness and firmness . . . a recognized impartiality," and they were failing if they did not gain "the confidence, the affection and the respect of the students." Finally, they were "not to forget that their vigilance and their labors were of no value if God did not bless them, and so they will not neglect to pray frequently and fervently for the students confided to their care."[32]

While teaching or instruction *(enseignement)* was one of the functions of the schools, training *(éducation)* was even more important, and all the surveillance was part of that training. Religion was supposed to be its greater and more influential part. It was taught, of course, as an academic subject beginning with the simplest catechism in the lowest classes and going on to a course in apologetics in the highest. But it was far more than a subject of study. It was part of the texture of the schools, and was meant to be their very soul and animating spirit.

A spiritual retreat, which was a time of conferences, meditations, and prayer, opened the school year for all the students; another special retreat for those finishing their studies closed the year. The daily Mass, spiritual reading, and prayers have

31. *Ibid.,* p. 870, Rule 16 for Prefects.
32. *Ibid.,* Rules 22 and 23 for Prefects.

already been mentioned. Opportunities for the sacrament of confession were provided every day and it was obligatory once a month. Many of the students received Communion once a month and some few oftener, a very rare occurrence in a France still tinged with the Jansenism of Arnauld's *Frequent Communion*. Each school had one or more "spiritual fathers" or directors available whenever the students wanted to consult them, and the *Rule* urged on every Jesuit a concern for the student's spiritual state.

The means most favored for furthering religious spirit and practice was always the Congregation of the Blessed Virgin, a relatively small and elite group of students, admitted to the organization only after probation.[33] They met once a week, were given further religious orientation and training and a more personal direction for their own religious lives. By rule the members promised to spend a period of time in meditation and prayer and in an examination of conscience every day. The Congregation asked a more committed Christian life of them. They were not only to set a good example themselves but also to set the tone of the school. They were to lead the way in the few external works of charity that a school boy could engage in, especially in help for the poor and the sick of the area.

Many of the external forms of piety and the devotional prayers in vogue would strike the observer now as sentimental or overblown, and some surely were so even for their own period. The grand processions, such as that for Fête-Dieu especially, while being a true gesture of religious homage, tended in addition almost to resemble military maneuvers, with several hundred of the students engaging in a variety of marching formations. Hardly anything illustrates the deep military bent of the early nineteenth-century Jesuits better than the elaborate plans and directives for those processions.[34]

33. See Charles Clair, S.J., *La Congrégation de la Très Sainte Vierge à St. Acheul, 1815–1828* (Paris, 1897).
34. PSJ, 2220, "Annales," 783. There are, for example, five pages of detailed

Not everything ran as smoothly, however, as might be implied from the close attention paid to every moment of the students' lives and from the seriously religious emphasis of the house. Loriquet said that the "Annales" would recount both the good and the bad, and if there was such innocence that "there were several here who at the age of eighteen did not yet have any idea of the difference of the two sexes," there were also such, he avers, as the nine-year-old corrupter who "tried to pervert others" and "gave marks of a perversity as profound as it was precocious."[35] All the schoolboy pranks occurred too, from midnight feasts in the bell tower with more than ample cakes and wine, "with deplorable results for the digestive system," to dummies in the bed with the students, to the shock and horror of the discovering prefect.

More serious were the problems of "particular friendships." "Rivalries, jealousy, affectionate notes, secret meetings, presents, and tokens of attachment" were the mode, and some would come "to meditation in the morning solely to encounter there the objects of their affection. They could be seen misusing the most sacred emblems to express their mad and foolish passion, drawing hearts wounded or in flames, which they would send to those who had put them into this state."[36] With *affairs de moeurs* the schools were ruthless; perhaps, indeed, they even saw them where they were nonexistent. Expulsion was supposed

plans for this procession, with march formations, command signals, and thirty-six different symbols for the participant groups outlined extensively. It was indeed a grand spectacle for all the surrounding area, a procession, a parade, and a review all in one.

35. *Ibid.*, 175–176, 529–530. In one case, a student asked a professor what distinguished men from women. The professor thought the matter grave enough to ask the Father Rector what to do, who in turn asked the Father Provincial. The answer came back down the line to tell him the truth in a "secret, solemn, and serious interview." Loriquet then has remarkably sane advice on being exact, open, and frank, and hard words for the ridiculous parental accounts often heard. But all this he puts in writing, he says, only because this "work was not destined for printing."

36. *Ibid.*, 471. The wounded or enflamed heart was, of course, the symbol used for the devotion to the Sacred Heart of Jesus, especially popular in nineteenth-century France.

to be the last sanction for these and other serious faults, but it was readily enough used. At Aix, in 1821, there were twenty-five within a few months; in 1824, Delvaux, another new rector at Aix, started his tenure of office with forty dismissals. And "there were hardly any years when Saint-Acheul did not see expelled twenty or thirty students, who were most assuredly not treated thus for peccadillos."[37]

Despite all the internal problems, despite the lack of personnel, despite the hasty or nonexistent pedagogic training of the teachers, despite what now seems an excessive rigidity, the eight schools were immensely popular. It was the family spirit which reigned there and the religious and moral training given there which made them so. Letters of parents and recollections of former students are too many and too insistent to doubt this. They stress it over and over, a spirit that the word "patriarchal" describes, with all that it implies of severity and affection at the same time.[38]

This training was not always successful, during or after the school years. Father Gury, the stern annalist of Montrouge, wrote to the Superior General in 1828 that "of more than two hundred young men graduated from Saint-Acheul and now in Paris, there are hardly twenty or thirty who have held out against the seduction of disbelief and dissoluteness."[39] Though the figures may be exaggerated, it is true that these later lapses were a grave and regular problem for the schools. The problem was more acute in Paris than elsewhere. There were few external supports there for the young men of sixteen to eighteen who left the overprotected atmosphere of the schools to live in the high Restoration society which, for all its external religiousness, was still often deeply skeptical and equally immoral.

But for all that the minor seminaries were on balance a

37. *Ibid.*, 3.

38. See for example, Jean-François Bellemare, *Le Collège de mon fils* (Paris, 1827), for one such testimony.

39. ARSJ, Franc., Gury to Fortis, Dec. 18, 1828.

success for the Jesuits of the time. They actually educated only a fraction of the French students in private schools. But of that fraction, among 3,000 students educated at Saint-Acheul alone in fourteen years, came 70 Jesuits, 550 priests, and 8 bishops. These figures indicate that the seminary aspect of the schools was well in evidence.

Other influences are less easy to measure, but for the Society, certainly, these foundations provided a link, makeshift though it was at times, between the presuppression educational establishments, almost fading from living man's experience, and the schools to be established in 1850. This is evident not only in the Jesuits to whom they gave an apprenticeship, but also in the laymen who, from all sides, asked for Jesuit schools after the passage of the Falloux Laws. Over and over, it was a group of former students of these minor seminaries, willing to make any sacrifice, who begged for such a school for their own sons. In the period between 1828 and 1850, many such former students were among those who turned much of the French nobility back to a Catholicism that was sincere even though too closely linked with a class and too tightly tied to a political form.

Charles X signed the Ordonnances on June 16, 1828. Godinot, the provincial, wrote to the superiors that for the closing of the school year in August they were "to proceed to the distribution of prizes without any noisy display and without speeches tending to make allusions or to arouse regrets."[40] Of course, there were strong feelings anyway, and speeches were not needed. The last acts of these schools were a testimony of how closely they linked throne and altar, and how deeply they felt about the king. They were more eloquent even than the enthusiastic ceremonial visits in these years of the Duke or Duchess of Angoulême and the Duchess of Berry to Saint-Acheul and Bordeaux and Sainte-Anne d'Auray. At Saint-Acheul in 1828, for example, the students, who used to hang in the chapel

40. *EJF*, III, 492.

the crowns they received for achievement, decided, now that the Jesuits were to be banished, to give them to the Duc de Bordeaux as "signs of the love which all the youth of Saint-Acheul have vowed to him."[41] At Aix they arranged to have carved on a statute of the Virgin Mary: "Lily of our kings, lily of Mary, together grow in our hearts; / You both have been nurtured there by the Fathers whom we mourn."[42] Finally, at Sainte-Anne d'Auray, the arch through which the Duchess of Berry had passed at her visit there (after Charles X had signed the Ordonnances) bore the legend: "Long live the King: All the Same."[43]

No sooner had the doors closed on the Jesuit minor seminaries in France than parents requested that the Society in some way provide religious schools for their children. As one father wrote to Sainte-Anne d'Auray: "Send my son to a college of the Université—never will they get that from me. I would rather that he be ignorant than irreligious."[44] In August 1828 the provincial and consultors agreed on the principle of schools abroad.[45]

The first but unsuccessful negotiations for "exile colleges" looked to the isle of Jersey and to Chambéry in Savoy. Finally the Spanish government gave permission for a college at Le Passage, a town near San Sebastian, only a few kilometers from the French frontier. In November 1828 it opened with about one hundred students and the faculty of the former minor seminary at Montmorillon near Bordeaux. For six years the school led a crisis-plagued existence, troubled by repercussions of the 1830 revolution in France, by poverty, by inadequate

41. PSJ, 2220, "Annales," 651.
42. *EJF*, I, 92. "Regia pectoribus Marianaque lilia nostris,/Crescite: quos flemus vos coluere Patres."
43. *Ibid.*, I, 400. "Vive le Roi: Quand Même."
44. *EJF*, II, 1104.
45. PSJ, "Liber Consultationum," Aug. 4, 1828. Hereafter, "Lib. Cons."

accommodations, and finally by the Isabellist-Carlist civil strife in Spain. When the Isabellists finally triumphed, the liberal government closed the school in 1834 and expelled the Jesuits from Spain.

Meanwhile other French families sent their sons to the Jesuit colleges at Mélan and Chambéry in Savoy, and at Brigue, Sion, and Fribourg in Switzerland, where members of the French province were also sent to teach. Of these schools Chambéry and Fribourg were the most important.

The Savoyard Jesuits had started the Collège Royal at Chambéry in 1823 with the sustained encouragement and influence of Joseph de Maistre.[46] The original French intent in 1828 of a separate French college there met government disfavor. However, the number of French boarding students at the Collège Royal increased regularly, and stopped at two hundred only because there was no room for more. By 1837 there were nineteen French Jesuits on the teaching staff. The college enjoyed its golden age, in association more or less close with the state schools of law, medicine, and art at Chambéry from 1830 to 1848, only to be suppressed in the latter year in the aftermath of the revolutionary upheavals.

Even more flourishing than Chambéry was Fribourg. Here, too, a Jesuit college had existed from 1580 until 1773, and even after the suppression the cantonal government obtained permission for the former Jesuits to continue to teach. They did so until the revolutionary armies arrived in 1798. In 1818 the

---

46. De Maistre had been a student at the Jesuit college at Chambéry before the suppression, supported the Jesuits in Russia at their college in St. Petersburg, and strongly urged the new foundation at Chambéry. Later, four of his great grandsons were to become Jesuits. Also involved in the establishment of Chambéry was Fr. Luigi Taparelli, brother of two leading figures of the Risorgimento, Roberto and Massimo (Taparelli) d'Azeglio. He was later also one of the founding editors of *La Civiltà Cattolica*. Finally, Charles Felix, the king who had given permission for the college, was successor to his brother Charles Emmanuel, king from 1796 to 1802, who entered the Jesuit novitiate in 1815 and died as a member of the Society four years later.

German-Swiss province of the restored Society came back to conduct the state college of Saint Michel.[47] In 1827 the Jesuits opened a *pensionnat* for the students from afar, then numbering about thirty. One year later, in the wake of the Ordonnances there were approximately 400 boarding students, and a grand purge in 1829 of more than 150 of the less desirable among them only left room for more applicants. Within the next twenty years the boarding division received more than 1,900 students, 1,200 of them from France, 200 from Switzerland, almost 200 from Germany, and the rest from most of the countries of Europe, from the New World, and even from Turkey and Africa. When the nuncio came to visit in 1846, thirteen students greeted him in thirteen different languages.

The school belonged to the German province, but the 1828 Ordonnances brought large numbers of French Jesuit teachers as well as French students.[48] Eighty-seven of the one hundred and eighty priests and scholastics at Fribourg after 1828 were French, and much of the renown of the *pensionnat* was due to Father Joseph Barrelle, formerly teacher and prefect at Bordeaux and Billom, then preacher in Portugal, and finally director at Fribourg almost continuously from 1833 to 1841. He was to be also the first rector of the new college at Avignon, founded even before the passage of the Falloux Law.

For such an international community German or French were the languages of instruction up to the class of rhetoric. From then on, Latin alone held sway for all subjects—philos-

47. Besides the various Jesuit archives, there exist also a two-volume work, part history and part compilation of miscellaneous documents, *Les Jésuites du Collège St. Marie à Fribourg en Suisse* (Lausanne, 1834), and in the cantonal library of Fribourg a manuscript, "Historia Collegii Friburgensis." The accounts in *EJF* and in Burnichon draw upon these sources. The alumni were extremely faithful in after years to the memories and to the teachers of Fribourg. In *Le Livre d'Or des Elèves du Pensionnat de Fribourg en Suisse* (Paris, 1889, with supplements to 1896), one will find abundant details of the life there.

48. This material on the teaching and courses will be found also in *Documenta Germaniae Pedagogica*, XVI.

ophy, mathematics, science, law, agronomy (curiously), and theology for those preparing for the priesthood.

In the minor seminaries, and at Brugelette, the *arts d'agré-ment* and the theater had a difficult time making their way. At Fribourg, perhaps because of the more cosmopolitan makeup of the school, they flourished joyously. For the students, and for the bourgeoisie of Fribourg, the school orchestra, the band, and the theater frequently presented elaborate programs. Most unusual of all, but perhaps necessary because so many of the boarding students stayed the whole year through, were the vacation trips, when groups of twelve to eighteen students, accompanied by two Jesuits, spent six weeks to two months hiking in all directions from Switzerland, in Austria, Italy, and the Rhineland.

International in student body and faculty, the college gave rise to doubts about the patriotism of the students to Switzerland or France. "The cosmopolitanism implanted at the *pensionnat* and certain organizations foreign to our custom and to our republican politics have destroyed in a part of our youth the love of fatherland and of Helvetic institutions," complained a Swiss liberal. Thiers spoke for the French counterparts: "There are at Brugelette and at Fribourg—I cite these colleges because I know what is being taught there—there are evil establishments, dangerous for every citizen who must live under the laws of France. That the Swiss or the Belgians should send their children to Brugelette or Fribourg, where they are taught contempt for our laws and our government, that I can grant; but I say that good Frenchmen are not produced there."[49] Most of the French students did not have to be taught to scorn the government of Louis Philippe. They were scornful when they came, because they were in great part sons of

49. A. Daguet, *Quelques idées pour la réorganization de l'instruction publique dans le canton de Fribourg,* as quoted in *EJF,* II, 625; and *Moniteur,* Chambre des Députés, January 29, 1846, as quoted in Burnichon, *La Compagnie,* II, 56.

legitimist families, and in many instances, members of the old nobility itself.

This background of the boarding students, who had to be of families who were, at the very least, relatively well-off, produced its own problems in relation to the day students.[50] Most of these came from less affluent Fribourg homes, able to attend the school only because there was no charge by the Jesuits for the instruction itself. The very nature of a boarding division emphasized the distinctions too. The Jesuits came to know the boarders much more intimately, not only simply by living with them, but because the estrangement of the students from their homes and families stimulated the teachers and *surveillants* to try to create as much of a family atmosphere as possible. For the day students, however, there were only the briefer contacts of class, made briefer yet by the surcharge of activities on all the personnel. The school produced no effective adaptation to this situation. In another area, also, there was failure even to begin adaptation to emerging realities. It was in the insistence on an education strictly classical in every sense, and the refusal of the citizens' requests to open "an industrial and commercial section."[51] Perhaps the 1840's in Switzerland were too early for such moves, but the problem would occur again later.

For the future schools in France, this type of mixed establishment might have provided a hopeful model. But in France the Society, even if it had had the manpower, was not going to find municipalities prepared to finance such schools on a large scale. Nor would they find the climate of relative tolerance which would have allowed the Jesuits to be, as they had been, the schoolmasters of a city. In Switzerland itself, tolerance came to

50. "The sons of shipowners, of merchants, of French noblemen met there, the nobility of Germany, the greatest names of France and Polish lords. There were dukes, princes, English lords and 'Serene Highnesses,' youthful natures a little proud, a little independent, and accustomed to comfort and ease" (Leon de Chazournes, *Vie du R.P. Joseph Barrelle, S.J.* [Paris, 1858], I, 284). The author himself was an alumnus of Fribourg.

51. *EJF*, II, 628.

an end when the federal troops in the War of the Sonderbund took Fribourg. They pillaged the student residence, sacked the property, closed the *pensionnat* and expelled the Jesuits from the country.[52]

Fribourg in Switzerland was a partly French school; Brugelette in Belgium was overwhelmingly so. Before the revolution in 1830 which brought Belgian independence, there had been little prospect of starting a Jesuit school in the territories of William I of Holland, but soon after independence a decree inaugurated in the new nation the liberty of teaching that the French had been demanding unsuccessfully in their own land. The Belgian Jesuits opened their own schools. In the following years requests came from France, especially from the north, "on the part of several notable persons . . . that an educational establishment for French children be set up at Tournai or in the vicinity by our French fathers."[53] The French Jesuits themselves greatly desired such a school; with their banishment from the seminaries, the number of new vocations to the Society had been falling alarmingly.[54] Soon there was another reason—the expulsion from Le Passage. Meanwhile, both the Jesuits and their friends in France and Belgium had looked at several sites and conducted preliminary negotiations, until finally in the autumn of 1834 they found a suitable place, the centuries-old convent of Wisbecq, in the commune of Brugelette between Ath and Mons.

There were so many difficulties that the new foundation almost failed to get started. Some feared the dangerous situation it might create in Belgian relations with France. A consultors' meeting in February 1835 dealt with the inexact information

52. Even at this date, 1968, the Swiss constitution still contains a clause, imposed by the victors, forbidding the establishment of the Society of Jesus in Switzerland. Individual Jesuits live and work there, and do so with knowledge of the government, but attempts to remove the legal restrictions still meet with opposition.

53. ARSJ, Franc., Reg., Roothaan to Renault, May 13, 1834.

54. Nineteen alumni of Brugelette eventually became diocesan priests and forty-seven became religious, mostly Jesuits.

that the General had received, with the needed (and soon warmly given) approbation of the Bishop of Tournai, and with the Belgian Jesuits' worries about competition from the French.[55] Roothaan had specified some of the conditions of discretion for the new house: the French were to consult their Belgian confreres; they were to be slow about doing any building; no Belgian students were to be admitted as far as possible; inside and outside there was to be complete abstention from politics; and finally, the French Jesuits were to undertake apostolic work in Belgium outside the college only at the invitation of the Belgian provincial.[56] Roothaan was prescient; all these points were to occasion discussion and controversy in the years ahead.

The school was careful not to trumpet its existence, and so it took a week, from October 21 to 28, 1835, for the first students, fifty of them, gradually to arrive. After that there was only a problem of too great numbers. A year later there were 150, and a hundred more in 1838. By the earlier 1840's there were more than 300 students, and the total stopped here because, again, there was no room for more.[57] Most of them were French, but a large number arrived from other lands after the closing of Fribourg, and the problem of Belgian applicants, attracted by the allure of a truly French school, was continual. The rector, Delvaux, thought at one time that he would solve it and the building problem together. He demanded that the parents of any Belgian student become shareholders in the civil society set up to acquire construction funds.[58] The applicants and the money still came.

55. PSJ, "Lib. Cons.," Feb. 21, 1835.
56. ARSJ, Franc., Reg., Roothaan to Renault, Feb. 7, 1835.
57. PSJ, Brug. 12: 2248, Diarum, Oct. 21 and 28, 1835. Regularly there were a few students from England. One of them, from 1846 to 1848, was Herbert Vaughan, future Cardinal Archbishop of Westminster. He was known to his French-speaking companions as "Milord Rosbif." See *Lettres de Jersey*, 46 (1936), 143.
58. PSJ, Registre, Guidée to Roothaan, Jan. 2, 1839. Buildings were truly needed, but Delvaux had a passion for putting them up which Superiors

The few day students found themselves treated almost as boarders. By the rule they were to spend even Sundays at the school from 8:oo to 11:oo A.M., 12:oo to 3:oo, and 4:oo to 5:oo P.M. They were "not to associate with any comrade except the students of the college." They were to go home by the shortest route, not to stop to look at shops nor to play in the streets, not to smoke in the town or even in the country, "not to enter any cafe, cabaret, inn, theater, public spectacle, barrack, circus . . . nor ill-famed bookstore—that is where there are any and all kinds of books."[59]

It was evident what lay behind the spirit of the new college:

> The college of Brugelette proposes as its end to revive again the establishments which have ceased to exist in France since 1828, and which a large number of Christian families had honored with their confidence.
>
> Since Religion is the basis of education, this establishment will attempt to give to the students a solid knowledge of the dogma which it teaches, and to form them to a love and a practice of the duties which it imposes. In order to turn children from vice and bring them to virtue, we shall employ by preference the methods of kindness and competition. The vigilance of the masters extends to all places and to all times; it is less by punishment of faults than by prevention of them that one establishes in this house order and regularity.[60]

What the families wanted of the college was equally clear. In the words of Pillon, the prefect and later the rector, "On every

---

regularly had to watch over. Two brief remarks: "No, a thousand times no, I do not want you to build" (PSJ, Reg., Guidée to Delvaux, Aug. 9, 1839). When he was rector again: "Could it be true that Father Delvaux has bought a million bricks? If it is a fact, it could only be the effect of a complete delusion; the prohibition to build implies the prohibition to buy the material" (PSJ, Roothaan, Roothaan to Studer, May 20, 1852).

59. PSJ, Brug. 4, "Instructions Spéciales."
60. PSJ, Brug. 3:2253, Coutumier, "Prospectus," 63.

page of the correspondence with your devoted parents, in private conversations with them . . . I find again and again these words of faith: 'Father, above all, make of my son a good Christian.' "[61]

The educational methods of Brugelette were essentially those of Saint-Acheul. Exactly the same religious practices were developed and held in honor and the Congrégation was the principal organization in the school. A retreat began the year and, for those graduating, closed it too. The freedom of Belgium allowed pilgrimages to ancient shrines in the neighborhood, and they took place with great solemnity. Finally, a less crowded school and a larger faculty made personal direction and counseling more possible. Discipline was still expected to be strict and prompt. One of the early pupils, later the most successful director of the Jesuit school preparatory for Saint-Cyr, remarked on his arrival how struck he was "at the very first sound of the bell, to hear one hundred chattering voices stop, as if all of those who had been speaking had had their throats cut. It seems to me . . . on reflection that this, more than any explanation, gave me a very strong idea of the rules and of the authority which made them observed."[62] There were still expulsions, swift and irrevocable, especially for "offences against morals," but apparently no need for as many as had occurred in the minor seminaries.[63]

All the indications are that the life was somewhat less rigorous than in the minor seminaries, and a truly great holiday would test all the endurance of any twentieth-century schoolboy. One of the great benefactors of the college, Baron de Secus, from the first opened his grounds to the students for their weekly break in routine, for picnics and games, hunting and fishing. Later he donated to the college for the same purpose

61. Orhand, *Pillon*, 72.
62. Stanislas du Lac, S.J., *Jésuites* (Paris, 1901), p. xxiii.
63. For instance PSJ, Brug. 12:2248, Diarium, Feb. 7, 1841; five students were expelled on this particular occasion.

one of his properties, where the students enjoyed canoeing, billiards, and a big old stable that had been turned into recreation space. This site was inaugurated in June 1846 with a marathon holiday. The day-long picnic began with a 4:30 A.M. rising hour, warmed up with swimming before breakfast, continued with a parade with band music to the new grounds, paused for the erection of a statue and a long and fitting discourse by the then Abbé Dupanloup, and after that careened on madly through the day with a concert, a swimming meet, a choir performance, races on land and water, a literary seance, games, and two huge meals, until at 10:30 at night even the students had had enough.[64]

One cannot read the house diaries or the minutes of the regular conferences of the surveillants without seeing that the spontaneity of the schoolboy regularly came through, and that the genuine interest of the faculty softened what in theory looked like excessive rigidity. Marbles scattered on dormitory floors at bedtime, books (even novels) smuggled in, a "great dissipation at supper, occasioned especially by the repeated demands for beer," and the "frivolous and hardly suitable names that the students use to describe the Fathers," were all part of the eternal student.[65] That the teacher give reasons for punishment, that student explanations be listened to carefully, that kindness be the first recourse, were urged regularly on the faculty. That the faculty did not always observe these directions is also true.

The attitude to theater and music also gave evidence of change. Music found favor in a way that would have been inconceivable in the minor seminaries, and not only was individual instruction given, but grand concerts with full orchestra

64. *Ibid.*, Nov. 5, 1835 and June 4, 1846, and Ch. de . . . (Raymond-Cahusac), *Brugelette, Souvenirs de l'enseignement chez les Jésuites par un de leurs élèves* (Toulouse, 1879), 31–32.

65. PSJ, Brug. 12:2248, Diarum, March 9, 1840; Jan. 4, 1844; May 16, 1848; and PSJ, Brug. 4:225, "Conférence des Surveillants," July 18, 1849 and Jan. 9, 1850.

were the pride of the house.[66] The theater was held in disfavor; the provincial was concerned about its deleterious influence on school and student. "It is regrettable that the theater has been introduced. Try at least to cut down on it for some time if it cannot be suppressed entirely."[67] In truth the themes were hardly dangerous: religious tragedies such as *Joseph sold by his Brothers, Hermenegild,* and *Agapite*; once in a while a melodrama such as *The Man from the Black Forest,* biblical dramas such as the five-act piece, *The Maccabees,* by one of the professors, Father Marin de Boylesve, who regularly wrote plays for these student productions.[68] Still the General worried: "You see, Father, that I do not conceal my fears, theatrical productions—even religious, even pious, even holy ones—in my opinion, founded on experience, will always involve more harm than good. They will not be anything but a *lesser evil,* and, as a consequence only *tolerable* by *necessity*; without that *necessity* I would not want any of them at all."[69] In the end, productions were limited to two a year, one before Lent and one for the Father Rector's Day.

The program of studies also underwent some changes. In 1820 the General Congregation of the Society had ordered a revision of the old *Ratio Studiorum.* Provincials were to send to Rome two memoranda. The first was to contain a survey of non-Jesuit educators' views on modern curriculum material

66. This flourishing state at Brugelette was due especially to Father Louis Lambillotte (1797–1855), teacher there from its first to its last year. To him was also due, unfortunately, a portion of the more execrable French church hymns of the nineteenth century, and, much more happily, some of the very first historical investigation that led to the reinvigoration of the medieval Gregorian chant.

67. PSJ, Brug. 13:243, "Memoriale," Nov. 1, 1840.

68. The first two were written by Father Charles Porée (1676–1741), the great teacher at the Paris Jesuit college of Louis-le-Grand. He was Voltaire's teacher, and lived to see nineteen of his former pupils elected to the Académie Française.

69. PSJ, C-12, "Enquêtes Provinciales 1849–1860," copy of letter from Roothaan, Rome, April 28, 1842. The General would seem to have shared the fear of Pascal of several centuries earlier: "All great distractions are dangerous to the Christian life; but of all those which the world has invented there is none more dangerous than the theater" (Pascal, *Pensées,* no. 208).

and samples of actual courses in use, together with each provincial's own judgment on them. The second was to be an outline of actual curricula in use in the fledgling Jesuit schools, with special attention to the place held by subjects other than Latin and Greek. Reports were sent but no decisions were reached, and nine years later, the next Congregation ordered the new Superior General, Roothaan, to take up the work again as soon as possible.[70]

A commission made up of members from all the provinces (Loriquet was the member for France) met for a year in Rome to study the old definitive *Ratio* of 1599, to consider further observations sent from all the provinces, and to draw up their own conclusions for the General. After further study, Roothaan, on July 25, 1832, promulgated on a trial basis the revised *Ratio*. Much of it dealt with broad changes in the courses of theology and philosophy for the Jesuits themselves.

In the revised *Ratio*, the vernacular language gained recognition as a major subject for the "college" classes up to rhetoric, along with Latin and Greek, although the latter were still given pride of place and effort. History, geography, and mathematics, though previously taught, for the first time *officially* entered the curriculum as subjects in their own right, though they were still called "accessory studies," and had claim only to a total of about six hours of class a week. Other modern languages were still wholly optional, almost like the *arts d'agrément*. The humanities strictly so-called, Latin and Greek language and literature, were still *the* study of the college, though, as always, in and around them much other material was taught. The students learned mathematics and the natural sciences throughout the course, bit by bit, with a greater emphasis on them in the two or three years of philosophy that followed on rhetoric.

70. Allan P. Farrell, S.J., *The Jesuit Code of Liberal Education: Development and Scope of the Ratio Studiorum* (Milwaukee, 1938), 385–386, prints some of the excellent recommendations of the German Vice-Province, followed frequently in the 1832 revision. For the subsequent history of the 1832 revision, see *ibid.*, 365–421.

Loriquet's plan had included some of these provisions, of course, and all of it was to be subject to revision in later years in the light of experience, just as the early Society had elaborated the first *Ratio*.[71] Brugelette, founded two years after the new code, tried to put it into effect from the first, but said quickly that it was not specific nor detailed enough for implementation. It indicated no progressively graded or ordered course for the subjects newly included officially, such as the vernacular language or literature, mathematics, geography, or history. In 1838, Delvaux, the rector, described for Roothaan some of the problems with the new plan as it was then applied: "There has not been enough care for the division between upper and lower classes. There is too much [natural] science in the lower classes, where we try to produce demi-savants or precocious savants, and not enough in the upper classes; at the end of more years of study, less Latin is known, so little even that philosophy can no longer be taught in that language! . . . A return to the purity of our plan would be true progress even according to the modern usage of the word . . . As it assures to the humanities and to the [natural] sciences their true place, it brings the child to the threshold of the main state schools (the *grandes écoles* and the universities) at the only age where he could, with some security, face their dangers."[72]

Brugelette devised its own plan after 1839. Absolutely basic to it was the concept of *successive* teaching. This meant the placing of the scientific and mathematical (i.e. above elementary algebra and geometry) subjects together with philosophy in the later years of the student's course, when his reflective intelligence first became capable of dealing with them, in a clear division from the previous years of the classic humanities which were supposed to be most aptly suited to stimulate and

71. The 1832 version never became definitive legislation for the Jesuits, because it was never submitted to the consideration and vote of a General Congregation, the highest governing body in the Society.

72. ARSJ, Franc., Delvaux to Roothaan, Aug. 11, 1838.

exercise his memory and imagination.[73] Despite a large number of minor changes made year after year, this program remained remarkedly faithful to the original ideas of 1839, and the Jesuits hoped to continue it in France after 1850.

The preparatory course gave the elements of Latin and of French grammar, of history, geography, and arithmetic. The course of letters was basically divided into grammar, poetry and rhetoric, with grammar lasting up to the second form, after which poetry took over. Eloquence was the concern of the last or rhetoric year of this division. It continued to be a very classical eloquence and literature. Once in a while Romanticism secured a tenuous beachhead; some of the teachers had apparently been reading to the pupils from Scott and Hugo, and some of the students themselves had gone so far as to ask to hear *Notre Dame de Paris*, but the provincial ordered that such books be swept out of the library.[74]

As for the accessories, arithmetic occupied all of the grammar forms, with algebra and geometry taking up the last two years. The pupils studied geography up to the third form inclusive and history throughout each year. Finally, the course of philosophy and science took in the last two, or ideally three, years of schooling, though this last ideal was very seldom reached. Philosophy occupied the greater share of time, and in the remainder mathematics, physics, chemistry, and natural history (or biology or zoology) crowded each other about. Optional and at extra cost were courses in English and German, and in drawing, music, fencing, gymnastics, and swimming.

For the opponents of the Jesuit schools, history and philoso-

---

73. Jacques Cretineau-Joly in his *Histoire de la Compagnie de Jésus* (2nd ed.; 6 vols.; Paris-Lyons, 1846), VI, 434–437 accused Cousin, then Minister of Public Instruction, of copying the Brugelette plan almost detail by detail without any acknowledgment in his *Règlement* of August 25, 1840 and his circular to the Academies two days later. Copy or not, at least there is a great similarity in Cousin's plan as set forth in text and table in Clement Falcucci, *L'Humanisme dans l'enseignement secondaire en France au XIXe siècle* (Toulouse and Paris, 1939), 181–184, quoting V. Cousin, *Oeuvres*, cinquième série, I, 166, 225.

74. PSJ, Reg., Boulanger to Pillon, Oct. 1, 1843.

phy were the neuralgic points. The history texts were still basically Loriquet's, though the Jesuits themselves had some misgivings about them as, with the growth of the Napoleonic legend, they became ever more anathema in the eyes of their opponents in the July Monarchy. The provincial, in 1839, was glad to see a history course in which "especially there was nothing in the comments which seemed [to indulge in] personalities."[75] One of the students, however, remarked later of this course: "How often did I not desire . . . less of the sterile fracas of battles, [and] a more vivid study of customs and habits, of the teachings which gave rise to them, of the institutions which were their reflection, of the general elements of politics . . . and also a chronology which was wider in scope."[76]

In philosophy, in the basic but rather eclectic (not Cousin's variety!) courses which became somewhat less ambitiously numerous in the latter years of Brugelette, the aim was quite frankly apologetic. They sought to prepare the young men for the objections of the unbelievers whom they were going to meet in the Université or among their associates after they had completed their college years. For some time there was a course in the philosophy of history, but "as for that vague science . . . , it would be necessary to be a St. Augustine or a Bossuet in order to teach with assurance, clarity, and fullness the reason, the overriding reason, for facts, in the manner of the *Discourse on Universal History* or of the *City of God*, and one would need auditors who possessed at one and the same time history and philosophy."[77] Thus wrote its teacher, Father Marin de Boylesve, to the provincial in explanation of several changes. To judge from examination programs, the former course surely was ambitious; observations might be called for on the methods of Bossuet, Voltaire, Vico, Herder, Hegel, Schlegel, Cousin, and Chateaubriand, and all this in the preliminary section

---

75. PSJ, Reg., Guidée to Delvaux, Jan. 4, 1839.
76. Ch. de (Raymond-Cahusac), *Brugelette, Souvenirs,* 72.
77. Marin de Boylesve to Rubillon, June 19, 1850 as quoted in *EJF,* I, 960.

alone.[78] The new offering was a series of "Lectures on Religion, History, and Literature." A former pupil recalled them: "He spoke to us as often of one subject as of another, little of literature, but much of philosophy '*à la de Maistre*,' of history, morals, politics ancient and current, in a word what he condensed into his first little work: *Appeal to Catholic Youth*."[79]

Most of this preparation was for meeting the kind of objections popular among the eighteenth-century philosophers, and still the current coin of the middle- or upper-bourgeois rationalist. There seems to have been little or no treatment of any more recently original problems, other than once in a while a brief reference to socialism, which was so utterly and self-evidently wrong in the eyes of these students that it presented no danger to them.

Thiers had remarked that Brugelette did not produce good Frenchmen; in any case they were surely convinced Frenchmen. In a day when frontier controls were less exigent than now, the pilgrimage to Notre Dame de Bon Secours across the border was not only a religious occasion but a patriotic one too, a time of joy in crossing the frontier, of stepping on French earth, of breathing French air. During the 1848 revolution in France, the rector introduced a revolution itself in the life of the college; he read newspaper accounts, formerly absolutely forbidden, to the assembled students, so that they might know the sufferings of their dear land and pray for her.[80] And after the 1850 Falloux Law, even the Jesuits at Brugelette stayed only out of duty, but felt deeply their exile in a foreign land —a few kilometers from France.

The closing of the school was almost inevitable once the state monopoly ended in France and Jesuit colleges were opened there. Besides, Father Pillon, the true mainstay of Brugelette, was transferred to Vannes in Brittany as first rector of the

78. PSJ, Brug. 13, Examens—1er Semestre, 1840.

79. Letter of Th. de Regnon in H. Fouqueray, *Le P. Marin de Boylesve,* as quoted in *EJF,* I, 954.

80. PSJ, Brug. 12:2249, Diarum, Feb. 26–29; March 6, 1848.

school there. Roothaan declared that "we certainly should not of ourselves dissolve our beautiful and dear college," and that he did not have the fear that "Amiens would be the death, now or soon, of Brugelette."[81] But Amiens as a boarding school, and Vaugirard in Paris as the same, were the final blow. In October 1853 there were only 190 students; at the end of the school year in 1854 the college was closed.

For eighteen years Brugelette was both the symbol and the reality of French Jesuit colleges. Approximately 1500 students had enrolled there, and while perhaps not quite as distinguished in later life as the alumni of Fribourg, they were even more devoted to the school and to the furtherance of the new colleges of the Society in France. But most important was the effect of the school on the Jesuits themselves. On this model they founded their new schools, in teaching, in discipline, in religious exercises, in spirit, even in problems. This was the baptism of experience for the greater number of them—for those who staffed the first colleges, their only previous teaching experience. Many of the former teachers later became prefects of studies and college rectors often in one school after another. To cite briefly but two examples, Father Olivaint, later killed by the Communards, was responsible for the early and great success of the preparatory school of the Rue des Postes; Father Pillon founded Vannes and Lille and was rector, besides, at Amiens and at the same preparatory school in Paris. Several of these Jesuit teachers, among them Fessard, Ponlevoy, Studer, Dorr, Grandidier, Mertian, and, again, Pillon, presided as provincial superiors over the organization and destinies of all the new colleges in the provinces of France.

81. ARSJ, Franc., Reg., Roothaan to Rubillon, Dec. 4, 1850.

III

THE TIDE OF NEW
FOUNDATIONS

Three weeks after the passage of the Falloux Law, the provincial of Paris informed the secretary to the French Assistant: "I have already refused six establishments, one of which is in Paris." A week later the provincial of Lyons wrote about seven or eight requests that he thought he had to accede to: "As you well foresaw, they are asking for foundations from every side. It is an absolute impossibility for us to refuse gently and politely the larger number. Where are we going to find the personnel?" Before the enactment of the new law, the two provincials had agreed on how they were to proceed; they were going to answer all requests kindly and to hold out at least some hope to the bishops already asking for colleges. But the first need was to prepare teachers; nothing was to be hurried. They were going to get together to follow the same program in each province.[1]

1. PSJ, Reg., Rubillon to Villefort, April 5, 1850; and LSJ, Reg., Maillard to Villefort, April 13, 1850.

By August, in the face of the avalanche, the good intentions remained, but their fulfillment became precarious. It was not quite four months after the Falloux Law when the Superior General wrote concerning the fifty-two foundations already refused in France: "I am at one and the same time happy and sad at the large number of requests which have been made and to which you could give no answer but a refusal. Father Rubillon for his part had turned down twenty-two foundations; you have refused thirty of them, and how many other requests were stopped by those refusals!"[2] The common program broke down when it came to acceptances. The north limited itself to two colleges in 1850, despite pressures on all sides; Lyons, by the end of the year took on nine schools, to the consternation of Rome and Paris.

These acceptances by Lyons were not the first cause for worry on the part of the other French provincial. Even before the Falloux Law had been voted, at the very moment of its discussion in the legislative committee in January 1850, the Jesuits in the south of France opened a college in Avignon.[3] The provincial of Lyons at the time, Father Jordan, had already suggested such a possibility in 1848. In September 1849 a group of Avignonese Catholic laymen publicly announced the new establishment as an independent, nontuition secondary school, and they pledged sufficient funds to maintain the school and its professors for ten years. They had the words of Father Jordan urging them on: "You do not ask for freedom; you take it."

The Paris Jesuits were amazed and fearful. Rubillon begged Jordan, "as a favor, for the love of the Society and the interests of the Catholics of France, do not go any further until the General comes and is well informed. Judge what will be done if the

2. ARSJ, Lugd., Reg., Roothaan to Maillard, Aug. 3, 1850.

3. See especially the account in *Le Collège des Jésuites à Avignon, 1565–1950* (Avignon, 1950), 41–46, and the letters in ARSJ, Lugd., Jordan to Roothaan, Sept. 10, 1849; Ribeaux to Roothaan, Oct. 28, 1849; Ribeaux to Roothaan, Nov. 20, 1849; Cade to Roothaan, Oct. 5, 1850.

Jesuits open colleges. The obstacle is not from your good people, but from the side of the Université and its Voltairian centralization." A week later he wrote again and said that "several salesmen have already come to see Father Coué [the treasurer], so the police, too, are well informed."[4] Ravignan, who knew the temper of the government, wrote in agitation to ask: "When everything is still in question, when an incident can cause the loss of everything and compromise it for an indefinite future, is it good for us, or wise or right for our friends and devoted advocates that we should put ourselves out in front, right in the face of the Université, still armed with all its tyrannical laws?"[5] Jordan answered that the move was not a complication or aggravation, that Lyons knew that the Paris Jesuits were working for the same goal by a different route, and that he [Jordan] asked as a favor that the other province not openly oppose the steps already taken. "If you are not for us, do not be against us."[6] A new Lyons provincial, Louis Maillard, and a new Avignon rector, Joseph Barrelle, became fearful. Fortunately for the college, the General, Roothaan, now in his exile from Rome, arrived at Avignon at this time, and after a review of the situation he decided in favor of opening the school, which already counted eighty prospective students.

On a cold January 5, 1850, the college began, in part of an old convent of Cordeliers, in the middle of "work suddenly interrupted. Several classrooms were without doors or windows, full of debris; others, though finished, were empty and without heat. The mistral blew chilly and strong across the courtyards."[7]

The physical setting was not the only improvisation at the new school. The necessary funds were guaranteed by good will, but by nothing else. At first an Abbé Bonnet was the legal

---

4. PSJ, Reg., Rubillon to Jordan, Sept. 17 and 24, 1849.
5. Cited in Ponlevoy, *Ravignan*, II, 173.
6. *Ibid.*
7. *Le Collège des Jésuites à Avignon*, 44.

director, and the Jesuits came to the house only to teach. The fathers of the students even took up places in the classrooms as teachers on the occasion of the official visit of the state inspectors, who were not slow in coming. The fathers said that since parents by right and by law could educate their own children, they were so doing at the moment, and that when they had to go to their ordinary occupation, they arranged to be replaced by men who had their entire confidence and who had agreed to be available whenever asked for. The inspectors caused no problem, the school turned out to be no hindrance to the Falloux Law, and after the March vote the province of Lyons ever prided itself on opening the first of the new Jesuit colleges in France.

The provincial of Paris had thought, even a year before the law, that it would be best to take colleges at three angles of the province, in Brittany, Alsace, and Flanders or Picardy. After reviewing a flood of requests, the previous first choices of provincial and consultors remained the same, Vannes and Amiens. The committees from these cities had been among the first to ask; the places were well located; the colleges were to be day schools and free of charge; but, it seems, one of the strongest reasons was that the "cities [were] remarkable for their spirit of order and for their affection for us."[8]

At Amiens, former pupils of Saint-Acheul, wanting to resurrect their old school, had taken the initiative, seconded by the archbishop, Monsignor Salinis. The College of Providence which opened in October 1850, with 150 students took its name from its buildings, part of a prerevolutionary convent of the Sisters of Providence. Here too, to begin with, the physical facilities were an improvisation, with three old buildings separated by two streets and a court. There were not even enough rooms to house the Jesuit community, and classes were sometimes held in the few available ones, or in "some dark little corner, once a kitchen, or a narrow passage previously a

8. PSJ, Reg., Rubillon to Roothaan, April 22, 1850.

corridor, and for sleeping rooms an attic or garret. No garden at all to go to for a little rest after the hours of work; almost no books to help the teachers in preparing their lessons. The library of the commune was the library of the school, as the boulevards were its garden."[9]

From the beginning, the purchase of property and the building of additions were a constant concern. There are records of such transactions in 1850 itself, in every year but one until 1858, and another in 1862. Finally, only in 1869 was the physical plant brought to completion. This same process was true in general of all these early foundations. But there was no improvisation with regard to studies or to the internal life of the college. Father Guidée, former prefect of Saint-Acheul, brought intact to the new college all the educational usages of the old school, somewhat modified by the experiences of Brugelette and Fribourg. He himself, as rector for fifteen years until his death in 1866, assured the continuity of these methods.

Indeed, the one feature of these older schools which the Society wished above all to avoid made its appearance too. The college had started as a day school; it was not several months old before it was clear that a boarding school was inevitable. This unfortunate development, common to Amiens, to Avignon, to Vannes, to almost all of the newly founded colleges, will reappear in the following chapters. It was one of the most persistent concerns of the new educational experience and it profoundly modified the character of that experience as originally planned.

As at Amiens, so too at Vannes in Brittany, a group of laymen took the first step in formally requesting a college. They were fathers of families from that city and from Nantes, Rennes, Quimper, Saint-Brieuc, even from Laval, Angers, and Rouen. On April 4, 1850 a petition arrived from the Municipal Council:

9. *EJF*, I, 222, quoting François Grandidier, S.J., *Vie du R. P. Achille Guidée, S.J.* (Amiens, 1877).

Morbihan wants religious schools. It today hopes to raise up again the institutions with which piety had previously endowed it.

We would like to have a completely gratuitous day school at Vannes, to which all the children would be admitted without payment, as they are in the numerous colleges which your holy Society has founded.

Learning is not a thing to be feared when competent teachers, imbued with respect for children, know how to win over their hearts and how to direct without effort the reason as also the will toward that which is beautiful, noble and elevated . . .

A specific subscription will cover all the necessary costs of this establishment and will assure its duration during at least five years.[10]

Rubillon told Roothaan that the offer came from "not only the most distinguished men of the city, but also the majority of the municipal council."[11] A planned request for a boarding school was for the moment left in abeyance, and negotiations with the council began on the following points in view of a final agreement by mid-June.

Only the "Course of Letters" was to be complete; there would be no philosophy and science course for the moment, in order to spare expenses in case the municipal college should close and its science equipment become available. The committee of founders would pay into the Society's training fund for the support of younger Jesuits still in studies a sum of eight hundred francs for each Jesuit teacher in the college. In addition the committee would maintain the Jesuit brothers and the domestics, and would provide all expenses of furniture, linen, library rent, and separate chapels for Jesuits and students. "It is important that the committee sees just how high

---

10. Orhand, *Pillon*, 106–107.
11. ARSJ, Franc., Rubillon to Roothaan, April 12, 1850.

the annual expenses will be, the expenses of a first-rate establishment." The bishop was to be asked for approval before anything was settled, and finally: "It is understood that the rector will have full and entire freedom for the admittance or dismissal of students, and for the whole direction of the college."[12]

All of this was a fine ideal, and it was what the Jesuits wanted in all of their new foundations. But it was hardly ever fully realized, and even less so at the beginnings of the colleges. Surprisingly, the gratuity of this day school was the feature which most often drew criticism at Vannes. One reason was identical with that which raised a storm for the very first colleges of the Society in the sixteenth century—the unfair competition that free education brought to the official establishments of the day, then the Sorbonne, and now the *lycées*.[13] This question of gratuity was another of the major problems facing the new schools, and, linked with the problem of the boarding school, it will also be treated more fully later. In particular, Vannes found for some time an unusual solution to the boarding problem. Many of the students came from the small towns in Brittany, and before six months were over, the pressures were so great that forty boarders had to be accepted in an arrangement unique for the time, but very similar to that of the ancient Jesuit colleges. The students from the country villages lodged in small groups in private homes in Vannes, paid six or seven francs a month for bed and one light meal a day, and received from their parents the rest of their food by packages. They came to the college only for classes, and had a sort of subprefect among the Jesuits to visit their lodgings, to look to good order, and to provide for their special needs.[14]

12. PSJ, Reg., Rubillon to Leve, April 14, 1850.
13. See J. Fouqueray, S.J., *Histoire de la Compagnie de Jésus en France* (Paris, 1910), I, 385.
14. For all the details of life at Vannes, told with interest and affection (perhaps too uncritically) by an alumnus, see Fernand Butel, *L'Education des Jésuites: Un Collège breton!* (Paris, 1890).

Father Adolphe Pillon, former prefect, then rector, prefect again, and always the moving spirit of Brugelette, became the first rector of this new college of St. François-Xavier at Vannes.[15] He, too, brought with him all the usages of Brugelette, and saw them firmly implanted during his stay of eleven years as the head of the college. He once remarked, even after being in charge for a decade, "I truly have much to do; sole trustee of the tradition of this house which I founded, I am consulted all the time by everybody on a whole crowd of things."[16] The school opened on October 15, 1850 with a benevolent audience of church and state, headed by the bishop and the prefect, and with more than two hundred students on hand.[17] By 1854 at the end of this first wave of foundations, the number of pupils at Vannes had doubled to more than four hundred, almost two thirds of them boarding students.

The Paris province held firm in 1850 with these two schools, plus the already heavy burden of Brugelette. Lyons finished the year with nine establishments, at Dôle, Sainte-Etienne, Bordeaux, Toulouse, Mende, Sarlat, Montauban, and Yseure, with Avignon already a going concern. Some of these schools were poorly located, and in total they were far more than the province could do justice to, but they were pressed upon and accepted by the provincial nevertheless.

At Dôle, in 1850 a small city of about ten thousand inhabitants and the former site of one of the Jesuit minor seminaries,

15. The appointment occasioned great consternation at Brugelette, already fearful for its life as the French colleges opened. Many letters went to Rome especially from the most generous of Brugelette's benefactors, Baron de Secus. There is a sheaf of them in ARSJ, Franc., Brugelette—1850.

16. Orhand, *Pillon,* 171. It should be recalled, too, that after Vannes Pillon went as rector to Sainte-Geneviève in Paris, then to the Champagne province as provincial superior, and finally to Lille as the founder of the college there in 1872.

17. Here the Université, too, was benevolent. Pillon lacked one of the five years as "stagiaire" required in order to be the legal director of a school. The rector of the Academy at Vannes, the Vicomte de Kergaradec, with the support of the deputy from Morbihan, Monsignor Parisis, sought and obtained a dispensation for him.

the provincial agreed to start a very modest day school with three or four classes. They included the seventh, sixth, and fifth forms, that is, for boys of about 9 to 12 or 13 years old.

It was a day school because this was the system that "divine providence seemed to have in mind." "Should a child, placed by it [Providence] in the very heart of the home, be completely cut off from the enlightened affection of a father and mother, from their good example, their tender words, their wise advice, their devoted care of health?" The answer was in the negative, but even so, the students came at six or seven in the morning, and stayed until at least seven in the evening, except for an hour and a half at home for the midday meal, all of this (on the other side of the coin), "so that the direction might be unified, and to relieve parents of a supervision which, if continuous, could be troublesome and sometimes even impossible."[18]

Here, not only teaching but also supervision were to be free of charge. Parents of the few possible boarders were to make their own arrangements without any financial involvement of the Jesuits. All of this was somewhat naive. Even more so was the hope that the officials of the city, seeing the benefits of such an establishment, would voluntarily undertake to maintain it. In 1852 there was briefly question of the city confiding to the Society the municipal college housed in the building taken from the Jesuits in 1828, but the proposal came to naught. At the beginning there were 80 students; two years later there were 164, including 40 orphans. In 1854 the total was 250, again 60 of them orphans. The following year the province thought of closing the place because of its location near other schools and because of the scarcity of teachers, but slowly the Collège de Notre-Dame-de-Mont-Roland made its way to something more than 400 students at the height of its prosperity.

Dôle was very much a country town; Saint-Etienne, on the

18. *Prospectus du Collège de Dôle* as quoted in Burnichon, *La Compagnie,* III, 391.

other hand, already had an industrialized urban character, with some reputation for "socialism." In 1849 Father Amédée de Damas preached a series of Lenten sermons there with great success, and, "as a result, the most influential families of Saint-Etienne . . . ask with great insistence for a residence for the direction of apostolic works, and for the establishment of congregations, especially congregations of gentlemen and of workers."[19] At this time, May 1850, there was no question of a college; by November one was in existence, again at the insistence of the "gallant Catholics," especially of the "unreservedly Christian families of employers."[20] Here, too, there was originally no question of any but a day school, but within another six months a half-boarding school (*demi-pensionnat*) existed, and by the beginning of the second year the inevitable result, a full boarding school. That second year also began with Father Damas, of the Lenten sermons of two years before, as the new rector. If, at some of the other schools, one could reproach the rectors with being far too old, here it was the opposite. Damas was only thirty, a man with ideas even larger than his youthful enthusiasm.

At first, all went well, even if the apostolic Catholics who had formed the corporate association and advanced their 400,000 francs to buy the needed building, were rather exigent about prompt payment of interest on their shares, and even if it was necessary to do a lot of repairing on the huge old structure formerly belonging to the Brothers of the Christian Schools, so as "to satisfy the students and their parents if we wish to overcome a sort of repugnance which the families living in the nearby departments feel for a city that is purely industrial."[21] The provincial, after his first official visit in October 1852, wrote that "Saint-Etienne was progressing very well . . . 153 boarding students at the present moment; there

19. ARSJ, Lugd., Maillard to Roothaan, May 5, 1850.
20. *EJF*, IV, 656.
21. ARSJ, Lugd., Damas to Roothaan, July 23, 1852.

will [soon] be more than three hundred students. The preparatory courses are going to be organized there."[22]

This last sentence referred to one of Damas' more grandiose ideas, the establishment of a series of classes in addition to or after the ordinary secondary school and immediately preparatory for the "Grandes Ecoles" of the state such as Saint-Cyr, Ecole Navale, and Polytechnique. The concept was excellent in itself; one of the most fruitful and imaginative works which the Society undertook in France was the institution of such a school in Paris in 1854, Sainte-Geneviève or L'Ecole de la Rue des Postes. But Saint-Etienne was hardly the place and these very early years of the college were hardly the time to venture on such a project, although for several years a small beginning was made. Damas said that he "could not forget that his father had been a soldier, nor could he resign himself to bringing up nothing but young men of industry and trade."[23] He even adopted as school dress for the students the uniform of officers of the French army.

With all the directness of a military man the rector approached the new master of France after the coup d'état of December 2, 1851. The attitude of the Prince-President was all important now for the future of the independent schools. Louis-Napoléon had little reason to love the Université, which furnished all too many of his critics, and in 1848 he had spoken out for independent schools. But enough of his advisers were convinced opponents of the new establishments, and a single state system presented so many temptations to easy control, that many Catholics were troubled. Damas, with permission of the provincial, Maillard, asked for an interview with the President, and exposed the concern of the independent schools, especially the Jesuit ones. Louis Napoléon at this juncture was happy enough to be waited upon by a member of one of the most

22. LSJ, Reg., Maillard to Roothaan, Oct. 28, 1852.
23. *EJF*, IV, 657.

openly legitimist families in France.[24] He reassured the rector of Saint-Etienne, and asked how he would be received if he came to the city. Damas replied frankly that he thought the reception would be poor.

When the tour did take place, Saint-Etienne received the Prince with *éclat,* and Damas, presented to a benevolent Louis Napoléon at the official reception, asked a favor of him. He wanted "to be able to write directly to the President of the Republic in case we would have some complaint to make about any too zealous an administrator."[25] The President acceded, again more than willing, on his way to full power, to be pleasant to such a group as the conservative Catholics. The next day Fortoul, the Minister of Public Instruction, sent a personal note to Damas, telling him that "the Prince-President . . . is happy at the efforts which in the ecclesiastical establishment of Saint-Etienne you are making to better the education of youth. His Highness will regard with satisfaction the relations established between the directors of the college and the various administrative officials of the State."[26] The word cannot have been slow in getting around; Damas wrote to Rome: "Our relations with the civil and military authorities are perfect. What do these gentlemen think of us at the back of their minds? I do not at all know, but their benevolence is perfect and their kind attentions without number."[27]

But a year and a half later the college was all but extinct, suppressed by an imperial decree. The incident is strange, but it will help illuminate in this one particular what is to be said

24. It will be recalled that Baron de Damas had been governor of the Duc de Bordeaux (Comte de Chambord) in 1828, and it was he who had suggested the Jesuits in 1833 as tutors at Prague for the young heir to the throne of France. The baron was Father Amédée's father. All six of his sons were educated at Fribourg. One other besides Amédée entered the Society of Jesus. See Comte de Damas d'Anlezy, "L'Education du Duc de Bordeaux," *Revue des Deux Mondes,* 11 (1902), 612–620; also Joseph Burnichon, S.J., *Un Jésuite, Amédée de Damas* (Paris, 1908).

25. Burnichon, *La Compagnie,* III, 401–402.

26. *Ibid.*

27. ARSJ, Lugd., Damas to Beckx, July 23, 1852.

later in general about the reactions of the Jesuit schools to the government. In May 1853 an incident known as the "Plaster Statue Affair" took place. Several students had bought from an itinerant salesman at the school small statues of the Virgin or of saints, but one of them had chosen a bust of Napoléon III. It seems that it was broken in the jostling usual to boys on a playground, and the pieces were kicked about playfully by some of them. The rector heard of it, inquired, decided that the incident had had no ulterior significance, and simply said nothing.

Of course, the story eventually got around, helped by a disgruntled former teacher. On December 29, 1853 the *Moniteur* published a decree suppressing the college "in consideration of the fact that it has tolerated, without repression, disorders which are a veritable insult to the Constitution and to the laws of the Empire."[28] The Paris provincial, Studer, in a circular letter, said that the reasons given to the Society for closing the college were (1) the statue affair, (2) an academic séance "wherein we had let prominence be given to the heroism of the Vendée, thus reviving memories of a civil war," and (3) pronounced tendencies "out of harmony with the laws under which we live and the authority which governs us."[29] The school was given eight days after formal notification to get the students back to their families.

The shock was great, among both the general Catholic public who heard for the first time of the incident and among most of the members of the Society, who had been equally ignorant of the whole affair and who now feared the beginning of another Jesuit hunt. By this time Damas had not been rector for some months, because the school needed a steadier hand once the waves of debts he had contracted began to build up menacingly behind the grandiose enterprise. In the circumstances, there was no use in his trying to write to the Emperor

28. *Moniteur,* Dec. 29, 1853.
29. PSJ, "Litt. Encycl. PP. Prov.," Studer, Jan. 11, 1854.

directly. Various demarches took place; finally the archbishop of Bordeaux, in favor with the imperial family, went to the Elysée Palace as did Father Ravignan.

Ravignan gave a curious account of his interview in January 1854 with the Emperor whom he found now benevolent and who had at that time only two complaints against the Society. There was "in the direction followed in the teaching in your colleges a spirit of opposition to the government," and two of the Jesuit mission directors "had preached the revolt of the poor against the rich."[30] Ravignan said that if definite names and places were given and proven, proper steps would be taken. Without requesting directly the reopening of the college in Saint-Etienne, he only asked that the Society be not judged and condemned in any future matter without having first been heard.

The Emperor knew how to use carrot and stick. Three months later, in response to a petition from a delegation of parents, he allowed the school to open again. The only restriction was that it change its name from Collège Saint-Michel. It officially became Sainte-Marie, but the old name survived in usage. For many years the college itself survived only precariously in the wake of this incident, epidemics, and, especially, ever present debts.[31] A good measure of success finally came when it began to take frank account of its industrial and commercial location; the average of 200 students up to 1864

30. Ponlevoy, *Ravignan*, II, 179, transcription of Ravignan's account of the interview; and II, 182. This is almost ironic; as Ponlevoy said (II, 183), "Just a moment before, the Jesuits had been condemned as legitimists in the colleges, now they were accused as socialists in the mission preaching." Jean Maurain, *La Politique ecclésiastique du second empire de 1852 à 1869* (Paris, 1930), 122 and 145–146 treats of the matter, and thinks that the sermons in question may have been preached at Aurillac. (See *AN*, F[19] 5.859, Delfour). Maurain says that "this reproach was made rather frequently of preachers" (122n). As a matter of fact, the Jesuits were afraid of disorder at any time, and in 1851 they had been just as concerned, or more so, about the possibility of revolt as had been the whole group of conservatives who saw in Louis-Napoléon the only hope of order and peace.

31. Most of these woes, from the "Emperor's Statue" on, are detailed in letters in ARSJ, Lugd., 4–XXI.

rose rapidly in the four or five years after that to more than 350 as the school concentrated especially on a careful preparation for the science option in the baccalaureate program.

Saint-Etienne was not the only college of the Lyons province to have a rector well known for his legitimist tendencies. At Toulouse, the founder of Sainte-Marie, Father Pie de Blacas, was of like mind, but no incident such as that to the north marred the progress of this school.[32] The Society itself took the initiative here in founding the college. It bought property in 1850 which had long before been a Cistercian college, and which had later become a factory for the manufacture of porcelain and faience. There was little question here but that the establishment would start with boarders. Four fifths of the first group of pupils were such, and all lived and studied in the midst of a construction site which by the end of this first year contained 250 students.

For those who lived the history, the progress of the school was without any spectacular incidents. It was perhaps somewhat more militarily orientated, somewhat more legitimist than several of the schools (and less so than others), but apart from these factors, its very ordinariness has made of its history a good source of information on the day to day operation of the typical nineteenth-century French Jesuit college.[33] The only slight check to prosperity and growth occurred from 1857 to 1865, perhaps because of the nearby Collège de Sorèze, conducted by Lacordaire in his latter years.

A former factory in a six-hundred-year-old building in the middle of town was not the best place for what were soon more than 400 students. By 1860 hopes were raised for a transfer to a better site at Caousou on the edge of the city. It took twelve years to realize the hopes, but in 1868 a section

32. See ARSJ, Lugd., Cardinal de Bonald to Beckx, Jan. 18, 1854. Blacas was considered by some as "an imprudent devotee of the Bourbon family." The college was also called a "center of legitimism."

33. See especially TSJ, Tolos.: Ste. Marie, "Diarium P. Ministri" and "Diarium Praefecti."

preparatory for the Grandes Ecoles was opened, later to become the independent Preparatory School of Caousou, the brother and rival of Sainte-Geneviève in Paris.

Ancient abbeys were all too ready at hand when it came to founding Jesuit schools. At Bordeaux, for example, in late 1849 the Society had finally, at the fourth request, acceded to the wishes of Cardinal Donnet for a college. The Jesuits would have started the school even before the passage of the Falloux Law, as at Avignon, but the cardinal himself made the decision to wait. It settled at the old abbey of Grand-Sauve, about fifteen miles from the city, and so, like the others could be nothing but a boarding school.

From 80 students in 1850, living, as usual, in somewhat minimal physical conditions, the school grew to 300 boarders and more than 100 half-boarders in 1859. Fortunately, from the beginning all understood that Grand-Sauve was temporary, and so there was none of the improvisation of facilities that went on at other schools from year to year until it became decade to decade. In 1857 the old château of Tivoli, at the edge of the city, was bought from the proceeds of the sale of Grand-Sauve for 198,000 francs, and in August 1858 the first stone was laid for "one of the marvels of Bordeaux."[34]

The Father General marveled too. He had ordered all work suspended the previous year until plans were reviewed and the first expenses in hand, but the plans still were rather grandiose, and he wrote to the provincial: "The journals have announced that a college in gothic architecture is going to be built. I do not know what truth there is in this, but I beg you, Father, to forbid the expenses of pure trimmings and of useless ornamentation."[35] In 1861, when the central part was finally com-

---

34. *EJF*, I, 796.
35. ARSJ, Tolos., Reg., Beckx to Studer, Aug. 28, 1858. All through 1858 there had been misunderstandings about financing the project. The provincial cautioned the rector: "Promises, however solid they might seem, are not resources. The money should be in the till, at least the greater part of it" (TSJ, Reg., Studer to Ribeaux, March 5, 1858).

pleted, another letter came from Rome, a severe one, strongly censuring "the worldly and luxurious look of the facade. The rules of the Society for [the construction of] buildings have been forgotten or, to put it truthfully, violated."[36] Perhaps fortunately for the Jesuit authorities in Bordeaux and Toulouse, the money ran out or else the two wings would have been built also and in equal grandeur.

Up to now, the Society had founded its colleges as independent institutions. At the time of the passage of the Falloux Law there had been some talk of taking on municipal or communal schools that might be offered to the Jesuits, but in fact superiors accepted only one such institution, at Mende in the department of Lozère. It was hardly one of the more promising situations, in a small town of six thousand inhabitants, not even as yet linked by railroad with the larger centers. The city signed the proper agreements with a Jesuit native of Mende and turned over to the Society for the opening of classes in the autumn of 1850 the College of Saint-Louis. It had thirty-seven boarding and 140 day students.

Since the contract involved a communal school, it came up for approval before the Conseil Supérieur de l'Instruction Publique, and there was a dangerous moment when not only this school but the whole future of the Jesuit colleges could have been compromised. For, most imprudently, the contract was drawn and signed between the city and the Jesuit, Valentin, *as representative of the Society.* "The discussion was lively and long . . . The members of the Commission who feared the invasion of the Jesuits into education told off again on the subject everything which had been said in 1828 and 1845."[37] Fortunately, there was no will to disrupt the whole Falloux

36. Burnichon, *La Compagnie,* III, 428. The problem of inadequate facilities versus the problem of debts was of long duration. See for instance TSJ, Reg., Rouquayrol to Beckx, April 2, 1864.

37. Beugnot, *Rapport au Comité de l'Enseignement libre sur l'exécution et les effets de la loi organique du 15 Mars 1850, par une Commission spéciale* (Paris, 1852), 32, as quoted in Burnichon, *La Compagnie,* III, 423.

settlement, still tenuous in its novelty. The Conseil approved the contract with the "Abbé" Valentin as an individual, and with the option of renewal at the will of the parties involved.

From that time on, until 1864, the life of the college was peaceful enough, and it functioned as all the other Jesuit schools in these first years, growing slowly to 200 students in 1855, equally divided between boarders and day students. For quarters, it had the buildings of the old communal college, and for partial support, 4,000 francs each year from the municipality. This was enough to cover the deficit, but not enough to take care of the inevitable additions. Providentially, a generous diocesan priest of the town gave 20,000 francs for that purpose. Fourteen years after the city invited the Jesuits to Mende it was, in effect, forced to invite them to leave, but that part of the story will be of concern later in this account.

As if six colleges were not enough for the Lyons province in 1850, it also had in its charge the three minor seminaries of the dioceses of Montauban, Moulins, and Périgueux. In actual practice, they too became full-fledged colleges. But they had all the special and additional problems of a responsibility shared by the Society, the diocese and, in some cases, the departmental or national governments. Each of these schools, too, serves as an example of some specific problems that had to be met.

At Sarlat the greatest problem was a set of legal entanglements. The bishop of Périgueux, an alumnus of Sainte-Anne d'Auray, invited the Jesuits to his minor seminary in the old and former episcopal city of Sarlat. This was the second such school in one and the same diocese, by special permission of the Prince-President, given in 1849. In 1850 Monseigneur Massonais entrusted the school to the Jesuits and classes started in November with forty-nine boarding and twelve day students, all less than fourteen years old. An increase in numbers after 1852 to a final average of more than 300, brought a problem which dragged on for fifteen years. More room had to be provided, but at Sarlat no one knew for sure to whom the room would belong because of the tangled juridical and financial state of the property. In 1818 the buildings and grounds had been given to the city for a diocesan seminary, with the provision that, failing such an establishment, the revenue from the property was to go to the hospital of Sarlat. Through the years the bishop and, in 1852, finally the Society, made additions to the buildings.

But when it came to repairing the original seventeenth-century ruins, for that is what they were becoming, no one knew who was to pay for them. All the way to 1867 there were many words, little money, and falling plaster, until, when the Jesuits threatened to leave, the city handsomely and generously sold the whole place to the bishop.[38] But for lack of special imperial acquiescence to the transaction, the problem flared up anew in 1880, at the time of the Ferry decrees. Sarlat provided in all this a good example of one of the difficulties which arose when the Jesuits were not masters of their own houses.

Another example was the minor seminary at Yseure, at the edge of the city of Moulins.[39] There, too, the property, originally a priory of Benedictine nuns, underwent confiscation during the revolution, and finally was turned over in 1823 to the new diocese of Moulins for a seminary. In 1850 the bishop, Monseigneur de Dreux-Brézé, asked the Jesuits to take over the school, and they started in that first year with 180 students, 18 Jesuits and 7 auxiliaries. Four years later there were 400 students.

Uncertainties did not wait even that long. By 1851, the Conseil Général of the department lodged a complaint that "the school of Yseure having been changed in large part by the

---

38. By 1864 the problem had become acute. The archives from then until 1867 (TSJ, Reg., *passim*) record letters to the general, the bishop, the mayor of Sarlat, and even a special provincial consultors' meeting in the presence of the French assistant to the general (TSJ, "Lib. Cons.," July 13, 1865).

39. Also spelled at various times Iseure or Yzeure.

Jesuits into an educational establishment appropriate to life in the world, the building had ceased to be exclusively consecrated to the public service for which it had been handed over, that is to say, for use as a minor seminary."[40] The national government answered that the bishop was simply taking advantage of the provisions of the Falloux Law. In later years the Conseil held to its position. The reply of Jules Simon, then Minister of Public Instruction and Cults, to a renewed complaint in 1872, is lengthy but important in the light it throws on the then current view of the government on the minor seminaries:

> We are no longer today living at the time of the Ordonnances of 1828, which meant to impose on children with a vocation the ecclesiastical garb from the fourth form on. The legislation in force is more liberal. It does not exorbitantly seek to lead to the priesthood all the students of the minor seminaries, nor to involve them in the path of irrevocable decisions before they are old enough to appreciate the seriousness of these resolutions. From the point of view of society, it sees without dissatisfaction the young aspirants to the ecclesiastical ministry forming themselves in the milieu that they are destined to return to after their theological studies. A clergy which from childhood would be completely isolated from the society in which it must live, would not be able to give an exact account of the needs of the time. Vocations thus prepared in an absolute confinement would not be, perhaps, sufficiently tested, and could lack that complete liberty which gives them their sincerity and force. The French clergy which receives in almost all the minor seminaries that "worldly" education which is a cause of complaint against the school of Yseure, is incontestably the best clergy in the world with respect to morality and piety.

40. Conseil Général, Aug. 31, 1851, as quoted in *EJF*, V, 218.

I do not hesitate to say, with my predecessors, that this establishment, in 1872 as in 1861 and 1840, is still an ecclesiastical secondary school because it fulfils the essential purpose of these establishments, and that we do not have the right to inquire into the means employed to arrive at this end, except for the conditions of the law of March 15, 1850.[41]

Simon's enlightened view did him credit. But, to be honest, neither the bishop nor probably the Jesuits shared the sentiments of that part of the letter which dealt with the disadvantages of isolation of the seminary students. Monseigneur de Dreux-Brézé had specifically asked that the students for the priesthood be separated from the others, and so they were. After 1864 the seminarians even had their own building, and there were in reality almost two establishments at Yseure, the college for lay students, much the larger, and the Residence of St. Louis for seminarians.[42] The two groups were together only for classes and for some of the religious exercises.

The school at Montauban provided one of the reasons for this concern for separation. There the Jesuits directed from 1848–1849 both the major and the minor seminaries. In the beginning, so the *Litterae Annuae* said, it was "rescue work . . . no discipline, the studies more than weak, money lacking for everything." Here, as everywhere, the usages of Brugelette and Fribourg were called upon.[43] The school prospered, but success was, perhaps, too great. For in one matter, that of vocations to the priesthood, Montauban experienced a great decline.

41. *EJF*, V, 218, 221. A copy of this letter is in ARSJ, Lugd.

42. For instance, in 1854 there were already 300 students in the Grand Pensionnat (i.e., the college), including thirty day and half-board students, and 150 in the Pensionnat St. Louis. By 1860 it was 350 to 100.

43. LSJ, *Litterae Annuae Lugdunensis*, 1850. Curiously, "bad books" (without exact definition) were a problem at first in the minor seminary. Since the source of supply was a peddler with "remainders" that were not going to be reprinted, the problem was solved directly. His whole lot was bought for 1600 francs, and the school authorities "made of it a vast auto-da-fe" (*ibid.*).

The place was too much a college, and not enough a seminary; at least so thought some. Father Blacas, the rector for thirteen years from 1854 to 1867, described the change in 1858: "The number of ecclesiastical vocations has much diminished in the house since we have been here. Eight or ten years ago, almost all the students of rhetoric would enter the major seminary for philosophy; this year only one of the boarding students has gone there, along with two day students." He thought the principal cause was "the mixing of the ecclesiastical and lay elements." As a result, "several on whom we were counting in the lower classes have fallen in love with the world and with its lucrative and brilliant careers, and they have abandoned their ideas of a future in the Church, to the great astonishment of their families and of the priests who knew them."[44] Another reason was the relatively high cost of attendance. It stayed high in order to lessen the burden of the deficit which fell on the bishop each year, but it prevented boys from the poor families from attending the school.

In saying that experience showed that it was not good to mix with the children of the world those whom God called specially to his service, and that priestly vocations were tender growths liable to be choked out by less delicate plants in the same garden, Burnichon only echoed in the twentieth century what the French Jesuits of the previous century were sure of also.[45] But to this view the serious objection arises: what about those Jesuit colleges, the greater number, which were strictly for lay students? It was precisely in them that most of the Jesuit vocations germinated, took root, and grew up vigorously.

There was no time, however, in 1850 for any such debates. By the end of that year, nine months after the Falloux Law, the Jesuits had eleven colleges operating in France. The Paris province had held back the tidal wave of applicants fairly well; besides the already flourishing Brugelette it had opened only

44. TSJ, Reg., Blacas to Beckx, Jan. 26, 1858.
45. Burnichon, *La Compagnie*, III, 417.

Amiens and Vannes. Lyons to the south was engulfed in the other nine schools, and the Father General at the beginning of 1851 observed justly, *"Festina lente* [make haste slowly] seems to have been completely forgotten. Perhaps ten years will not be enough to set up properly those [colleges] which have been started."[46]

46. ARSJ, Lugd., Reg., Roothaan to Maillard, Jan. 30, 1851.

IV

SUCCESS AND ITS

DIFFICULTIES

In the four years following the passage of the Falloux Law more Jesuit schools were opened, but fortunately the pace was much slower. In 1851 three colleges were begun; in 1852 two, and in 1854 one college and one institution of a special type. After this there were no new foundations until 1870, and with the cessation of new colleges, the Jesuits could also look at the problems raised by the schools.

The province of Lyons took on the first additional schools, near Villefranche-sur-Saône, at Saint-Affrique, and at Oran in Algeria. In 1842 the wealthy Countess de Barmondière, who was interested in helping noble families impoverished by the Revolution and in providing for Christian education, had given to the Jesuits her château of Mongré near Villefranche for the establishment of a college when that would be possible. In 1849 the locale figured, along with Avignon, in the letters from Paris to Lyons, beseeching the Provincial of Lyons not to open a school before the adoption of the Falloux Law.[1] Avignon was begun then, but Mongré had to wait until 1851.

The new college was like the others in its need for buildings, but unlike them in the resources it had at hand. If necessary, and of course it was, part of the fine park of more than twenty-seven hectares could be sold to pay construction costs. At the beginning, only the lower college classes existed, but by 1855 the course was completed, all the way to philosophy. Perhaps the spirit of the noble benefactress continued to preside over the place, for, from the first, Mongré had an aristocratic allure, and more than its share of students from unreconciled legitimist families.

If Mongré was a gift, Saint-Affrique was an imposition. As had happened at Saint-Etienne, a popular mission in 1850 gave several families the idea of founding a Jesuit college. A small inaccessible town of six or seven thousand inhabitants with a relatively large Protestant minority would seem to have had little chance for a college even after three or four requests. The provincial, Maillard, in a letter some years later explained the unexpected acceptance. "Vanquished here, [the families] turned to Rome and went directly to our Very Reverend Father General. Letters, requests, entreaties were presented to him; highly placed persons became petitioners, in such a way that, finally giving in to so many solicitations, Father General wrote to me: We must accept. His word was an order. I accepted."[2]

Among those highly placed personages was General Gémeau, commander of the French forces stationed in Rome to help sustain the papal rule. He was a good friend of one of the members of the Saint-Affrique committee, and he made a request for the college to Pius IX personally. From there the matter took the foreseen course, to the establishment of the College of Saint-Gabriel. Everything had to start from the ground up. Initial expenses were met by a subscription of 100,000 francs,

---

1. PSJ, Reg., Rubillon to Jordan, Sept. 17, 1849.
2. LSJ, Reg., Maillard to Beckx, May 7, 1855.

on which the city agreed to pay the interest charges for the first years, and by authorization for a lottery, a method seldom used by Jesuit institutions.[3] The school at Saint-Affrique, in a simple and sometimes somber part of France, was to distinguish itself mainly by a hard and poor life for teachers and students. The number of students never reached 300, but even in circumstances often different from those of the schools in the larger centers, the program of studies and the daily round of life were still the same here as elsewhere.

The studies and the life of the college were even the same, with but a few adaptations, in the school founded at this time in one of the colonies. The Jesuits had come to Oran in Algeria in 1843 to work in the prisons and as missionaries, especially among the French colonists. The storm of anti-Jesuitism in France in the late 1840's had its counterpart in Algeria too, but the government, and especially, again, the military, were in general favorable to the Society's work.[4]

Even before 1850 the provincial at Lyons had promised his support for a college. In 1851, with the backing of the governmental prefect, who was an alumnus of the Jesuits in France, and of General Pélissier, the governor of the province, the modest college of Notre-Dame d'Oran was opened. A year later, the growth of the school required a location other than the small Jesuit house and, due to the exertion of the general, an unused jail was turned over to serve as the new school. Burnichon remarked piously that thus again was verified the proverb: "To open a school is to close a prison."[5] With this establishment the Lyons province completed its roster of schools until the new wave of foundations twenty years later, after the fall of the Second Empire.

Now in 1852 it was the turn of the Paris province. Two colleges were opened in that year, at Metz and at Paris, and one in

3. Burnichon, *La Compagnie*, III, 434.
4. *EJF*, III, 990–992.
5. Burnichon, *La Compagnie*, III, 451.

1854 at Poitiers. All of them were to rank among the most important of the French Jesuit colleges. Just as important, but outside the direct scope of this study which deals only with the colleges, was the special school opened at Paris in 1854—Saint-Geneviève, or the "Rue des Postes," preparatory to the Grandes Ecoles of the state.

As at Oran so at Metz, the bishop and the general were among the firmest friends of the new establishment.[6] In the diocese of Monsignor Dupont des Loges, a secondary school, the college of St. Augustine, was run by an Abbé Braun, former student of Fribourg and soon to become a Jesuit novice after accomplishing his and the bishop's dearest desire, that of turning over the school to the Society. A Jesuit residence had been in existence in Metz since 1832, and much educational and religious work had been done with the soldiers throughout all these years. In 1850 the bishop had asked for a college, and Rubillon gratefully replied that he recognized the many advantages there, but that he did not have enough men and the province had for the time "adopted as principle not to establish [a college] where there already existed resources for a Christian education."[7]

In February 1852, the province finally accepted the already existing school. Again the building was an old convent, this time put up almost 700 years before for the Augustinians and partly rebuilt in the eighteenth century. In October 1852 the Jesuits took over the classes after a solemn Mass attended by the commanding general of the military district, the prefect, and the magistracy, and celebrated by the bishop.

The school began with 240 students, up to the class of rhetoric. The final class of philosophy was added the next year, with 40 more students. In 1854 there were 300 students, with the

---

6. The college and all its antecedents, in both the pre-suppression and post-restoration Society are treated at length in L. Viansson-Ponté, *Les Jésuites à Metz* (Strasbourg, 1889).

7. PSJ, Reg., Rubillon to Dupont des Loges, May 8, 1850.

unusual proportion of more than half of them day students. Two years later, in 1856, as the reputation of the place spread abroad, the balance was changed, with 200 boarders out of a total of 330. The college at Metz soon needed new quarters, or rather, it had needed them from the beginning. Of two possibilities, an already acquired country place at the edge of the town, or the ancient abbey of Saint-Clément in the middle of the city, the latter was clearly preferable. But the buildings had belonged to the army since 1791, as a barracks and artillery equipment depot, then as a storage place for army rations, and later for army cots.

For three years a letter-writing campaign by the bishop attempted to persuade the Ministry of War to sell the place. The bishop even approached the Prince-President. When the reply came, it was from the Emperor, advising the bishop that the request had been sent to the ministry.[8] The ministry's terms were exorbitant; more letters followed. In March 1853 the bishop asked for the Emperor's personal action. "Everything is possible, Sire, if one of those powerful words, which have already raised up so many things from the ruins, [should] come from your lips."[9]

Finally, on June 28, 1855, the Jesuits acquired the property for 401,000 francs, payable in fifths, every half year. With help from the bishop again, with a bank loan of 300,000 francs, and with the proceeds from the old property, the Society undertook the restoration of the abbey. It had been founded in A.D. 613, rebuilt several times, was almost abandoned for a hundred years, and was in such a state that it took three years to make the place habitable and until 1870 to finish a project which finally cost 1,600,000 francs.

The Jesuits thought the money well spent. Saint-Clément's lived up to all their hopes in the short years of its existence,

---

8. Dupont des Loges to Louis-Napoléon Bonaparte, Nov. 27, 1852, and Napoléon III to Dupont des Loges, Dec. 10, 1852, in *EJF*, III, 324.

9. Dupont des Loges to Napoléon III, March 11, 1853, *ibid.*, III, 325.

until the German occupation of Alsace-Lorraine. From the simple point of view of numbers, in 1858, the first year in which the whole college was in its new quarters, there were 400 students. Five years later there were eighty more, more than 500 before 1870. Possibly only Vaugirard in Paris had a more international clientele than Metz, where there were Belgians, Russians (thirty of them), as many Luxemburgers, a hundred Poles, and dozens of Germans, Englishmen, and South Americans. Within the city of Metz itself the college was one of the centers of Catholicity. The chapel, or in reality the church, of Saint-Clément was popular; the bishop was enthusiastic. Since Metz was a garrison city, the military played a large part in the life of the place, and they were among the most devoted supporters of the schools. In turn, they wanted something special. In 1853 the superior, Turquand, a former army officer himself, wrote: "Before long, we cannot doubt, they will ask for a school preparatory for the military schools of the government."[10] Such a course began in 1858, but it took almost another five years of negotiation and hesitation before Rome finally gave definitive permission for it. In the years that followed, until the Germans closed the school in 1872, more than 350 future officers were admitted to the government schools from Saint-Clément, almost 60 percent of them to Saint-Cyr.[11]

In the same year of 1852, Paris at last had its Jesuit college, ninety years after Louis-le-Grand had been taken from them at the time of the banishment of the Society from France. Though all recognized the importance of a college in the capital, there had been great hesitation about such a foundation. Roothaan was not at all eager to stir up trouble with a Jesuit

10. Burnichon, *La Compagnie*, III, 442.
11. See Viansson-Ponté, *Les Jésuites à Metz*, 304. The other successful candidates went to the Ecoles Polytechnique, Centrale and Forestière. The Jesuits and the alumni never forgot at the time of the First World War, and never allowed the *"cartel de gauche"* to forget later, that General Foch was one of these former students of Saint-Clément's.

establishment right under the gaze of opponents, and he feared also the difficulties of giving a "true Christian education" in such a place as Paris.[12]

However, from early 1851 an opportunity had been presented that was hard to pass up. An Abbé Poiloup offered to sell to the Society his already existing college at Vaugirard, a small village situated at the edge of the city near the present Porte de Versailles.[13] Poiloup had himself founded the school, and had worked for its success for twenty years. After more than a year of difficult negotiations, the Society bought the college, the grounds, and the country house at Moulineaux for something more than 800,000 francs, with part of the cost being met by a loan from the Crédit Foncier. The Jesuits had feared some trouble at first, and the consultors worried about a new restrictive educational law in 1852.[14] But "the government, [and] the archdiocese are not looking at us at Vaugirard with a jaundiced eye, as had been said. The little storm raised by some of Abbé Poiloup's associates has calmed down."[15]

On October 19, 1852 the Collège de l'Immaculée-Conception received its first students under the Jesuits. There were almost 170 of them that first year, one hundred more the next year, and from then on through the 1870's despite the efforts to keep the numbers down, the school never ceased growing, even after the day school at the rue de Madrid was founded in 1874. In 1861 there were 400 students, 600 in 1867, and 700 in 1872; there were approximately 800 in 1875–1876.

Contrary to the original intention for the other colleges, Vaugirard was meant from the first to be almost exclusively a

12. ARSJ, Reg., Franc., Roothaan to Studer, June 19, 1852.

13. PSJ, Paris: C³12: "Lib. Cons.," Jan. 6, 1851. Right from this first news of the opportunity, the provincial and consultors were favorable but also cautious.

14. *Ibid.*, April 21 and Nov. 29, 1852. Interestingly enough, the Crédit Foncier, had just been founded this same year; Vaugirard must have been one of its very early clients.

15. ARSJ, Franc., 8-II, 8. There was a controversy for a while over Poiloup's legal proprietorship and the financial arrangements that followed. Some of the former teachers thought that part of the money from the sale should go to them.

boarding school. Paris was too distracting a city for a young man to be abroad in and get a full Christian education at the same time. Even the Parisian students, with a few exceptions approved by the provincial, had to live at the college.[16] In fact, more than half of the students came regularly from outside the capital; during the first twelve years, for example, 37 percent of them were from Paris, 56 percent from other parts of France, and 7 percent from colonies and foreign countries.

Vaugirard was, at times to the annoyance of other Jesuit schools, *the* college of the Society in France during these years. Its very location in Paris could not help but make it so. It was even a place to visit, and the Father Minister's diary lists through the years everyone from the mayor of Vaugirard to the Apostolic Nuncio, the Duchess de Rochefoucauld, the Veuillots, Prince Lucien Bonaparte, Father de Smet from the Rocky Mountain Missions, Cardinal Patrizzi, Count de Mun, the bishop of New York, who talked rather long "in English and very successfully owing to several political allusions" (December 8, 1861), Prince Gallitzin, Montalembert, and even Villemain, no particular friend of the Jesuits.[17]

Equally interesting were the people who wrote to the rector or prefect, often about getting students into the school—or keeping them there. The Prince de Broglie inquired about his son's progress (March 2, 1864); Germiny, one of the governors of the Bank of France, did the same for his son (June 29, 1861). Dom Gueranger made inquiries for a friend (December 27, 1864), as did the Carmelite Prior in London for an acquaintance in Hamburg (September 23, 1865). The Count de Palikao recalled his services to the Jesuits in China, and asked the Jesuits in Paris to admit the son of a friend of his (July 5,

16. *EJF*, III, 1380. The consultors regularly had problems with requests to attend family festivities such as weddings or First Communions. In theory, permission was to be denied to leave the school even for such occasions; in practice, it was often almost impossible to refuse. See for example, PSJ, Paris: C³12: "Lib. Cons.," Jan. 19, 1855; May 9, 1858.

17. PSJ, Paris: C³13: Vaugirard: "Diarium P. Ministri," *passim*.

1863). General Trochu wrote in July 1864; and if in that same month legitimism was summoned up in the name of one of the correspondents, Rochejacquelein, no less a good Bonapartist than Baron Portalis wrote the next month (August 10, 1864). Berryer was sure that the Jesuits could do something "with a young man who knows that at his majority he will come into an important fortune and . . . believes that he has no need to be concerned with serious study" (December 30, 1861).[18]

In 1869, a delicate case arose which the rector described to Beckx: "Her Majesty the Queen of Spain wanted to entrust to us her son, the Prince of the Asturias. We believed that it was better to suggest to her a different catholic college, even in the interest of her son. The evil-minded journals would not have missed the chance to howl. Her Majesty so well understood the wisdom of this advice that she sent to me one of the Spanish Grandees to thank me."[19] But more immediately delicate were the cases of ill-suited students who had been recommended by bishops, "for a Parisian education." Even yet more delicate were those suggested by the Father General, of which there were frequently several.[20] Happy the day when the school could say they were doing well, but sometimes even the General's support was not enough to keep a boy in school. "A consultors' meeting was held about dismissing a certain student whom Father General much favors, but who has such disgraceful grades that all decided he should be expelled. But in view of his mother's financial situation, Father Rector will grant her a small pension."[21]

Almost from the beginning the college was in the fortunate

18. PSJ, Paris: C^{3}1: Vaugirard, *passim*.
19. ARSJ, Franc., Argout to Beckx, Jan. 25, 1869.
20. For example, ARSJ, Franc., Argout to Beckx, Dec. 3, 1867, mentions among those recommended by the General, "Leopold Torlonia, nephew of the nuncio, Msgr. Chigi, Jean Sanfelice, son of the Marquis de Monteforte" and goes on to remark that the Father General will probably "receive a visit from the Marquis of Roccagiovine, brother-in-law of Lucien Bonaparte; you can tell him that his son Napoleon is in good health."
21. PSJ, Paris: C^{3}12: "Lib. Cons.," Dec. 31, 1867.

position of being able to pick and choose among prospective students. In 1859 forty applications were rejected, in 1862 the same number.[22] By 1867 the rector wrote that never were parents so eager to get their sons into Vaugirard; of 380 applications for admission that year, the school had accepted just less than half of them, and "many of the children confided to us belong to the families of the high public officials of the State."[23]

Undeniably, there existed a certain tone of society about the school from the earliest years. One small item is illustrative; the consultors, debating whether the students should wear white trousers when they entertained their parents, decided that though it was a problem to keep them clean, still it was desirable "because it was more elegant." On the other hand, the Jesuits tried to discourage, limit, almost forbid contact with the Parisian world during the school year. "The one thing that we have to complain about is basically the Parisian frivolity, born in the milieu in which our students live and nourished by the frequent visits in the parlor."[24]

By no means were all of the students rich. The needy mother mentioned earlier was not an isolated example, and the college regularly gave a large number of reductions in the fees for the boarding school. After 1870, when the number of day students increased, there was even more scholarship help for them. For example, "almost one half of the day students [116 day students out of a grand total of 670] follow the courses gratuitously."[25]

For rich or poor, life within the college itself was not luxurious. It was not until after many years of construction that the splendid buildings were finished, and they never really kept

22. PSJ, *Litterae Annuae Parisiensis*, 1859–1860 and 1862–1863.

23. ARSJ, Franc., Argout to Beckx, Dec. 3, 1867. In 1865–1866 even the son of the director of the Ecole Normale Supérieure was listed among the students. *Litterae Annuae*, 1865–1866, and PSJ, Paris: C31: Vaugirard.

24. PSJ, Paris: C312: "Lib. Cons.," July 14, 1854; and ARSJ, Franc., Argout to Beckx, Dec. 1867.

25. ARSJ, Franc., Chauveau to Beckx, Jan. 26, 1873.

sufficiently ahead of the needs of the student body. By modern standards, accommodations were Spartan, and in 1867, fifteen years after the school was started, parents were still deploring the severity of the students' life.[26] The rector, too, wrote in that year, perhaps however to add conviction to his plea to finish the building program, "I do not doubt that if, unfortunately, the public health commission were induced to make a visit to our establishment, it would condemn and close several of our dormitories and classrooms."[27]

However spare some of the physical facilities might have been, they were surely as good as and probably better than those in most secondary schools of the time. One need only read the volume dealing with the nineteenth century at the best lycée of Paris, Louis-le-Grand, by its great and devoted historian, Gustave Dupont-Ferrier, to realize this.[28]

Louis-le-Grand had been the most famous college of the Jesuits in France before their expulsion. From it had come as alumni, for example, Fleury, Crébillon, Molière, Malesherbes, and characters as diverse as St. Francis de Sales and Voltaire. Among its most famous teachers had been the theologians Petavius and Maldonatus, Hardouin, the still enigmatic historian of the councils of the Church, and Porée, the teacher of literature to a generation (1708–1741) of Frenchmen, many of them later Académiciens.

Vaugirard had no illusions of occupying the same position in nineteenth-century France. The course of studies was that of all the Jesuit colleges. Vaugirard concentrated on implementing it as fully as possible, especially in the classical languages. But the school was fortunate in having some of the better Jesuit educators and administrators of its time, and they helped much

---

26. PSJ, Paris: C³12: "Lib. Cons.," March 5, 1867.
27. ARSJ, Franc., Argout to Beckx, Dec. 3, 1867.
28. Gustave Dupont Ferrier, *Du Collège de Clermont au lycée Louis-LeGrand, 1563–1920* (3 vols.; Paris, 1921–1925), II, *passim*. The author says (III, Foreword), that it took him fifteen or sixteen years to research and write the three volumes of the history of this one school.

to make its reputation. The mention of a few of them and of their previous and subsequent positions helps to make clear the continuity that developed at Vaugirard, and the interrelationship of personnel between it and other Jesuit colleges.

Most important in creating the traditions of the new school and in starting them on their way was Father Pierre Olivaint, one of the most gifted members of the Society in nineteenth-century France. A graduate of the Ecole Normale Supérieure, professor in the lycée of Grenoble and the Collège Bourbon, and *agrégé* of the Ecole Normale before his entrance among the Jesuits, he was the first director of studies at Vaugirard under Father Eugène Coué, and then his successor as rector from 1857 to 1865.[29] Olivaint's successor as rector was Father Gustave Argand (1865–1869). He was a priest and canon of the cathedral of Rennes before he became a Jesuit and, together with Olivaint, he saw the great years of the college in the Second Empire.[30] During the early part of Third Republic and the sad period of expulsion of the Jesuits from the school Father Emile Chauveau was rector (1872–1883). In 1835 Chauveau was, as a scholastic, one of the first surveillants at the new school, and in 1859 for a short time prefect of studies there under Olivaint. Before returning to Vaugirard he spent ten years as teacher in several of the colleges, and was for a brief period one of the Jesuit hostages of the commune. As prefect of studies after Olivaint came Father Charles Heriveau. Later prefect at Bordeaux, he returned to that position at Vaugirard in 1865, and occupied it for fourteen years until his death in 1879, thus assuring with the rectors a remarkable continuity in the direction of the school.

29. See Charles Clair, S.J., *Pierre Olivaint* (Paris, 1878). Coué himself, before his tenure at Vaugirard (1853–1857), was treasurer of the Province of Paris; after his rectorship he became assistant to the provincial, and then successively rector of the colleges at Poitiers (1861), Metz (1867), and Vannes (1871).

30. Argand later became rector at Poitiers from 1869 to 1875. While there he was confessor and counselor of M. Legentil, the originator of the project for the Basilique de Sacré Coeur on Montmartre, "the act of reparation reared as a monument by a penitent France."

Such a continuity existed, too, with several of the more important professors. Father Marin de Boylesve was professor of philosophy for sixteen years, from 1853 to 1869. Among the teachers of these upper classes as professors of history were, again, Olivaint, and also Father Eugène Marquigny, later chosen by the Countess of Chambord herself to write the life of the last Bourbon claimant to the throne, "Henry V."[31] In the rhetoric and humanities classes, Father Georges Longhaye was for long an excellent teacher and almost the official arbiter of literary tastes for students and fellow Jesuits, tastes quite a bit too classically inclined for modern times and perhaps for his own too.

Even among the surveillants, often young Jesuit scholastics who occupied that post for only a few years between the study of philosophy and theology, there were examples of continuity in priests who stayed at the task for years. Most notable was Father Charles de Nadaillac, surveillant from 1868 to 1880, the author of Jeux de Collège, a handbook of recreation in the colleges.[32]

The province catalogues bear record to other long tenures, as they do to the number of Jesuits at Vaugirard. In 1853–1854 there were 40 members in the community and 270 students; three years later there were 51. By 1865 there were 58, and by the end of the Second Empire, in 1870, there were 66, 25 priests, 22 scholastics and 19 lay brothers, occupied with a college of somewhat more than 600 students.

It was no wonder that with 40 Jesuits at Vaugirard in 1854, the vigorous Bishop Pie of Poitiers, later to be a cardinal, thought that there were enough men available, and kept pressing the provincial for a college in his episcopal city. In 1850 Rubillon had refused the first request, and through that sum-

31. See *EJF,* II, 631–634, "Frohsdorf."
32. Charles de Nadaillac, S.J., and J. Rousseau, S.J., *Les Jeux de collège* (Paris, 1875).

mer letter after letter went to Poitiers with the same refusal to ever more insistent demands.[33]

The bishop wrote to Rome too, and in answer to an inquiry from the General, the provincial sent a long reply which illustrates the impossible situation in which the French Jesuits found themselves. Rubillon admitted that he had refused a day school in Poitiers because of the bishop's already existing Catholic college, and because of the state faculty. He said that he also had turned down a boarding school proposed by Pie at the small town of Thouars, for it would have involved an inextricable tangle of four interested parties, the city, the diocese, the stockholders, and the Society. Then he recalled the demands on personnel for Brugelette, Amiens, and Vannes, and went on: "besides, your reverence has reminded me that our residences need to be strengthened; you have recommended that I set aside Breton Jesuits for Quimper, that I give help to the bishop of Toronto and to China; [you have urged] the full two-year period of studies for the rhetoricians, special preparatory studies for professors of physics and mathematics, and encouragement and formation of writers. In truth, I cannot keep up with all the present obligations; on both knees I beg you not to involve us in new ones, especially in these stormy times, and to leave to my successor a little liberty of action."[34]

Rubillon's further remarks on the particular and quite basic matter of finding a suitable place at Poitiers is an exasperated commentary on how little those who wanted a college knew what it involved: "to find a locale . . . for him [the representative of the bishop] that is an easy thing; he is thinking of the garden shed and the chicken coop at the back of our property, or of a tiny rented house, where there is nothing in the way of yard, chapel, prefect's office, or classroom. Next year, if the at-

33. PSJ, Reg., Rubillon to Rousseau, April 9, 1850, and *passim* throughout 1850.
34. PSJ, Reg., Rubillon to Roothaan, Aug. 22, 1850.

tempt succeeds, some space nearby will be rented, but at a distance from our residence; and, he says, *if the attempt succeeds, you will go on further,* if it doesn't succeed, you can pack your bags, *you are accustomed to that.* Just what does your reverence think of that way of acting and speaking?"[35]

The pressure continued. By 1854, though "there would be plenty of grave reasons to put it off again, . . . Monseigneur Pie wants us to take his college beginning this year, and for that he has serious reasons."[36] One of them was the closing of Brugelette that summer, with a whole faculty now supposedly free. On October 10, 1854 40 Jesuits and 155 students made up the new community of the college at Poitiers, heir of Brugelette.

Memories of Montmorillon had helped to bring the college to Poitiers, and within a few years an alumnus of another of the former Jesuit minor seminaries, Sainte-Anne d'Auray, helped it purchase a suitable location for new buildings. Meanwhile, however, the place was having more than the usual financial troubles, and the minutes of the province consultors' meetings are instructive reading. By early August 1857 Poitiers was so deeply in debt, space so lacking, and students so relatively few to meet the financial charges, that there was talk either of closing the college or of getting extra help from the province. Should a new superior be appointed? A visitor? Perhaps some of the Jesuits might ask their relatives to help the college. A few days later a bank loan was decided on, with stock certificates as security. The loan finally came from the Banque de France, with railroad stock of the province as collateral.[37]

Then in 1858 the new building program began, too ambitiously, and through the next two years money trouble again was a topic of several of the meetings. Under a new rector the first move to part of the new quarters took place in 1860. Later

35. *Ibid.*
36. PSJ, Reg., Studer to Beckx, June 26, 1854.
37. PSJ, "Lib. Cons.," Aug. 6 and 9, 1857, Feb. 8, 1858.

that year he was sure that there was an underhand attempt to keep the college from moving into the whole place. As a result, there was also trouble with the contractors, and so more money was needed.[38]

By 1861 there was a third rector. The next year "the terrible temporal [i.e. financial] state of the college at Poitiers" was again up for discussion, and it was suggested that three good treasurers of other houses in the province examine the situation and see what was to be done.[39] Finally the college managed to get all the buildings completed and itself out of debt, and although the number of students rose regularly, to 300 in 1860, and to more than 400 in 1865, echoes of this trouble still resounded beyond these years.

Poitiers was the last college founded by the French Jesuits during the reign of Louis Napoleon. Once the Second Empire had firmly established itself, the fundamental disagreements of papacy and regime in religious policy broke through the covering of political solidarity against disorder or revolution in France and the Papal States. The French state, still basically Gallican in religious affairs, stood firmly for the prerogatives of the Napoleonic concordat, organic articles included; thus it was inevitably opposed to a papacy ever more centralized, ever more disinclined toward local autonomy in the Church, and ever more resolutely set against interference by the state in religious matters.

Within the French Church, the most powerful supporters of such Ultramontanism were, of course, the religious orders and congregations, especially those with headquarters in Rome. They were regularly a source of watchful concern to the government. "The congregations and religious associations were

---

38. *Ibid.*, Nov. 9, 1860. The rector was justified in his suspicions of official opposition. Maurain, *La Politique ecclésiastique,* 465n, says that Rouland, the Minister of Cults, tried to prevent the move (AN, F19 6.288 and BB18 1.535).

39. PSJ, "Lib. Cons.," Nov. 1862.

not only contrary to the administrative authoritarianism and the Gallican tendencies of the government. It saw in them a political danger."[40] The government regularly asked the prefects for information on the congregations established in their respective departments. They were to report on the directors and professors in schools, on superiors, and especially on the political opinions of the latter.[41]

Of all these congregations, the Jesuits were universally reputed to be—and probably were—the most ultramontane. Consequently they were the objects of even more detailed prefectorial reports than were the other congregations.[42] Maurain, who has done the most thorough investigation of the government archives, confirms what seems true from the Jesuit records also.

> All the reports are in agreement in recording the extreme reserve in matters of politics on the part of the Jesuits, who preoccupied the government more than all the other religious orders. In general, they abstained from voting, confirming thus to the traditions of their order, except when the bishops suggested that they vote. Certain ones among them willingly expressed their gratitude for a government which assured the liberty of their order. But others belonged to legitimist families. Above all, the legitimists made up the main clientele of their ministries, of their chapels, and of their colleges. They were thus obliged to keep on good terms with them. The general of the order, seeing the danger, put his religious on guard against a solidarity which would compromise them in the eyes of the government. He reiterated his instructions in

---

40. Maurain, *La Politique ecclésiastique,* 122.

41. For example, Fortoul made such requests in 1853 (AN, F19 5.589 and F19 5.768 to 5.877) and again in 1856 (AN, F19 1.948, 6.092, 6.247, 6.253, 6.313); Rouland did the same in 1859 (AN, F19 6.244 and 6.283).

42. Maurain, *La Politique ecclésiastique,* 121. See AN, F19 6.288.

several letters, a fact that is enough to show what resistance they encountered.[43]

After 1854 new colleges continued to be offered to the Society, but the burdens of staffing and paying for those already in operation, and administrative vexations on the part of the government hindered further acceptances. Finally, "from the end of 1859, the imperial government decided not to allow the nonauthorized congregations to found new establishments except when the government itself recognized their usefulness."[44] This was a simple abrogation of Article 60 of the Falloux Law which stated that "any Frenchman at least 25 years old . . . can open an establishment of secondary instruction" on the condition of making the proper notifications to the local, prefectorial, and state officials, and it was a veiled return to the old system of preliminary governmental authorization.[45]

43. Maurain, *La Politique ecclésiastique,* 118. The problem of "keeping on good terms with the legitimists," and the neutrality of some of the Jesuits are both illustrated in the case of the liturgical invocation "Domine, salvum fac Imperatorem" (Lord, protect the Emperor), which was the modern version of the old "Domine salvum fac regem." Whether, at Vaugirard, to sing it at Mass, or add it to other prayers, or sing it at Benediction, or just forget it completely, appears explicitly in consultors' meetings from at least 1858 to 1864, with all sorts of qualifications, hesitations, and referrals to the provincial. See for example, PSJ, Paris C³12: Vaugirard, "Lib Cons.," Feb. 8, 1858 and Sept. 6, 1864; and PSJ, Paris C³2: Vaugirard, Fessard to Olivaint, Feb. 11, 1858, referring to Cardinal Morlot's letter and prescriptions of the Holy Father.

44. Maurain, *La Politique ecclésiastique,* 443. On March 9, 1852 the government had already supplanted the election of members of the Conseil Supérieur de l'Instruction Publique by direct nomination. On June 14, 1854, a new law suppressed the departmental educational councils, reorganized France into sixteen academies and put into the hands of the ministry the nomination of members, a long step back toward the *"monopole universitaire"* at least on the administrative level.

45. A "veiled return" in the sense that no law was so passed or even introduced. It was simply a decision of the emperor's Privy Council. Maurain traces it to 1859–1860 through various ministerial references in later letters: e.g., AN, F¹⁹ 6.288 Baroche to Ravinet, Feb. 27, 1866, and F¹⁹ 3.972 Baroche to the Prefect of Sarthe, Dec. 21, 1868. De Rochemonteix, *Souvenirs de Notre Dame de Sainte-Croix* (Le Mans, 1883), 43, also quotes a letter of Victor Duruy,

While the government was thus regularly occupied with the politics of the congregations and especially of the Society of Jesus, the Jesuits were concerned about their standing in the eyes of the government. At first, on the educational level, there was some fear of how the provisions for inspection in the Falloux Law would be applied. This fear may have been aroused by the emphasis which the Catholic opponents of the law placed on the unacceptability of inspection of religious schools by nonreligious, even antireligious, minions of the Ministry of Education. In actual fact, there seems little evidence that many real problems developed, until perhaps the later years of the empire. In many instances the academic councils were benevolent, and at the minimum, both sides learned to live with one another.

On the political, and no longer on the directly educational, level, the Society always felt some tension. The example of Saint-Etienne loomed ominously in its memory. At the least incident which the government might construe as a hostile act, immediate measures of repression or of explanation were taken. A letter of the provincial of Lyons to the Superior General in 1857 furnishes a vivid example of this.

> We have had these days at Mongré a little alarm. One of the students posted up on a door a picture of the Emperor which came as a prize in a new year's puzzle gift, and another student spat on it. As soon as I was informed of the incident I started for Mongré, and the two students (13 and 14 years old) were expelled on the spot. The rector of the Academy at Lyons, to whom I made my report, at first found the punishment a little severe . . . The Cardinal of Lyons, also informed, told me that it [the incident] was nothing. However, I asked him to write to the Minister, and he judged it prudent to do so. Lastly, I

Minister of Education, to the rector of the Academy of Caen, Jan. 13, 1870, on this quiet decision.

immediately sent Father Périé to Paris to see, with Father Studer and Father Ravignan, what else was to be done. I believe that at Mongré no one of the Jesuits is at fault, that everything possible is being done to forestall other incidents such as this, and that the stopping of the whole thing was prompt and exemplary. But what a problem with children whose parents are themselves so imprudent, so extreme in this way.[46]

Often the local officials were friendly; in the early years, especially, even the representatives of the central power were gracious. The prefect of Lozère would personally bring to the college at Mende an invitation to a concert in the salon of the prefecture. At Avignon the archbishop, at the distribution of prizes at the end of the year, would find himself in the company of the prefect, the mayor, and the rector of the academy.

But even with such benevolence, one could not be too much at ease. Again at Avignon, for example, in 1852, the prefect, M. Durand Saint-Amand, aware that the municipal councillors, the founders of the college, and the fathers of families were all openly known as legitimists, gave a panegyric of Napoleon III at one of the assemblies, and at its end invited the students to cry "Long live the Emperor!" This they most fortunately did, "urged on by the attitude of their teachers, by their gestures, and by their looks."[47]

In Paris, so close to the center of power, precautions were constant. The records of the house consultations at Vaugirard testified to this concern. Should a student be dismissed "for a certain antipolitical manifestation? After taking into account the stupidity of this particular student, and in order not to spread abroad the news [of the incident] all the consultors thought that a dismissal was not imperative. But a severe punishment was to be inflicted." This was early in 1854. Later the

46. LSJ, Reg., Jocas to Beckx, Jan. 4, 1857.
47. *EJF*, I, 486.

same year, the consultors saw more malice in another case, and the student was dismissed. In the following years, there was more than one emergency consultation about such matters. In 1865 when the atmosphere was threatening for the Jesuits, all the consultors agreed on immediate dismissal of a student who, in the presence of two policemen, had shouted out a remark against the Emperor, despite the fact that the boy's father was an officer in the imperial guard; the rector himself went that very evening to report the incident to the prefect of police.[48]

The provincial consultors had even wondered, some years before, whether it would not be good to go directly to the Emperor to try to clear up calumnies being circulated within the government about the Society, but they could not agree on the opportuneness or effectiveness of such a move.[49]

From Rome came letters cautioning against politics such as those mentioned by Maurain. One of them, to all the French provincials on January 10, 1855, was made public by wish of the General himself:

> In fact as in law, the Society of Jesus is and declares itself to be apart from all political parties, whatever they might be. In every country and under every form of government, it confines itself exclusively to the exercise of its ministries, not having in view anything but its purpose which is quite above all human political interests.
>
> Always and everywhere, a member of the Society will fulfill loyally the duties of a good citizen and of a faithful subject of the government which rules his country.
>
> Always and everywhere, he says to everyone by his teaching and by his conduct, "Render to Caesar the things that are Caesar's, and to God the things that are God's."[50]

48. PSJ, Paris: C³12: Vaugirard, "Lib. Cons.," May 16, 1854; Nov. 20, 1854; Nov. 23, 1865.
49. PSJ, "Lib. Cons.," April 18, 1859 and June 11, 1860.
50. ARSJ, Franc., Reg., Beckx to Provincials in France, Jan. 10, 1855.

These are fine sentiments, but they seemed to need much re-calling. The Roman archives contain private reiterations of these themes to the individual provinces.[51]

The Jesuits certainly were ultramontane, but within the privacy of the community not all were legitimists. Even as late as 1866 when, for some time, relations between France and the Holy See had been anything but cordial, there was a curious incident at Lille where two of the Jesuits were greatly at odds on Napoleon III, one arraigning the other for his support of the Emperor. The superior, too, wrote that "the good Father V . . . is affected by a sort of delirium on the subject of the ever increasing prosperity of the Church, thanks especially to the services rendered to it by the new Charlemagne, the idol of his heart."[52] Though the Emperor would have been gratified by such a tribute if he had known of it, he and most of his government would probably still have been convinced of the fundamental opposition of the Jesuits.

Each party had different limits for God and Caesar. The number of alumni of Jesuit schools who volunteered for the pontifical military service could do nothing but irritate the French government after the mid-1850's and convince it that Caesar was getting less than his due. To mention only one school, Vannes alone had thirty-two students among the papal troops at Castelfidardo, three of whom were killed there. Between 1860 and 1870, more than 130 alumni were members of this pontifical army. Sometimes students even interrupted their schooling in order to enlist, but this was rather frowned upon by the Jesuits. Bishop Mermillod of Lausanne, one of those who ardently recruited for Pius IX, reported the Pope's

51. For example: ARSJ, Franc.: March 13, 1856; August 30, 1857; Jan. 21, 1860; ARSJ, Lugd.: Feb. 25, 1856; July 17, 1856; Feb. 25, 1859; May 27, 1859 (on this occasion one of the Jesuits had said from the pulpit that the war then in progress in Italy was unjust. He was severely reprimanded). ARSJ, Tolos.: July 17, 1856, renewed Oct. 25, 1856.

52. ARSJ, Camp., Possoz to Beckx, June 14, 1866, and Dubois to Beckx, July 2, 1866.

words, "The college of St. Francis Xavier at Vannes . . . Ah, of all the colleges of France, that is the one which is dearest to me, for no other has given me so many defenders."[53]

As a result, through all these years the Jesuits felt insecure about their schools. They worried about the reactions of the government, and were most reluctant in general to engage as Jesuits in any kind of discussion in the colleges which might touch on what they conceived to be the political order.[54]

A problem more immediate and more internal to the schools was the uncertainty whether they should be boarding or day schools. The Society originally wanted to found only day schools after 1850. Every pertinent document gives evidence of this. Yet by 1854 when the roster of colleges was closed, not one of them was exclusively such an establishment, and this failure was to weigh heavily upon the future of the Society in France in all the years to follow.

The Jesuit colleges, from the earliest ones in the sixteenth century up to the suppression in the eighteenth century, were in the very great majority day schools. Boarding colleges were held in disfavor mainly because they would have conflicted almost necessarily with the complete gratuity of Jesuit education, a practice based on concern for the living of the vow of poverty as conceived by the Society. Instruction could have been given freely, even in a resident school, but the Society would surely have had to charge for room and board in such a place, and thus the basic principle of free teaching would always have been threatened or at least confused by the resi-

53. *EJF*, V, 49, and *Souvenir du 10 mai, 1876* (Vannes, 1876).
54. The question of the possible dissolution of the Society by the government came up every once in a while in the province consultors' meetings. Even though the Jesuits were prepared to engage the best lawyers possible to handle such a case, it was still thought most likely, if it came to the alternatives of official government recognition or dissolution, that certain conditions would be imposed that the Society could never accept.

dent charges. As a result, where boarding schools did exist, the residence was almost always a separate entity.

After the restoration of the Society in 1814 there were precious few rulers or cities or wealthy individuals able or willing to set up foundations like those which had existed previously and had provided the funds which made free teaching possible. Reluctantly the Society asked the Holy See for a dispensation in particular cases from the provision in its constitutions which forbade the acceptance of tuition. In France, day schools had been in practice impossible for the Jesuits before the Falloux Law. The minor seminaries of 1814–1828, supported at least minimally by the diocese, had been by law boarding schools. The exile colleges could have been no other than that.

The whole question of boarding schools was thought serious enough to be discussed formally in the presence of Roothaan at Brugelette, in September, 1849. Major superiors from France, Belgium, Italy, and Spain conferred on the future of the schools in general, and on boarding schools in particular.[55] The General wanted boarding schools to be very limited in number, thought they were not at all ideal, and agreed that since the constitutions themselves did not define clearly the nature of this type of school, one would have to look to the history of the Society for such information.

The two French provinces had decided that the first schools founded after the Falloux Law were going to be day schools. Some minor adaptations might have to be made, but day students, hopefully, were going to be in the great majority. Within a few months of opening, the plans and the hopes were in ruins. Everywhere without exception, a Jesuit-staffed boarding section had to be opened and all too soon the majority of students were of this type in each of the colleges. By the end of 1850 it was clear that future schools could be no other than

55. PSJ, C-12: "Enquêtes Provinciales 1849–1860."

residential. Finally, the history which was consulted in order to determine in the concrete the organization of such schools was very recent history; the colleges in fact modeled themselves on the minor seminaries.

To follow the case of Amiens as an example is to know what happened everywhere. In July 1850 Philippe Villefort, the French Jesuit subsecretary, wrote: "I much fear that the desire, universally shared by our fathers, of having very few boarding schools and many day schools will not be able to overcome the numerous obstacles in its way." A few days later, Rubillon already had to make a partial concession. "From a religious and scholastic viewpoint, pure day schools would be more advantageous, but a day school encounters such opposition in [current] ideas, and some central parts of cities and some family circles offer such dangers that boarding or half-boarding schools have become necessary almost everywhere. After resisting a long time, I have just granted permission for a half-boarding school at Amiens."[56]

Financially, ruin was inevitable even with this partial concession. "It is impossible to meet our charges with a day school and a half-boarding school [*demi-pensionnat*]. We shall have to settle our affairs and withdraw in solemn humiliation for the Society and for the faith, or we shall have to establish a boarding school." The provincial was speaking of Amiens in particular, but he and the provincial of Lyons might have said the same for all the schools. Roothaan agreed. "To abandon the college which we have just opened at Amiens would be, in a way, for us to commit suicide, but without the opening of a boarding school, we would be forced to abandon the college, for lack of means of subsistence."[57] Even with the permission to charge tuition for the teaching itself, there was not enough

---

56. PSJ, Roothaan, Villefort to Fournier, July 10, 1850; and PSJ, Reg., Rubillon to Villefort, July 13, 1850.

57. PSJ, Reg., Rubillon to Roothaan, Dec. 6, 1850; and PSJ, Roothaan, Roothaan to Rubillon, Dec. 10, 1850.

money to make a go of a new foundation simply because there were not enough students. Most of the families did not want day schools and would not send their sons to them. This was the basic problem.

Often, fathers of families had themselves been boarders at the Jesuit minor seminaries or exile colleges, and they wanted that type of school for their sons, or they were of such a social class that a free school or even a minimally expensive day school was demeaning in their eyes. Then too, parents were in many cases landed proprietors from small towns or villages. Of necessity, they sought a boarding school. Perhaps even more common, ever since the creation of the Napoleonic lycée the whole experience of a generation of French secondary schools had been of the residential type. The tradition of the old Jesuit day schools had vanished and was forgotten. The prospect of new Jesuit day schools was stillborn and disappeared.

What this meant for the colleges of the Society after 1850, and what it was going to mean in the future, was described with clarity in a document of 1858.[58] In pleading for day schools its basic arguments went as follows: The *petite bourgeoisie* and the ordinary people of city and country, that is, three fourths of the population, had no resource but a day school. Yet they were not coming to the Jesuit schools, the day sections of which were insignificant. The constitutions of the Society urged on Jesuits work for the less-favored classes. Reason itself counseled such work, for while the Jesuits said that they hoped to act on the leading elements in a society, they should have taken account also "of that ordinary child of the people, who would by his talents arrive at the highest positions in the state, and that army of civil servants who are recruited almost entirely from among the bourgeoisie."[59] The history of the Society

58. PSJ, C-12: 6040, "Des Externats dans les collèges de la Compagnie," Sept. 1858. No author's name appears on this long handwritten report.
59. *Ibid.*, 2.

showed, too, that such students had come to the Jesuit schools in the past. It was wrong, then, to resign oneself to the isolation in which the colleges currently existed.

Even the experiences of the revolution in 1848 had shown that the Jesuits had been popular where they had had residences that occupied themselves with the ordinary people. To the objection, sometimes seriously raised, that it was "an evil service rendered to the children of the lower classes to take them from the occupations of their fathers, and it was favoring a disastrous tendency of the present age, that of rising out of one's social condition," the only response possible was that closing the Jesuit schools to such "disordered ambition" would not stop it. The students would simply go to those "pestilential schools which do not give along with instruction [in secular subjects] the antidote of a religious education."[60]

Why was there so little success with the day divisions that the Jesuit colleges did have? The Society did not know how to deal with the susceptibilities of such students, who were both timid and resentful in the presence of the obviously rich class of boarders. On the one hand, the boarding section devoured the time, energy, and attention of the Jesuits, and, on the other, "the day division was for some of them a new institution that brought into our school rooms a class of society which they had never before dealt with on close terms, and for whose needs they were not prepared."[61]

The author of the report thought that a day division would never flourish as long as it was part and parcel of the boarding school, because it supposed what did not exist, that is, at least a relative equality in backgrounds, taste, and exterior conditions of life. One could not present day students with the sight of abundance, superfluous expenses, joyful carelessness, and family influences on the part of the boarders, in contrast to their own daily privation and worries, and the preoccupa-

60. *Ibid.*, 3.
61. *Ibid.*, 5.

tions of their families. In the classrooms and the academies an equilibrium could, perhaps, be maintained, "where talent itself assigned the ranks," but this was true nowhere else in the college. Ideally, the solution would have been a completely separate day school, but in the present, practical order at least several moves were possible. First, one or several of the priests on the faculty were to be appointed to work exclusively with day students in all fields, in an attempt to create a true family spirit. Second, special recreational, social, and educational facilities were to be prepared for the day students. Third, the Society was to enter into closer relations with the diocesan clergy and the directors of primary schools, giving them the right to designate regularly as holders of scholarships students of poorer or more modest means.

> Our colleges will [then] stop seeming to be reserved for a privileged caste; they will take on the aspect of more generous, more disinterested institutions, more devoted to the welfare of the poor.
>
> They will even gain more boarding students, by losing that caste mark, that air of colleges of nobles, which contributes to holding at a distance from us the newly rising classes, civil servants, civic officials, men engaged in finance.
>
> Thus the Society will situate itself, as it rightly hopes, in the midst of the Christian people . . . and to the profit of the faith, will have put down deep roots among a Christian population. This will be its recompense for having carried on the mission of its Master—"The poor have had the Gospel preached to them."[62]

Unfortunately the Jesuits never did, perhaps never could, attract a large number of the *petit-bourgeois* families. More and more through the years of the Second Empire, in addition to the aristocracy, the upper middle and the upper classes came to the schools. Only after 1870 did new day schools and the

62. *Ibid.*, 11.

day divisions in the older schools begin to flourish. Even then, there was still not enough success in attracting pupils from the lower ranks of the financial and social ladder.

Eleven colleges in one year, a total of eighteen institutions in less than five years, cannot be founded on hope and good will alone, even though those may seem to have been the principal resources in the first few months. Next to men, money soon became the most pressing need. To get the schools started, the Society tapped a variety of resources.

At first some of the Jesuits seemed to have thought that financing would not be a great problem since local governmental bodies could take care of it.[63] They relied in part on a provision of the Falloux Law which stated that "the independent schools can obtain from communes, departments or the state, a locale and a subvention, without this subvention exceeding one tenth of the annual expenses of the establishment."[64] They foresaw also the possibility of the Jesuit school becoming the communal college. In such a case the municipal council would have entered into a contract with the Society, which would have had, thereafter, no concern for the finances. It quickly became clear that such hopes of official help were almost groundless. As it turned out, only Saint-Affrique received a real subvention, and only Mende was founded as a communal college.[65]

Some saw the colleges being supported by the spontaneous alms and gifts of faithful Catholics, much as the residences

63. PSJ, C-12, "De la possibilité et des avantages des collèges proprement dits." Again, there is no author's name on this report and no date, though it seems to have been written at just about the time of passage of the Falloux Law.

64. *Titre* III, c. I, art. 69.

65. Though the Jesuits did not become involved in communal colleges, within a few years almost fifty of them had passed from direct state control to the direction of religious groups. This, as Rubillon said, when the movement began in 1850, was hardly calculated to put the Université in good humor, and he worried about possible reactions (PSJ, Reg., Rubillon to Maillard, Nov. 23, 1850).

were supported. This was totally to misconceive the differences between the usually small and simple residence of Jesuits and the large, complex entity that a college would be, with all its requirements of a stable, solidly guaranteed future. In several cities, friends of the Jesuits grouped themselves in a loosely organized fashion and promised financial help to the prospective schools. Avignon was a case in point, and it taught an early and needed lesson. No contract had been signed, no formal engagement entered into; once the school was barely established, the inevitable result was that both sides had to muddle through a difficult period of financial misunderstandings.

Finally, two sources of initial funds were most commonly employed. First, a form of corporate stock organization under civil law was set up, which issued and sold annual interest-bearing shares in the particular educational enterprise. Amiens is again an early example, where the money thus realized from the shareholders was used to buy land and buildings in the name of one or several Jesuits who were the legal proprietors. Each year, after interest charges and the expenses of community and college had been met, any profit was to be used to buy back the capital stock to the benefit of the Society.[66] In case of liquidation of the whole enterprise, the building would become the property of the shareholders, with no further obligation on the part of the Jesuits. If by *force majeure* the Society was again to be forbidden the right to educate, the establishment would go to the bishop who would carry on the place as a school, reserving to the Jesuits the right to resume its direction when possible. With modifications to suit the individual cases, some such contract was most commonly entered into by many of the schools. A second usual source of funds was a loan, most often from a bank, as, for example, for Vaugirard from the Crédit Foncier, or for Poitiers from the

66. See PSJ, Reg., Rubillon to Roothaan, June 21, 1850. Except that their owners were not legally creditors, these shares would seem to have been more like bonds, in present day parlance, than stocks, but at the time, in the eyes of the law, they were the latter.

Banque de France. Sometimes, too, individual friends of the Society or families of particular Jesuits would loan money, often on property mortgages.

These sources of capital funds were used throughout the period from 1850 to 1880. A résumé of the financial situation at Marseilles in 1879, five years after the founding of the school, can serve as an illustration.[67] A total of 400,000 francs for the purchase of property for the new college were obtained by the sale of stock shares to families of Jesuits and to friends. Another 300,000 francs came from an issue of bonds at three percent; 100,000 francs from a mortgage loan by a friend at three percent; another 100,000 from a five percent mortgage loan by the fathers of two of the Jesuits; and finally, 30,000 francs were borrowed for a current account on a short term loan at five percent. This second total of 530,000 francs was used to help pay for construction and furnishing of the building. The rector reported that "all were in agreement that our borrowing was done under favorable conditions with regard to the interest due, which is lower than the ordinary rate."

Once in a while there was another source of funds. Before pronouncing final religious vows as a member of the Society of Jesus, a Jesuit makes a renunciation of personal ownership of goods, and what he has or might have as patrimony he wills finally and irrevocably as he chooses. He need not designate the Society or one of its works as beneficiary, but he may do so. Sometimes such a renunciation was made in favor of the schools. Father Damas is one example of a Jesuit from a wealthy family asking that part of this fortune be applied to a particular school, in this case 300,000 francs to Saint-Etienne.[68] But such a bequest was hardly a frequent occurrence.

The Society could not legally hold ownership of property and buildings since it was not a recognized congregation. So, at first, individuals, or small group of Jesuits in partnership, be-

67. ARSJ, Lugd., Clairet to Beckx, Jan. 16, 1878.
68. ARSJ, Lugd., Damas to Roothaan, July 23, 1852.

came the legal proprietors. Later, a type of tontine arrangement was set up, and still later, the Society took advantage of
the passage of further general financial legislation to constitute
a series of corporate ownerships, the members of the boards
of which happened, as individuals, to be Jesuits. A typical instance was the "joint-stock company" set up at Toulouse on
December 31, 1864, by nine Jesuit shareholders, for "the instruction and education of youth, the publishing of new works,
and in default of these purposes, for the profitable exploitation . . . of the properties engaged by the contractants." These
properties, the capital of the company, had a value of 890,000
francs, and were made up of the college of Sainte-Marie, the
day-school building, the villa-farm outside the city, and the
residence and church at the rue des Fleurs.[69]

The revenue of the colleges came mainly from the fees paid
by the students. The day students paid nothing or were
charged a relatively small sum; the gratuitous instruction at
Toulouse, or the sixty francs per year at Sarlat or the seventy-
two at Amiens were typical of the early 1850's. By the late
1870's such fees were higher. The money was supposed to cover
the expenses of these students and a small part of the general
expenses of school and community. The fee could not very well
be far out of line with the sums charged by the state schools
if the colleges hoped to compete for day students.[70]

The boarders really supported the schools. Without their
numbers, no one of the establishments during the Second Empire could have existed, and even when the day schools were
increasingly emphasized after 1870, it was not the simple day
scholars but the half-boarders and the all-day students [*externes
restants*] who provided a great part of the revenue. Brugelette

69. TSJ, Tolos., Collège Ste. Marie et Mont Blanc, "Société par Actions,"
Dec. 31, 1864, art. 2 and 5.
70. Sometimes the lycées were more expensive, e.g., at Louis-le-Grand, 120
francs after 1845, up to 300–375 francs by 1860, between 450–700 francs in the
years up to 1900. See Dupont-Ferrier, *Le Lycée Louis-le-Grand*, II, 90. The
Jesuit school at Lille in 1877 proposed a fee of 450 francs for a day student;
ARSJ, Camp., Sengler to Beckx, Jan. 1877.

had asked a total of 790 francs from its full boarders for ten and a half months in 1849–1850. When Vaugirard was founded in 1852 the price was close to 1000 francs. Sainte-Marie in Toulouse on the other hand charged only 750 francs in the early 1860's. By the late 1870's the cost was 1400 francs in Paris for boarders, and the same amount for them at such a school as the one at Lille, new, provincial, and peopled mostly by nonboarders.

These fees, and whatever extra was received in the way of gifts, were to meet all the expenses of the school, support the Jesuit community, pay the interest on loans and dividends on stock, retire the shares if possible, and, it was hoped, provide some profit to be set aside as capital investment funds.[71]

Despite these various sources, money was never easy to come by, and Mongré was the only school that had few or no financial worries; in later years it could even help some of the other establishments. There were not many really wealthy Jesuits, loans had to be paid back, interest charges fell due regularly, and building and maintenance seemed never to end. Through all these years, worried correspondence went on between rectors and provincials and Rome on the subject of debts.[72]

One example will illustrate how deep a concern the debts were. In 1858 the Mignon family offered as a gift to the Paris

71. A detailed letter in 1874 on the management of investments began by remarking that "the introduction into modern society of anonymous, transferable securities, exactly at the moment when the laws deny to the Society a juridical personality, and when they hinder in a thousand ways the [administration of the] real property of religious orders is, without doubt, a benefit of Divine Providence which lessens our difficulties." Human prudence was then called on to aid Divine Providence, with detailed advice for the rectors and treasurers of the various communities. Purely speculative investments were absolutely forbidden as contrary to canon law and to the rules of the Society. Then there were instructions which started with choice of stocks or bonds (the latter were preferred), and ended with ways of protecting investments, in ordinary and in troubled times. LSJ, "Litterae Encyclicae Patrum Provincialium," P. Jullien, "Sur l'emploi des valeurs immobilières, titres de rentes, obligations, actions," Oct. 20, 1875.

72. In 1869, almost twenty years after its foundation, the college in Toulouse still had some debts going back to 1852, debts to single creditors as low as 3000 francs and as high as 60,000 francs; TSJ, Tolos., Collège Ste. Marie.

Jesuits for a day school a magnificent piece of property near the Parc Monçeau, 14,000 square meters of land worth approximately one million to one and a half million francs. Another benefactor offered to gather the funds for the building. Despite this opportunity to open a day school, and despite the fact that the General was strongly advised that the Society should accept or be left out completely as far as such a college was concerned, he refused absolutely, because of the frightful debts weighing upon the other colleges.[73] He may have known from experience that inevitably the venture would cost far more than the most generous estimate. Most of them had. In any case, the day school in Paris only came into existence sixteen years later, in 1874, after several renewals of the generous offer.

These financial worries were no different in many ways from those of other private schools. But perhaps they weighed more heavily on superiors as they remembered the disaster that had befallen the Society in the eighteenth century. Bankruptcy charges had been the occasion of the grand assault in the old *parlements* against the Jesuits immediately before their expulsion from France. The current situation, too, was itself enough cause for concern. Any public crisis, any generalized depression, might bring on a particular ruin for the heavily indebted Jesuit schools and open the way to further complications. Thus, here was another reason that within the colleges one was not going to try something venturesome, financial or scholastic, which might jeopardize one school—or even the whole system.

Boarding schools were necessary in order to attract students. But boarders required many more facilities than did day students. Along with the added money which they brought in, came the added expenses which they necessitated. Heavy expenditures in the form of money were worrisome enough. They were worse when they took the form of men.

Most unfortunately, this is just what the boarding schools

73. ARSJ, Franc., Fessard to Beckx, April 28, 1858.

did; they devoured personnel. The relationship between the total number of Jesuits available and the number of colleges to be staffed, not even to speak of other ministries of the Society, was completely out of proper proportion. The boarding schools created problems that were both current and long-range, for colleges and Jesuits alike.

The problem appeared right at the beginning of the work of the restored Society, with the eight minor seminaries, all boarding schools, taken on by a province in which the members were all newly recruited. The second chapter of this study treated briefly of the situation, an impasse from which the only exit was the violent one of the expulsion from those schools in 1828. This gave at least a breathing spell to the renascent Society. An organized course of studies could at last begin to function for the younger Jesuits. The exile colleges, too, while not so numerous as to make overwhelming demands on personnel, did give an opportunity for the formation of future teachers if and when schools were again to be allowed in France.

The year 1850 brought back the old difficulty, and the following years to 1854 compounded it. Eighteen day schools started in so short a time would have been a difficult enough burden; eighteen boarding schools were an almost impossible burden, especially if it is remembered that, as far as could be, their entire personnel was Jesuit.

The makeup of that personnel and the particular functions of its members will be treated at length later. Here only a few clarifying remarks will be made. The number of actual teachers would have been approximately the same in either day or boarding schools. For the former, the Society could probably have furnished enough men so that the individual teacher would not have been overwhelmed with work. Even then, any rapid growth in numbers of pupils would have created problems. But boarding schools added a whole new dimension to the situation. Several hundred students were present day and night, every day and every night, and it was part of the system of education that one or more surveillants or prefects or masters on duty were with them at all times. Besides, this was not just one undifferentiated group of children. A cardinal principle of the system was the separation of the students into several divisions, according to age, maturity, and class year. Each division had its own prefects, thus doubling or tripling the number of men needed for this function. These prefects were for the most part younger Jesuits, still engaged in their training in the Society.

Between the completion of novitiate, classical studies, and philosophy, and the beginning of the study of theology, the Jesuit seminarian or "scholastic" usually spent some years in one of the colleges, in a period known as "regency." The Society's intentions for the period were clear; it was then, as now, to serve as a time in which "the practice of virtue is acquired, habits are formed, individual talents are manifested, and the young men themselves make progress in their studies."[74]

What too often happened was that the overwhelming needs of the school took precedence. Scholastics were sometimes sent to the colleges as prefects before their studies preliminary to philosophy were completed; all too often they were sent there to act as prefects and study philosophy at the same time; regularly they were kept in these posts for four, five, six, seven or more years. One example will illustrate what this came to in practice. Adrien Carrère, later rector at Pau and Toulouse (1874–1882) and provincial (1882–1887), entered the Society after completion of his baccalaureate studies in 1852. Even before he finished his novitiate of two years, he was sent as second prefect to the minor seminary at Montauban, and pronounced there his first vows as a Jesuit (November 13, 1854). In 1855 he was first prefect and professor of mathematics. For the next year and a half he was on the sick list. From 1858 to 1861 he

---

74. *Epitome Instituti Societatis Jesu* (Rome, 1949), part 4, sect. 3, chap. 1, no. 295.

taught mathematics, physics, and chemistry at the college in Bordeaux, and from 1861 to 1863 natural history and chemistry at Toulouse. Only in 1863, nine or ten years after the beginning of this regency, did he start his study of theology, and that without the period of formal philosophical training specifically enjoined by the rules of the Society. Those studies he had to get up on his own. His case was not exceptional.[75]

This was a total perversion of the purpose of regency, and a great harm in future years for the individual and for the Society. The General recognized the danger. To a newly appointed provincial he wrote in 1857: Let this question of the training of scholastics be "the object of your concern. Let not our scholastics be committed to an exterior ministry without having received a solid training, both in learning and in the religious spirit. I insist on this recommendation because on it depends the preservation of the Society."[76] The provincials saw the problem too, but saw no way out of it, and so the practice of sacrificing the future for the present continued to go on.

As one report of around 1850 put it, to mention only studies for the moment, this period of regency, as then constituted, formed a lacuna "at the time of life most favorable to intellectual development. It is a mortal blow from which they [the scholastics] never recover; let them have the finest of talent, they will never be other than just passable."[77] If this seems a harsh judgment, as yet in 1850 unsupported by facts from the new schools, there was a harsher one yet, and more complete, from the provincial of Lyons in 1871. He gave a long list of reasons, after twenty years of experience, for the immediate suppression of several of the boarding schools of the province. The life of a surveillant in such a school was detrimental to the religious life of the young Jesuits. It not only ruined the health

75. TSJ, *Catalogi Provinciae, passim.*
76. ARSJ, Lugd., Reg., Beckx to Fessard, April 15, 1857.
77. PSJ, C-12, "De la possibilité et des avantages des collèges proprement dits."

of many of them, with the constant demands and impossible hours, but it ruined, too, the future of good men. It prevented the proper training of the scholastics. It made them lose their taste for study and their love of work. "This incessant concern for the behavior of the students little by little strips away their strength of mind and makes it incapable of any other thought; it is a sad thing to say, but that is the way it is; it *dehumanizes* them."[78]

By 1870 there may have been some hope of ameliorating if not of solving the problem, because the number of Jesuits had regularly increased during the previous twenty years. But the new wave of schools in the early years of the Third Republic dashed that hope. Between the Falloux Law and Ferry Decrees no real solution was found. Only the expulsion from the schools in 1880 brought temporary relief, as it had in 1828. But as the Jesuits gradually returned to their posts from the late 1880's on, the problem reappeared.

The definitive expulsion in 1901 was also a definitive solution. The few colleges, again in exile, provided a regency that was capable of fulfilling its purpose. In addition, because the colleges were few, the scholastics could begin to enjoy the full complement of studies, while the priests permanently assigned to teach at last had some of the minimum leisure necessary for further scholarly work. From these two imposed solutions of 1880 and 1901 can be dated for the Society the beginnings of a fresh and more open approach to its educational work, and, even more important, the beginnings of the concentrated work on the highest level of scholarship and research which the French Jesuits were to do in the twentieth century and which had long eluded them in the nineteenth.

78. ARSJ, Lugd., Gaillard to Beckx, March 12, 1871.

V

WHAT AND HOW

TO STUDY

The *Ratio Studiorum* set forth a simple and explicit purpose for the Jesuit colleges. Let the teacher so instruct the youth who were enrolled in the educational establishments of the Society that together with a knowledge of the liberal arts they would also acquire especially the character worthy of a Christian.[1] This chapter and the next will treat of the teaching and the studies in the colleges, the first part of that twofold purpose. To separate learning from the acquisition of a Christian character is precisely what the Jesuits sought *not* to do, but the importance and the place of each of the two parts will be more clearly put in relief and better understood if each is at first seen separately.

The studies in a college of the Society of Jesus were first of

1. *Ratio Studiorum,* "Regulae Communes Professoribus Classium Inferiorum," no. 1. The 1832 revision of the *Ratio* is the text which is used here for citations and paraphrases, unless otherwise indicated.

all regulated in accord with the norms set down in the *Ratio Studiorum* of the Society. But through the years those norms were particularized even more in the curricular plans which the French provinces elaborated in accord with the recommendations of special ad hoc commissions and in the letters on studies which the provincials sent to their respective provinces. In addition, the schools always had to take account of the official state programs, especially in view of the wholly state-regulated examinations and of the increasing need to acquire the official baccalaureate degree. It was within the context of these three factors, the *Ratio,* the study plans, and the government programs that the theory of teaching was elaborated and then reduced to practice.

The *Ratio* of 1832 was intended to serve as a tentative revision of the 1599 version, and to be perfected in the light of actual experience. What kept the General from carrying out this intention is not certain, but when the wave of new schools broke over the French provinces after 1850, the *Ratio* of 1832 and the Brugelette *Plan of Studies* were the only existing anchors for their pedagogy.[2]

What was the *Ratio?* It was not in itself a philosophical exposé of general views on education, nor a declaration of education principles, nor a treatise on pedagogy, but rather a series of quite specific, concrete, and ordered directives, intended for the practical guidance of those to whom particular functions in the schools had been confided. This in part explains its formulation in sets of rules. Behind those rules, of course, was

---

2. Farrell, *The Jesuit Code of Liberal Education,* 394–395, suggests among other reasons the "disrupting influence of so many expulsions" and the "impracticability at the time of attempting to prescribe a uniform curriculum for all parts of the Society." A completely reorganized curriculum which greatly interested Roothaan was worked out between 1849 and 1851 by an Italian Jesuit named Vasco. Discussions on it were carried out in his presence in France in 1849. But it was not ready to be put into practice in 1850, and even if it had been, there was very little likelihood that the restored Society, fiercely jealous of its "old traditions" would have adopted it. After Roothaan died in 1853, the project seemed to have gone no further. See Henri Vasco, S.J., *Il Ratio Studiorum adattato ai tempi presenti* (Rome, 1851).

a precise aim or purpose, and this precision of aim greatly contributed to the unity of the ensemble. The general aim of the whole system, from the lowest class of grammar to the highest philosophical or theological discipline, was something which has become a truism, but which until the Society first enunciated it explicitly had not at all been so clearly put for the Christian schools: "the harmonious development of intellect and will, of mind and spirit," not only, however, simply for their own sakes, but also in their function of preparing "educated apostles of Christ's Kingdom on earth."[3] There is no question that the schools were to serve an apostolic purpose.

Within the humanistic disciplines, for the lower or college classes, the more specific goal was the "perfect eloquence" of Quintilian's *Institutio Oratoria*. An ordered education brought the student first to study and acquire thoroughly the basic elements of a language in the classes of grammar. Once these were acquired, it led him on to experience that language in literature. Finally, in the class of rhetoric, all this was to result in that "finished power of utterance" (*ad perfectam enim eloquentiam informat*), which to the Renaissance, to the Jesuits who formed the *Ratio* at that time, and to their successors in the nineteenth century was supposed to be the union of knowledge and the ability to put that knowledge into apt words. Crowned by the philosophy and science classes after rhetoric, such an education was to bring about a union of "the right use of reason joined to cultivated expression."[4]

The unity of such an ensemble was strengthened by the concentration of the subject matter in the classical Greek and Latin literatures, regarded as the perfect models of style and language. In the nineteenth-century schools the classical French literature of the seventeenth century, which the Jesuit schools of that time had done much to form, was added to the canon

---

3. Farrell, *The Jesuit Code,* 356.

4. See *Ratio,* "Regulae Supremae Classis Grammaticae," no. 1; "Regulae Professoris Humanitatis," no. 1; "Regulae Professoris Rhetoricae," No. 1; and Farrell, *The Jesuit Code,* 356.

of works to be studied and imitated. Other subjects antecedent to the years of philosophy had been, at least in theory, treated in relation to those classics.[5] In the nineteenth century, however, these "accessories" had specific times and texts allotted to them in the curriculum. This unity of subject matter, and also the unity of method in actual practice, will be treated more thoroughly later in this and the following chapter. From the beginning, superiors from the General on down urged the application of the *Ratio* in the schools. "It will always be easy for you, in case of doubt, to know what I would prefer, and it is what you would prefer certainly just as we ourselves do, that is to say, what brings us closest to the *Ratio*, taking into account the exigencies of our present position."[6] The principals of the individual schools, too, were insistent that the teachers put the *Ratio* into practice.[7]

Descending to the immediately practical order of all the details that go into the actual curriculum of a school, the Brugelette plan was the model which the schools after 1850 followed. A comparison of it with the general plans of 1852, 1868, and 1875 immediately makes clear the basic continuity in subject matter and the uniformity in provincial regulations.

In the study of grammar and literature there was little change. Some of the Christian classics, such as the Acts of the Apostles and works of St. Basil and St. John Chrysostom, both Fathers of the Church, were included, as the result of the tempest of "Gaumism" to be described in the next chapter. In the philosophy and science courses there were a few more

5. Here again, it should be mentioned that whatever the theory might seem to impose in the way of rigidity, practice could be quite supple. The teaching of a quite modern geography in the context of *Ratio*-directed schools is but one example of the continually adaptive work that went on in a variety of subjects. See again François de Danville, S.J., "L'Enseignement de l'histoire et de la géographie et le *Ratio Studiorum*," *Analecta Gregoriana* 70 (1954), 123–156.

6. PSJ, Roothaan, Roothaan to Studer, Dec. 10, 1852.

7. The check lists of topics in the Roman archives refer continually to the subject, as do the individual provincial archives. See ARSJ, Franc., Lugd., Tolos., Camp., "Rerum Series."

changes. The possible third year, mentioned in 1848, did not appear in later programs. The specifically literary and historical studies included in the earlier curricula had disappeared, including "philosophy as applied to modern history." The first year philosophy course stayed constant, although the terms used to designate the individual disciplines within it sometimes varied. For the second year, the philosophical studies themselves were almost as constant, but the rest of the programs reflected the increasing demand by parents and students for more express preparation for the baccalaureate examination.

Along with this continuity, there were, indeed, changes throughout the years, but a comparison of programs indicates that even though teachers and prefects often complained about a total lack of consistency, these changes never touched the basic assumptions or the basic plans. Often the changes consisted simply of moving from one class to another a particular work of an author. Often, too, there were mere changes in textbooks, always an occupational temptation for educators.

This strong continuity throughout the years was accompanied by a uniformity throughout the provinces. First, Paris and Lyons worked at coordinating programs, in which they were joined in 1852 by Toulouse, formerly part of Lyons, and by Champagne, formerly part of Paris, in 1863. Both continuity and uniformity depended upon regular provincial and interprovincial correspondence and upon meetings of rectors and prefects of the colleges, often presided over by the provincials. Classes had been in session but one month in 1850 when Rubillon wrote to Amiens, "Has he [the prefect] drawn up the program of studies, or have you, as at Vannes, simply adopted that of Brugelette? I want to have [a copy of] it." Two months later the General was asking the same question: "Have you been careful to establish a uniformity of studies between Vannes and Amiens?"[8]

8. PSJ, Reg., Rubillon to Guidée, Sept. 29, 1850; and PSJ, Roothaan, Roothaan to Rubillon, Nov. 20, 1850.

In the archives there is, for example, a detailed document, a "Summary of Remarks" on studies and classes sent to the provincial in 1850 by several Jesuits.[9] It dealt with method, content, textbooks, length of school year, time to be devoted to each subject, teachers and surveillants, and the cultivation of solid and manly piety. Its value becomes most apparent when it is compared with *La Pratique du Ratio Studiorum pour les collèges,* written "after the well-known decrees of 1880 forced us to leave the colleges where we had taught," to help "the numerous and zealous priests and laymen . . . who volunteered to continue our work and to maintain the traditions of our teaching."[10] The "Summary" of 1850 and the 1896 edition of this book demonstrate at every turn the continuity and the uniformity which extended over almost fifty years.

The *Ratio* made much of details. The correspondence and meetings, too, although rarely concerned with basic assumptions, did involve much questioning, rethought, and retouching of individual situations and practices.

In 1855 the Paris province sent a long questionnaire to all the schools.[11] It dealt with theology, philosophy, and all the college classes, and it wanted extensive details. Did the school keep to the order of classes as in the *Ratio Studiorum* of 1832? How long was each class, morning and afternoon? What were the divisions of time, material, and exercises? Which authors were used for each year of Latin, Greek, and French? What competitive exercises were held in class, or in public? What special remarks were to be made about examinations, vacations, religious exercises? The questions went on and on. Most of the schools sent fairly complete reports; their details appear in this and subsequent chapters. Here it is enough to note that the schools did try to correspond faithfully to the printed programs, with allowance for all the vagaries of human nature

9. PSJ, C-10, "Collèges secondaires, 1804–1860," "Précis des Observations."
10. François-Xavier Passard, S.J., *La Pratique du Ratio Studiorum pour les collèges* (Paris, 1896), vii, viii.
11. PSJ, C-12, "Enquêtes provinciales, 1849–1860," "Quaesita de Scholis," 1855.

which were often enough evoked in reports on individual persons and incidents.

Again in September 1858 a commission made up of men from the three provinces of Paris, Lyons, and Toulouse studied at length the running of the schools. By this time the desire for continuity was getting out of hand; the 1832 *Ratio* was no longer good enough for the commission. Its members were sure that studies had never been more flourishing than in the last half of the sixteenth and the first half of the seventeenth centuries, that the Society had given a great impulse to those studies, and that they had been less admirable since then, since the old methods had been forgotten in almost all of Europe. "The most certain means, therefore, of raising the level of education in our colleges would be, in our eyes, to return as fully as possible to the old methods of the Society, and in particular to the old *Ratio Studiorum* in its entirety. Thus, the first wish of the commission on studies is the complete return to all the requirements, to all the practices of the *Ratio,* a return which it unanimously recognizes as important, or rather as *absolutely necessary,* and which it earnestly asks be accepted in principle from this year on."[12]

Several examples will illustrate what the commission meant in practice. The *Catechism* of Canisius, from the sixteenth century, was to be retained without any changes. Greek and Latin grammar were to be taught from the books of Alvarez and Gretzer, because of the "unity of method and the authority of the old Society."[13] Nothing but the classical masterpieces of French were to enter into the vernacular language classes. Finally, when dealing with the time to be given to the subordinate studies, the commission declared: "We have set down as the principle and foundation of our . . . [college] studies, the

---

12. *Ibid.,* "Rapport de la Commission des Études pour les trois provinces de France réunie à Paris en Septembre, 1858."

13. *Ibid.,* III. The "grammar question" will come up again later in this study

most perfect possible observance of the old *Ratio Studiorum*. But, the *Ratio* says not one single word about the teaching of the "Accessories"; it does not devote to them a single minute of the two daily class periods, but it requires, on the contrary, all the time of these classes for work of a completely different type. Therefore, it seems necessary to find outside the ordinary classes some few minutes for the teaching of arithmetic, history, and geography."[14]

This was the kind of static literalness of which some had long accused the Society in its educational practices. Taking its stand on a pure form of words, the commission in reality denied the practice of the old *Ratio* which it so much wanted to follow.[15] In fact, the revered text itself dealt with the possibility of change. One of the rules for provincials stated that since differences of place, time, and person would arise, "adjustments may be made according to the requirements of the case, yet in such a way that they will be in keeping with the general system of our studies."[16]

The solicited comments on the commission's report were not at all unanimous. Boylesve thought that "on several points, the report was exclusive, partial and arbitrary," but he agreed that the "classes would not be strong until we follow to the letter the old *Ratio* in whatever concerns Greek and Latin . . . All the commissions in the world are unable to be better . . . [than the old Ratio on college classes]. There has been no progress in that part; there has been nothing but decline. Only the upper classes [of philosophy] have need of some change, because of the growth of the physical sciences and of mathematics, and also because of the growth of error in philoso-

14. *Ibid.*, V.
15. The denial may have been due in part to unawareness of what really went on in the former schools of the Society. The Jesuits of the mid-nineteenth century had ancient commentaries such as that of Jouvency, but they did not have the detailed studies of actual practice, which were only to appear later.
16. *Ratio* (1599), "Regulae Provincialis," no. 39.

phy."[17] On the other hand, Cahier, apropos of the desire to adopt the old grammars had some strong general remarks: "I fear a certain danger of sloth in the system . . . of reproducing the old works of our Fathers as the best possible way. Our elders did not claim to be setting up the pillars of Hercules, and something has been accomplished since Gretzer; it is only that we hardly know either of these facts. And I do not see many libraries in our houses carefully stocked with the serious works produced in Latin and Greek (especially in the last eighty years). One finds it more simple to suppose that that is all from another age, and that strangers have nothing to teach us. *All right!* But I have my doubts."[18]

The interprovincial recommendations were the subject of thirteen or more meetings for the Paris province in August 1859. These sessions dealt with details that ran from the admission and dismissal of students through subjects, textbooks, punishments, competitions, prizes, vacations, faculty, all the way to whether the lay custodial and janitorial employees should have one or two meat courses at dinner. In addition to such meetings, there were frequent general letters from the provincials to the Jesuit communities in the schools themselves. Lyons alone sent important ones in 1850, 1853, 1860, 1869, and 1871, and the other provinces acted similarly.[19] The observance of the *Ratio* was urged strongly, but there was never agreement on a return to the old version. Even by early 1861 Fessard, the provincial of Paris, was writing to Rome to ask which version was to be followed, the new, as Gautrelet of Lyons maintained, or the old, as the former Paris provincial,

17. PSJ, C-12, "Enquêtes provinciales, 1849–1860," "Observations," Boylesve, April 8, 1859.

18. *Ibid.*, "Observations," Charles Cahier, Feb. 12, 1859.

19. LSJ, Litterae Encyclicae PP. Provincialium, Oct. 10, 1850—Maillard: *Sur les classes et les études;* Oct. 17, 1853—de Jocas: *Sur les études et la discipline dans nos collèges;* Dec. 15, 1860—Gautrelet: *Aux recteurs et aux préfets;* Sept. 27, 1869—Gaillard: *Quelques observations sur les collèges;* Oct. 24, 1871—Gaillard: *Idem.*

Studer, had seemed to indicate.[20] Rome replied that Roothaan's *Ratio* of 1832 was still in force and obligatory, and it informed all the provinces of this.[21]

In any case, the possibility of going back to the old *Ratio* was purely academic, and grew more so every day. A note to the provincial, commenting on a long memoir which was another "victorious apology" for the old forms, put the matter succinctly: "But the difficulty—the impossibility—is in belling the cat. If our colleges constituted a little world apart, entirely separate, our method might be employed exclusively." But since the Université was an ubiquitous fact, it would be "supremely rash" to be "cut off from all the rest of the world."[22] Finally, a glance at an 1872 meeting of the Paris provincial, consultors, and rectors shows them discussing new ways of teaching the vernacular and current foreign languages, history, mathematics, and geography as integral parts of the ordinary curriculum.[23]

In 1874–1875 another long series of meetings took place among what were now four provinces, to investigate and, if necessary, to revise the list of authors used in the schools, in the light of the new study and examination programs of the state.[24] The attitude to be adopted toward *Ratio* and study plans in the face of such requirements was most sensibly expressed by the provincial of Champagne in a letter to the rectors. If the new baccalaureate examinations seemed to demand modifications in the Jesuit program, then such changes had to be honestly accepted, while trying to maintain fidelity to the

20. PSJ, Reg., Fessard to Beckx, Jan. 22, 1861, as copied in PSJ, C-12, "Emploi du Latin dans les classes et les drames, 1860 ss."

21. For example, ARSJ, Rerum Series: Tolos., Dec. 19, 1861.

22. PSJ, C-13, "Enquêtes collèges secondaires, 1862–1880," Letter of de Bonnio, S.J. (?) accompanying Couplet's "Mémoire contre le projet des modifications à introduire dans notre ancien *Ratio Studiorum*," Amiens, Oct. 24, 1862.

23. PSJ, "Lib. Cons.," Aug. 7–9, 1872.

24. PSJ, C-13, "Enquêtes collèges secondaires, 1862–1880," "Compte rendu des séances," Sept. 1875.

traditions of the *Ratio*. It was well to note, he said, that the *Ratio* "was conceived in a spirit comprehensive enough to lend itself to all really advantageous changes."[25]

The independent schools always had to take into account the official programs of the Ministry of Education. Although by the terms of the Falloux Law, the government did not have the direct right to impose its programs on such schools, yet, in fact, these schools by force of circumstances had to approach ever more closely the official norms. The most important of these circumstances was the increasing necessity of the baccalaureate diploma for career advancement after college, and the monopoly on granting that diploma maintained by the Université. A school might in theory set up its schedule fairly well as it pleased, but, for all that, there was an examination to be passed by the students on material set down officially by the Ministry of Education, before official boards constituted in each of the Académies or educational regions of the country.

The colleges of the Society were particularly susceptible to the pressure of these circumstances. They knew that any notable or continued failure of their students in the examinations would furnish extra ammunition for the opposition to religious schools, because both friend and foe watched the Jesuit colleges more closely than they did the other establishments. Even more important, in increasing number the clientele of their schools was of the type which would need the baccalaureate diploma not only for advancement but even for entree into a career. The days of Brugelette and Fribourg, when many of the students went on as alumni to be landed proprietors, were no more. Even at Brugelette, as early as 1838 the provincial had indicated in his instructions that it was "extremely important that those who finish their studies in our establishments be on the way to degrees."[26]

25. CSJ, 1011, "Litterae Encyclicae Patrum Provincialium," Grandidier to rectors, Sept. 23, 1875.
26. PSJ, Brug. 13:2243, "Memoriale P. Provincialis," Jan. 7, 1838, 7.

In 1850 the pressure for degree preparation was greater yet, but it was still slight in comparison with what it would become year by year. At Vannes in this first decade of the schools, Pillon sighed sadly: "Alas, with these [government] programs so poorly constructed and ever changing, what will become of the fine old method of the Society which formed so well the mind, and even better yet the heart? We shall have to handle the subjects . . . in the light of the examination. Farewell to those wonderful old declamations and orations in which France and the Church appeared so worthy of praise and affection."[27]

By 1855 Guidée, though he was fiercely attached to the old traditions, wrote that "because of the preparation for the baccalaureate (and this preparation is a *sine qua non* of the existence of our colleges), the public defense at the end of the year of the theses in philosophy cannot be held, nor many of the monthly philosophy disputations." The importance of the degree, even so early, is highlighted by an interesting statistic: when the new province of Toulouse decided in 1852 not to prepare for the baccalaureate until after the completion of two years of philosophy, it lost sixty students in a single year from two colleges alone. The option of preparing in the course of the first year of philosophy had to be restored.[28]

An 1861 complaint was only one of many such, that specific preparation for the examination took too much time from those most important last courses in philosophy.[29] Rome wrote thus to provincials and provincials to rectors, but no one could really come up with anything to ease the pressure. The best that could be done was to put off until as late as possible in the year the specific preparation for the examination. This the Jesuits did without the least hesitation; some of the teachers described how they ignored the official program as such until

27. Orhand, *Pillon,* 152.
28. PSJ, C-12, "Enquêtes provinciales, 1849–1860," "Quaesita de Scholis," 1855, Guidée, Amiens: response, May 22, 1855; and *ibid.,* letter of Maillard, Provincial of Toulouse, Oct. 13, 1853; copy included in responses.
29. ARSJ, Rerum Series: Tolos., April 20, 1861.

after Easter, and only then treated explicitly the material in it which was not contained in the Society's own program. To this degree, there were some grounds for the frequent charge that the Jesuits prepared their students for the examinations by cram sessions, by memory aids, by lifeless schematizations. The Jesuits justified themselves in the conviction that their program was better, that most of the examination material had, as a matter of fact, been treated at length in the ordinary classes, and that the degree preparation was simply a necessary evil.[30]

Problems arose not only from the immediate preparation for examinations but also from the "constant changes" in state programs which Pillon complained of. Such changes did occur all through the years, but in 1852, 1863, and 1873–1874 there were three official revisions which were more far-reaching than usual and which more directly affected the Jesuit schools.

In 1852, the Ministry of Education introduced the regime of "bifurcation" in studies, whereby an option for a baccalaureate in science or in letters took place at the beginning of the third form. Up to that form, all students in lycées or colleges were to follow the same courses; from third form on through rhetoric one section emphasized mathematics and the natural sciences, the other emphasized the classics, while both sections took their remaining courses in common, ideally together in the same classroom. Finally, the last year, a common endeavor now called "logic" instead of "philosophy" was to add to this education the crowning touch of an "exposition of the operations of understanding" and an "application to the study of science and literature of the general principles of the art of thinking."[31]

---

30. This "tyranny of the baccalaureate" did not bear down on the independent schools alone. Dupont-Ferrier describes the same phenomenon at Louis-le-Grand, speaks of the "triumph of the Manual of the 'baccalaureate merchants'" and quotes a ministry inspection report that "almost everywhere in the lycées of Paris, the handbooks of the preparators have replaced the regular lessons of the professors" (Dupont-Ferrier, *Louis-le-Grand*, II, 280 and note).

31. Decree of April 10, 1852 by Fortoul, the Minister of Education, as quoted by Falcucci, *L'Humanisme*, 232.

These changes were brought about "to satisfy the wishes of families and the needs of society . . . at a moment when through scientific discoveries and heavy industry the systematic exploitation of natural resources was going to develop on a scale hitherto unknown." Yet, the committee of men of letters, scientists, and some representatives of industry which established norms for the courses, said that "in according to each [of the two sections] its own importance, [it] puts literary studies in first place: . . . second place it gives to mathematics, third to physics and mechanics, last to chemistry and the natural sciences. This is enough to show that it understands that the literary studies of the science section are to be serious."[32] There followed a long eulogy of these literary studies which even their most passionate advocate among the Jesuits would have found sufficient. Finally, such studies were even in themselves an aid to industry: "Among the elements that make up her strength, our land puts in the first line that indefinable, intuitive perception called 'taste,' ornament of our civilization, immeasurable capital fund for our industries . . . Let us keep intact for our nation this delicate instinct of taste which characterizes it and which can be applied everywhere; let us treasure it, because it takes the place for us of the coal mines of England and the great natural resources of the United States or of Russia."[33]

Bifurcation was not instituted as a regular program in the schools of the Society; the great majority of their students had no desire to prepare for the science baccalaureate in itself.[34] But the Jesuit course of studies could be adapted to provide its opportunities. In most places and increasingly as the years went on, some partial adaptations were made. At Saint-Etienne a full

32. *Rapport Thénard-Dumes au sujet de l'enseignement scientifique dans les lycées,* July 23, 1852, as quoted in Falcucci, *L'Humanisme,* 240.
33. *Ibid.,* 241.
34. The reform did not meet favor at all with the teachers in the lycées. The literary studies for the scientific section were called scornfully "grocery men's Latin." See Falcucci, *L'Humanisme,* 253–255.

and explicit program was set up. Sometimes, indeed, students who wanted to prepare in science would transfer to Saint-Etienne in their last year or two for this purpose. Heavily scientific and mathematical education in the Jesuit system usually took place at a school such as Sainte-Geneviève, preparatory for the Grandes Ecoles of the state.

In 1862, after ten years of bifurcation, Rouland, the Minister of Education, presented to the Emperor a dithyrambic description of the state of studies "since the adoption of the new plan . . . announced by your majesty in the decree of 1852 . . . The [students'] work, more regular, more sustained, becomes day by day more effective; discipline is excellent and, as it were, spontaneous. The students, occupied with studies in accord with their aptitudes, their future, and their tastes, accept their assignments without difficulty . . . Assured of the threefold support of the state, of municipalities, and of families in everything concerned with secondary education, the Université need do nothing to maintain and consolidate its progress but persevere in a way seriously put to the proof."[35]

One year later a complete reform was announced. The old system had in reality worked out poorly, and as Duruy, the new minister, said, "all the academic councils, . . . all the teaching corps in Paris . . . and public opinion too were protesting against the system of bifurcation." To begin with, he reinstated the class of philosophy as such. Comprising psychology, logic, moral philosophy, and theodicy, it was again the "necessary crown" of studies. Such a course put "back into place, in all their grandeur and magnificence, the moral verities which are the common ground of humanity and from which secular societies draw their life."[36] This reinstatement of philosophy could

35. *Rapport présenté à l'Empereur . . . sur l'enseignement secondaire . . . dans les établissements d'instruction publique,* June 14, 1862, as quoted in Falcucci, *L'Humanisme,* 303–304.

36. "Exposé par V. Duruy de la situation de l'Empire en ce qui concerne l'instruction publique," Nov. 5, 1863, as quoted in Falcucci, *L'Humanisme,* 304–305.

not but please the Jesuits, though the content of the courses as set down by the government was in their eyes hardly the life-source of society.

History, the physical and natural sciences, and mathematics were also reorganized as fundamental disciplines of the last year of secondary training and of preparation for the bacca-laureate. With the science changes the Jesuit schools had no great quarrel other than the need of refashioning courses and schedules once again. As for the history course, they would treat the required matter, but hardly in accord with the phi-losophy of history behind the general directives for the course as it was to be taught in the lycées. What these directives im-plied will be seen in the explicit treatment of history in the next chapter.

Finally, in 1864, Duruy suppressed the last remnants of bi-furcation, and in 1865 returned, without saying as much, to a system rather similar to the one which had existed during the Restoration. All lycée students were to be part of one group, with common literary, scientific, and philosophical training. After philosophy, special mathematics classes existed as prepa-ration for the Grandes Ecoles. Those who did not want a completely traditional training had the option of starting pre-paratory mathematics somewhat earlier in place of several of the accessory subjects. This arrangement, except for the last-named option, was much like the one which had existed in the Jesuit exile colleges before 1850.

The third important revision of studies by the French state took place between 1872 and 1874, partly as a result of an offi-cial examination of conscience in the wake of the Franco-Prus-sian War. Jules Simon, the new Minister of Education, started the process. He inaugurated a very short course in hygiene, added a few hours per month to the time given to history and geography, changed the time of the modern languages from study hours to class hours, and proposed that more time be given to the vernacular. With these changes a choice had to be made, obviously, between adding hours to an already crowded schedule, or taking hours from the traditional disciplines. Simon chose the latter course; in September 1872, he suppressed the writing of Latin verses and cut down on the number of Latin themes and other written exercises.

He thus brought down on his head the imprecations of every traditional classicist in France. Dupanloup, the bishop of Orleans, in most cases a moderate man, fulminated the first anathemas in writing to the personnel of his minor seminaries to ignore the minister's circular, because, he said, "as far as [these] radical changes go, . . . they will be the ruin of the humanities and the definitive overthrow of eminent intellectual training in France."[37]

A few months later, the bishop returned to the attack with a famous letter protesting the "disastrous innovations," the "worst attempt against the study of the ancient languages since the Convention." "These vigorous exercises, grammar study, written theme, written translation, Latin composition, all this robust and healthy gymnastic of the mind he abandons . . . He dishonors them as much as he can in the minds of students and teachers . . . No, no, it is a death blow which M. Jules Simon strikes at them, and, as a result at the education of the nation, at the French spirit."[38]

It was by no means simply Catholics who vigorously opposed this new system of "organized sloth."[39] For all his hard words, Dupanloup at least usually stayed with the pedagogical issues and had a case which, in terms of a particular conception of culture, was disputable. But other Catholics saw in the changes

37. Falcucci, *L'Humanisme*, 315. The official circular appeared on Sept. 2, 1872; Dupanloup wrote on Oct. 6.

38. Felix-Antoine-Philibert Dupanloup, *Seconde lettre de M. l'Évêque d'Orléans . . . sur la circulaire de M. le Ministre de l'instruction publique* (Paris, 1873), 10, 12, 15.

39. Some Catholics opposed Dupanloup also. François Lenormant begged his fellow Catholics not to defend "a system of teaching which is no longer made for our times." See Georges Weill, *Histoire de l'enseignement secondaire en France* (Paris, 1921), 164n.

another attack on the Church. The Assumptionist superior, d'Alzon, for example, wrote a furious diatribe, and even Dupanloup once allowed himself to remark, "If I must speak all my thoughts, I would here be more fearful of the dictatorship of M. Jules Simon than of M. Gambetta. With M. Gambetta, you know whom you are dealing with; with M. Jules Simon you do not know."[40]

In any case, with the fall of the Thiers government in 1873, Simon was no longer Minister of Education. The new government at first went back basically to Duruy's program of 1865, and then, in 1874, came out with another new program, accepting such innovations as modern languages, but retaining all the Latin that the former minister had wanted removed. As Simon said, "I had suggested a few additions and a few curtailments. They kept the additions and gave up the curtailments. That was the worst of solutions."[41]

These changes from 1872 through 1874 involved again the Jesuit schools, at least indirectly, for they had to take account of the new and more heavily charged program, and of a division of the baccalaureate examination into two parts, one after rhetoric and the other after philosophy. All the provinces met again, as mentioned previously. In general they discussed "what means were to be taken to prepare for the baccalaureate without sacrificing rhetoric and literary studies?"[42] In particular the exigencies of the new program were reflected in the topics presented. A few of them were: How shall the first year of philos-

---

40. D'Alzon, *Revue de l'enseignement chrétien*, IV. Earlier d'Alzon had written of the state system: "It is time to know who are the true authors of our defeats; whence came so weak an education of our officers, in the face of the incontestable knowledge of the Prussian general staff, . . . what teachers the mob of Belleville had had, and what teachers the sailors, the Breton militia and the pontifical zouaves had had" (*ibid.*, I), and Dupanloup, *Seconde lettre,* as quoted in Weill, *Histoire de l'enseignement,* 164.

41. Jules Simon, *La réforme de l'enseignement secondaire,* 302, as quoted in Weill, *Histoire de l'enseignement,* 165.

42. PSJ, C-13, "Enquêtes collèges secondaires, 1862–1880," Mourier to rectors, Aug. 28, 1875. See also *ibid.*, "Quaesita," Sept. 22, 1874; "Réponses des collèges;" and "Compte rendu des séances," Sept. 1875.

ophy be divided between philosophy, science, and history? How reorganize and when start the courses in English and/or German? Could a policy be formulated for the future of those rhetoricians who did not pass the examination the first time around? Significantly, there were no calls for an integral return to the details of the old *Ratio*.

The result of all the adjustments was the *Plan* of 1875. Slowly, under the pressure of necessity, the discrimination of what was basic and what accidental in the *Ratio* was making headway. A good number of years more would have been necessary to bring it to fruition, but after 1875 the battle lines began to stiffen again. In having to defend their right to teach and their pedagogic heritage against mounting anticlerical opposition to their schools, the Jesuits would tend to defend as basic every jot and tittle of that heritage.

It was particularly in the grammar and literature classes that the distinctive methodology of the *Ratio* was brought into play, but it could be and was adapted to other subjects too. This methodology involved a three-step procedure. In these classes the teacher would first state a precept or rule or proposition of grammar, for instance, or of rhetoric. Then he would explain, elaborate upon, illustrate it by examples from the particular literary author who was being studied at the time, this step usually involving a Socratic questioning of the students' grasp of rule and example. Finally, the students were set to applying the rule in written and oral exercises. In this procedure some were far more skilled than others, and in practice it had to be varied from subject to subject and even from class to class, but it was the fundamental basis of all of the Jesuit college teaching. This explains in the *Ratio* the whole series of practical rules on all the concrete details of the method, for example, on the "prelection," written assignments, memory work, repetition, competitive exercises, examinations, and public exhibitions of skill.[43]

---

43. Farrell, *The Jesuit Code*, 338 and 354, has a schematic analysis of these rules and indications of where they can be found in the *Ratio*.

The authors who were being studied at a particular time in class were the sources from which precepts were illustrated and from which material for oral and written exercises was drawn. In the lower classes the mechanics of style and composition were to be learned from these authors. In upper grammar, and in humanities and rhetoric, the same authors were used to teach an appreciation of literature and some theory of criticism. All of this was done so that ultimately the student could actively and correctly express himself in written and spoken word, in accord with time-honored principles of style and composition.

Since the literary author was so important in this process, the "prelection" was the keystone of the whole overarching method. Basically, it was the detailed explanation of a lesson given by teacher to student *before* the student set himself to study it. Simple as this sounds, it was something of an innovation when the presuppression Jesuit schools introduced it as a regular feature of their method.

Usually, the prelection would progress through the following steps.[44] First, there was a short summary of the content of the section or passage to be studied, plus an attempt to relate it to the material studied immediately previously. Then, the grammatical and syntactical difficulties of the passage were pointed out and solved. Next, the teacher would comment on style, explain difficult allusions, and introduce material from other disciplines such as history or geography which had a bearing on the subject. Finally, at least in early stages of learning, he would translate the passage, in whole or in part.

During the prelection itself, the teacher could call on students to explain some of the material. At the next class period, all students were responsible in public recitation for the whole passage, for a mastery of the rules it illustrated, and for an idiomatic translation. Through personal research, the student was

---

44. *Ratio,* Regulae Communes . . . Classium Inferiorum," nos. 27–29/ . . . rhetoricae, no. 6/ . . . humanitatis, no. 5/ . . . grammaticae supremae, no. 5/ . . . mediae, no. 6/ . . . infimae, no. 6.

also responsible for a further understanding of interrelations within the whole literary work and within the context of other disciplines. In addition, he was to give yet more proof of mastery by written compositions which reproduced the style of the passages studied. At the end of a week, he was then accountable for all the material studied during that time.

There were decided dangers in this method. It could turn into a lecture or a bare translation. It could be crashingly dull or an exercise in wide-wandering and barely relevant remarks. It could render the students utterly passive and confine the teacher to a rigid mold. Its immense advantage was that, together with the other parts of the method, it put order into the daily round of classes. At any time, brilliant teaching is not a common occurrence, and it is certainly less so day in and day out. A poor teacher, and they were not uncommon, at least had a framework of method upon which to rely, and a series of steps that could bring regular and orderly, even if uninspired, progress. In combining imagination and order, a good teacher could, with the prelection, be a very good one. A brilliant teacher had ample opportunity to make of his class a vivid experience in learning, and a means of true intellectual activity on the part of the students, while the cadre of the prelection aided him and his students in giving form to insight.

VI

THE PROGRESS
OF LEARNING

The several programs of study devised by the Jesuits for the colleges usually supposed a seven or eight year span during which the student, after progressing through a literary curriculum, would complete his education with philosophy and science. Each of the plans designed to reduce to practice the reputedly distinctive prescriptions of the *Ratio* on what and how to study provided ideally five forms, often five years, for literature and two or three years for the philosophical and scientific studies. In practice, the former studies usually took longer than this, and the latter were often shortened to two years at the most. In this, the Jesuit colleges were similar to the state lycées, though they often seemed to have more success in keeping students in school until they had completed the whole program.

The prospectus of the Jesuit college regularly reminded parents that "to be admitted to the preparatory [seventh] form, one must be able to write easily from dictation, must know the most important rules of the French language, . . . some notions of history and geography, . . . and the four fundamental operations in mathematics." For some years an eighth form or even a ninth existed in the colleges as an elementary course, but the more usual commencement was one year later.

"The purpose of the seventh form is to prepare for the study of Latin."[1] Right from the beginning, there was to be no question of what would occupy most of the student's working hours in the years to come. The child of nine or ten started Latin study in this year, sometimes with the formidable grammar of Alvarez. Little did he know what controversies had gone on to keep in his hands that Latin treasure from 1572. His *only* other subjects were elementary French grammar, exercises in reading and writing, explanation of a French author, usually La Fontaine, elementary arithmetic, Bible history, Church history, and some geography.

With the sixth form began the course in "Letters." Even this form was an extra one, added on to the original five-form plan. For the next four years the basic subjects were always the same, French, Latin, Greek, history, geography, and arithmetic. They were such in the *Plan d'Etudes* of 1852 and such they were in the 1890's in *La Pratique du Ratio*.[2] A summary schedule, necessarily composite, but not at all atypical of the class and study periods of an ordinary day would run as follows:[3]

Class and Study Schedule for Ordinary Days

½ hour	8:00– 8:30	Previously prelected lessons recited from memory: subject matter—rules of grammar and style and Latin author.

1. Passard, *La Pratique*, 89.
2. See *ibid.*, 221–238 for a complete sample of the *Plan d'études.*
3. This is an adaptation of schedules in CSJ, MsJB 980, "Plan d'études-Brucker"; PSJ, C-10, "Collèges secondaires, 1804–1860"; PSJ, C-12, "Enquêtes provinciales, 1849–1860"; and Passard, *La Pratique, passim.*

¼ hour	8:30– 8:45	Previous day's precepts recalled and new ones explained briefly.
½ hour	8:45– 9:15	Written assignments corrected publicly.
¾ hour	9:15–10:00	New prelection, usually of orator: explanation and summary of subject matter of Latin author.
½ hour	10:00–10:30	Vernacular and Accessories (history, geography, mathematics).
¼ hour	10:30–10:45	Recreation
1¼ hours	10:45–12:00	Study and written assignments, until dinner.
¾ hour	1:30– 2:15	Study and written assignments.
¾ hour	2:15– 3:00	Previously prelected lessons recited from memory: subject matter—rules of grammar and style for Greek and sometimes vernacular author.
¼ hour	3:00– 3:15	Written assignments corrected publicly.
¾ hour	3:15– 4:00	New prelection, usually of Latin poet or, on alternate days, of Greek or vernacular author. Dictation of theme for written translation.
½ hour	4:00– 4:30	Vernacular and Accessories (history, geography, mathematics).

¼ hour	4:30– 4:45	Rosary
2½ hours	4:45– 7:15	Study and written assignments, until spiritual reading and supper.

On two days a week, there was a full hour for Mathematics in the afternoon.

Variations for Saturday

1 hour	8:00– 9:00	Brief repetition of whole week's work on particular author and recitation from memory of week's prelections. Then, (Latin) historian read and explained at length.
1 hour	9:00–10:00	Prelection, or declamation by students of Latin speech, and/or contest among students of one class or among several classes.
¾ hour	2:15– 3:00	Explanation of Latin poet or, sometimes, catechism repetition for part of the time.
1 hour	3:00– 4:00	Greek and/or vernacular poet.
½ hour	4:00– 4:30	Pious exhortation or explanation of catechism.

One significant addition took place in the last years before 1880; the formerly optional modern foreign languages, German and English, became obligatory from the fourth or third forms on.

It was clearly understood that there was forever a hierarchy in all these subjects of study: Latin, Greek, and French were the heart of the course; the others were "accessory subjects."[4] The sixth through third forms made up the classes of grammar. The purposes and contents of these years can best be expressed in paraphrases from the teachers' rules in the *Ratio,* and from the content of the various plans.

For the lower class, the sixth and fifth forms, the aim was "the perfect knowledge of the rudiments [of Latin grammar]," and the beginnings of Greek. Cicero, Phaedrus, and Cornelius Nepos were the authors studied. The middle class sought "knowledge, though not exhaustive, of the whole of Latin grammar," and did further work in Greek. Cicero's works were again the chief text, plus "the easier of Ovid's poems, Aesop again, and selected and expurgated works of Lucian."[5] The actual plans also included Caesar, Quintus Curcius, and some of the *Eclogues* and *Georgics* of Virgil. In Greek, this class and the next studied selections from Xenophon and St. John Chrysostom.

Complete knowledge of grammar, idioms, figures of speech, and prosody was the aim of the third form or upper class. Sallust, Livy, and Cicero were the prose authors used, especially the latter in his dialogues *On Friendship* and *On Old Age,* and in some of his orations. In poetry the class read Ovid, Catullus, Tibullus, Propertius, and especially Virgil in several books of the *Aeneid.* Some material from mythology also received mention here.[6] The practical application of such rules underwent modifications from plan to plan. Some authors such as Catullus disappeared for a time, supplanted by Terence, only to show up again later. Plutarch and Homer and Herodotus

---

4. More than once a partisan of the old *Ratio* would devise an ingenious scheme to banish these intruding accessories altogether to the outer darkness of, for instance, half-holidays and even Sundays, but common sense prevailed against this. One such attempt can be seen in PSJ, C-4, "*Ratio,* XIX-XX," "Mémoire contre le projet des modifications à introduire dans le *Ratio Studiorum,*" Amiens, Oct. 24, 1862, R. P. Couplet, S.J.

5. *Ratio,* "Regulae Professoris Infimae Classis Grammaticae," no. 1; and ". . . Mediae Classis Grammaticae," no. 1.

6. *Ibid.,* ". . . Supremae Classis Grammaticae," no. 1.

appear also, and a little later Plato, and further selections from the Greek Fathers, especially, in 1852, St. Basil's treatise, *On the Reading of Pagan Authors.*

The humanities and rhetoric made up a separate section of the course in letters. "After the pupils had finished grammar, . . . the class [of humanities] was to lay the foundation for eloquence . . . by a command of language, some erudition, and a sketch of the precepts pertaining to rhetoric." This command of language "consisted especially in acquiring correctness of expression and fluency." The student gained such correctness by modeling his work strictly on the best of the classic authors, and since this was a preparation for eloquence, "the one orator used in daily prelections was Cicero." Among the historians, Caesar, Sallust, Livy, and Quintus Curcius were the models. Among the poets, it was "especially Virgil, except for the fourth book of the *Aeneid,* plus selected odes of Horace, and elegies, epigrams, and other works of the chief classic poets, provided that they [were] purged of every obscenity."[7] In Greek, the *Ratio* was rather general for this year, but the plans prescribed explicitly some dramas of Euripides or of Sophocles, and the *Philippics* of the greatest of the Greek orators, Demosthenes.

For rhetoric, although "the scope of this class could not be easily defined in exact terms," it aimed to train to "perfect eloquence." This involved the two elements of oratory and poetry, and was to be accomplished by learning and practicing the precepts of oratory, by stylistic exercises, and by complementary knowledge (*eruditio*). Such precepts were again to be drawn from Cicero, and also from Quintilian and Aristotle. As for style, although the best historians and poets could also be used, the class was again to draw overwhelmingly on the speeches of Cicero, works most suited to this instruction, in which the rules of style would be exemplified in all their clarity. For Greek studies the *Ratio* again generalized, saying

7. *Ibid.,* ". . . Humanitatis," no. 1.

simply that it included a fuller knowledge of authors and dialects.[8]

Selections from Tacitus, Virgil, Horace, and Juvenal also figured in the actual plans, as did, for Greek, Demosthenes again, together with St. John Chrysostom as the Christian representative of oratory. Sophocles, too, appeared with *Oedipus Rex*. In 1868 the exigencies of the baccalaureate brought selections from Thucydides and Aristophanes, and both then and in 1875 a brief line in the program for Latin, Greek, and French mentioned also "Authors required for the baccalaureate." The notice was there simply to reassure parents that this all important preparation was indeed taking place. Those authors were, with only minor changes, the same ones as were specifically mentioned.

Classicism was at the very heart of the educational philosophy and practice of the nineteenth-century French Jesuits. It meant for them, first, the adamantine conviction that the Latin and Greek literature of classical antiquity presented universal values for human development. The moral values developed by antiquity were, they maintained, radically incomplete and inadequate in themselves, and needed the advent of Christianity for their completion. But the literary and artistic values of classical culture presented fixed and immutable standards of the highest perfection. By long and intimate contact with those masterpieces of the human spirit, and through them with the classical culture in which those values were embodied, students were ideally to acquire for themselves personal but objective standards by which to appraise, to accept or to reject works of literature and art.

This immersion in the classics was not only to provide standards by which the work of another might be judged, but also, and even more important, it was to train the student to "eloquence," which for the Jesuits of these schools meant the

8. *Ibid.*, ". . . Rhetoricae," no. 1.

ability not only to speak but also to write correctly and effectively. The classics were to be the stylistic models; they were to help the student to "find in language the exact equivalent of the thought in mind, . . . the quality of fluency, . . . the capacity to order discourse with a sense of logic and thus endow it with force, and to compose discourse with the care that issues in elegance, which is a thing of restraint, propriety, polish, grace."[9]

To Latin and Greek were now to be added those French masterpieces which shared in the power of the ancient classics because of the genius of their authors, because of the universal values which they also expressed, and because of their adherence, too, to the immutable canons of literary composition first practiced and then set down once and for all in antiquity. What this meant is clear by a contrast with the French Jesuit concept of Romanticism. The excerpt is taken from the conclusions of several meetings of professors at the college in Poitiers.

> The fundamental rule of the romantics is to abandon themselves to their own whims and fancies; the inevitable result of this principle is, in their works, a ridiculous combination of the ugly and the beautiful, of the highest reaches of the ideal together with the most degraded aspects of reality. Here and there, romanticism does present beauty of the first order without doubt, but in that case, it is neither classicist nor romanticist who speaks, but it is the human spirit in a moment of true, noble and generous inspiration. Thus, what we can learn from the romantics belongs by the same title to the classics. Everything which belongs as their own to the romantics, that is, their principle and its necessary consequence, is contrary to the universal rules of common sense and good taste.[10]

9. John Courtney Murray, S.J., "On the Future of Humanistic Education," *Critic,* 22 (February–March, 1964), 38–39.
10. PSJ, C-12, Poitiers, "Réunion Académique St. Joseph, 1859–1860, Compte-

Classicism as understood by the Jesuits, and not by any means by them alone, included, first, the element of lasting and universal human values. But it quickly embraced also a second element of basically unchangeable stylistic laws for the apt expression of those values, and a canon of authors who so expressed them. Finally classicism came to include a third element, that of method, which has already been discussed.

The Jesuit schools defended classicism vigorously during all these years. They defended it because they thought it right and true, and because they found it in the educational heritage of their order as that heritage was expressed in the *Ratio*. But a confusion of ends and means often seemed to be involved. Stylistic law and pedagogical method were in themselves only means to the end of preserving and transmitting humanist classical values. Because, however, the Jesuits were convinced that the end could be attained only with those specific means, they not only defended the means as tenaciously as the values but they frequently tended to regard them as values in themselves. What was, and what was not an essential part of the classical heritage? The question was never seriously answered because it was never clearly asked.

The reasons for retention of the classics did not pose themselves as abstract questions to be discussed simply within the community of the Jesuit schools. These they accepted all too uncritically. But soon after the colleges began they underwent from the outside a far from abstract attack which maintained that classical literature was in itself a pernicious influence in the training of youth in the schools.[11] In 1851 Abbé Théodore Gaume published *Le Ver rongeur,* a passionate exposé of what

---

rendu des séances—au R. P. Fessard." It was not this clear-cut in practice, however. For example, one of the students at Bordeaux recalled how his teacher "inspired us with an appreciation of the poetry of Virgil, and at the same time gave us a share of his admiration for Châteaubriand" (*EJF,* I, 793).

11. PSJ, C-18, "Gaumisme-Classiques," and C-19, "Classiques Païens," contain material about this whole controversy, including clippings from *L'Univers,* in which both sides expounded their positions.

he conceived to be the true cause of the sickness of all modern society.[12] This cankerworm was the pagan education which at the time of the Renaissance had been introduced into Christian society through the medium of the classical authors studied in the schools, indeed even in the Christian schools. This education had paganized and corrupted literature, the arts, philosophy, religion, the family, and, most balefully, society itself. "Four centuries ago, throughout Europe, there was an open, a sacrilegious, an unfortunate break in the chain of Catholic teaching; the pure springs of truth were replaced by the fouled cisterns of error, spiritualism by sensualism, order by disorder, life by death." Paganism was the final result, and it brought with it in the social order war, unbridled liberty, exaggerated desire for freedom, despotism, and a drift "toward communism and social ruin." To the question of what had produced and nourished this abysmal state of affairs, education would respond, "It is I who make man and society. For the last three centuries, I have been pagan. I have made man in my image."[13]

Gaume ardently believed this thesis, and with equal ardor he was sure that the only cure lay in "making education Christian again. Here [was] the last word in the fight, . . . what must be brought about at any price." In the practical order this meant for him the replacement in the classrooms of the pagan authors of antiquity by the Christian authors; of Horace, Virgil, and Cicero, of Demosthenes, Homer, and Sophocles, by Augustine, Jerome, and Ambrose, by Chrysostom, Basil, and Gregory, to mention but a few names. Centuries of European students had been corrupted by their schoolroom pagan authors; they were to be regenerated by others who were Christian. But even Gaume could not get away from his own classical training, and with sublime inconsistency, he did allow, under

---

12. Théodore Gaume, *Le Ver rongeur des sociétés modernes ou le Paganisme dans l'éducation* (Paris, 1851).
13. *Ibid.*, 3–4, 289.

carefully controlled conditions, pagan authors as models of literary excellence in the upper literature classes.

Incredibly enough, there were a good number of adherents of this simplistic presentation of a problem and of its solution. Among the bishops, Gousset of Rheims and Parisis of Langres were warm partisans of Gaume; in praising the book, Veuillot and Montalembert were in accord. Dupanloup was ardently on the other side, and the long *Lettres,* so dear to French controversy, made their public way back and forth. Without naming Gaume or his work, Dupanloup described these views as "exaggerated, absurd, disrespectful to the church, and capable of troubling consciences."[14] Gaume did not back down one whit. He told Dupanloup and all who cared to listen that the system of classical teaching of the previous four centuries was "a blunder, an abominable custom, a source of corruption, a hellish nourishment, a bait for the passions of the young, a system which has lost Europe, an error which has done more harm to religion than Protestantism itself has done."[15]

Everyone knew what group had formally founded its colleges on a system of training in the classics and had, with those colleges, been the schoolmasters of Catholic Europe for so much of this period. Dupanloup made it one of his criticisms that Gaume thus accused the Jesuits of having worked zealously to make Europe pagan. Gaume replied that he accused no one; the teaching orders had not invented the pagan world; they had had to use it and could not prevent the awful results.

The Society was for a while in a quandary. The French Jesuits thoroughly disagreed with Gaume, but among his enthusiastic adherents were so many of the staunchest lay and

14. Félix-Antoine-Philibert Dupanloup, *Lettre de Mgr. l'Évêque d'Orléans . . . [aux] ecclésiastiques chargés dans son diocèse de l'éducation de la jeunesse par l'emploi des auteurs profanes grecs et latins dans l'enseignement classique* (Orléans, 1852).

15. Théodore Gaume, *Lettres à Mgr. Dupanloup, Évêque d'Orléans, sur le paganisme dans l'éducation* (Paris, 1852), 210. On the positive side of the ledger, under Gaume's sponsorship excellent editions of several of the Church Fathers were produced. Some are still in use by scholars today.

clerical friends of the Society, and so many of the Ultramon-
tanes.[16] Finally, the Society took up the pen for its traditional
educational procedures.[17] Of the works put out by the Jesuits,
the best was that of Father Charles Daniel, *Des Etudes classiques dans la société chrétienne.* Historically, he argued, it
simply was not true that only at the Renaissance did the pagan
classics start to be the educational fare of Christian youth.
When at that time they did take pride of place, the Church
itself encouraged their use. Besides, no one could be more
surprised than veteran teachers that from them in a direct line
descended all the wide world's evils, moral, political, and
social.[18]

The controversy went to Rome; the Holy See tried to quiet
it by exhorting to the use of Christian authors, and praising
the sane use of pagan authors. It flared up overseas in Canada
in the late 1860's, and had a brief revival in France ten years
later. As a result of the quarrel, though the programs of studies
in the Jesuit schools were not drastically modified, yet material
from several of the ancient Christian writers was regularly introduced. The incident had the effect of committing the Jesuits
even more fully to their traditional ways.

The commitment to tradition in the classical studies and the
confusion, at times, of ends and means was strikingly illustrated
in the "Grammar Question" which agitated the schools for a

16. Even before publication of *Le Ver rongeur*, Roothaan's approval of its
position had been sought. The General made no public statement, but in a
private letter he remarked rather acidly, "It is really remarkable that the thesis
upheld by M. Gaume has had successively as patrons Julian the Apostate,
Luther, and several prominent Jansenists" (ARSJ, Franc., Reg., Roothaan to
Studer, July 24, 1851).

17. Besides articles and pamphlets, three substantial books appeared at this
time: Arsène Cahour, S.J., *Des Études classiques et des études professionnelles*
(Paris, 1852); Nicholas Deschamps, S.J., *Du Paganisme dans l'éducation, ou
Défense des écoles catholiques des quatre derniers siècles contre les attaques
de nos jours* (Paris, 1852) and Charles Daniel, S.J., *Des Études classiques dans
la société chrétienne* (Paris, 1853).

18. One such veteran, and perhaps disillusioned, teacher remarked that the
whole controversy was useless because everyone knew that students never did
pay attention to any classroom text, good, bad, or indifferent.

good number of years. Right from the foundation of the minor seminaries in 1814, the Jesuits had restored not only Cicero and Virgil to their places of honor, but Alvarez too. He had been a Portuguese Jesuit, author of that indispensable first tool for acquiring Latin, a Latin grammar. Published in 1572, *De Institutione Grammatica Libri Tres* had been probably the most widely used grammar in Europe for two centuries, and down to the end of the nineteenth century continued to be republished, re-edited and translated.[19]

Although Alvarez had been used in the eight minor seminaries and in the few exile colleges, the revised *Ratio* of 1832 not only did not impose the work in Latin, but it authorized a translation into French, especially for the classes of beginners. When the new colleges opened in 1850, there was no unanimity of practice. In 1852, the idea arose at Brugelette that Alvarez, whole, entire, and undefiled in its latinity, should be imposed on all the colleges, and in the fall of that year, under the slogan of a return to sources, and to the *Ratio* in particular, (the ancient *Ratio*), a meeting of prefects at Vaugirard agreed to this.[20] The Paris provincial, Studer, was all in favor of the move, and vigorously pushed it.

Latin, and nothing but Latin in the classroom, from the very first day of class, was the ideal. Olivaint at Vaugirard described what would now be called the "direct method" of teaching a language. "Our youngest students begin by speaking Latin . . . We are taking up again the method of our bygone Fathers . . . ; we are treating as a living language this tongue which should by no means die; we are learning Latin by speaking it."[21] For some years the attempt to teach in this way went on. Unfortunately, the method seemed always linked in

19. See Sommervogel, *Bibliothèque de la Compagnie de Jésus,* I, cols. 223–245, for a list of the editions, translations, versions, and abridgments of this work for three centuries. A partial English edition was published as late as 1888, a Latin-Chinese one in 1869.
20. PSJ, C-16, "Grammaires," letter of Wagner to (?), Aug. 14, 1861.
21. Clair, *Olivaint,* 287.

the minds of all, partisans and opponents, with the use of the particular grammar by Alvarez. By 1860 the opponents of the system were becoming vocal. They claimed that it was almost impossible so to teach children of eight or ten years, and that even if this were the ideal, still there and then the Society was simply isolating itself and its schools from the educational situation of the times. Meetings, reports, memoirs, consultations followed in great number.[22]

The partisans of Alvarez might have based their case on the advantages of the direct method itself. This they seldom did. It is very revealing of the mentality of a fair number of the Jesuits that they put the greatest weight on an argument from tradition, or on an argument ad hominem or on both. They called on the age-old practice, the venerable tradition of the Society in using Alvarez, a tradition which, surely, the sons of the Society could not give up. The answer, not slow in coming, was that, as a matter of historical record, Alvarez had not even been used very widely in France in the old Society, and that as a matter of current practice, in other places, Rome included, the book had already for some time been translated.[23] The next argument was that to give up Alvarez was to concede a round to the enemies of the Church and of the Society. This viewpoint was most strongly put as one of the points in a long memoir of more than eighty pages against any change from the old grammar.[24] The author said that there were two methods in conflict, one which taught Latin as a living language and the other as a dead language. The first was that of the Jesuits. "The other, conceived at Port-Royal, under the in-

22. PSJ, C-4 in part, and PSJ, C-16 in whole, are archive dossiers of the Paris province alone which are filled with this material.

23. When Alvarez had been introduced into France in the sixteenth century, such an outcry was raised that the old grammar of Despauterius, by special concession, was allowed for the French provinces! See Farrell, *The Jesuit Code,* 441–452.

24. PSJ, C-4, *"Ratio, XIX–XX,"* "Mémoire contre le projet des modifications à introduire dans le *Ratio Studiorum,*" Amiens, Oct. 24, 1862, by R. P. Couplet, S.J. There is also a copy in PSJ, C-13, "Enquêtes collèges secondaires, 1862–1880."

spiration of Jansenism, is noteworthy only for the disasters which it has inflicted upon literature. In bringing on the neglect of Latin, it has impoverished Philosophy and Theology and, by that fact, has struck at morality and at the church itself. For a century now, it has reigned over the ruins which it has heaped up, giving every day to the world the visible proof of its powerlessness to rebuild what it has destroyed."[25]

After three years, in each of which the question was on the agenda of the meetings of rectors and prefects, the new Paris provincial, Fessard, made the decision to adopt French-Latin and French-Greek grammars, while safeguarding the use of Latin as a vehicle of instruction in class. The Superior General, Beckx, had been consulted and had approved this moderate decision.[26]

The whole problem may seem in itself a rather minor one, but it did not seem so to the Jesuits of the time. It is illustrative, in the terms in which it was carried on, of the weight which tradition and history had, and of the commitment not only to ends but also to specific means in the preservation of a classical heritage. It is also illustrative of what Burnichon called a "habit flowing from the national temperament, [in which] the French Jesuits pushed logic to its extreme consequences, and ended up by finding themselves all alone in their views."[27]

The controversy over the use of vernacular in the grammars serves to remind one that the French language, too, was officially one of the principal subjects of instruction, and not just an accessory. The *Ratio* did not deal with it at any length at all; it simply remarked in the schedules for all three grammar classes that the last half hour in the morning was to be devoted to the vernacular and to accessories, and in the afternoon to the same or to a scholastic contest among the students. For humanities and rhetoric, the notices were equally terse; in the

25. *Ibid.*, 80.
26. PSJ, C-16, "Grammaires," letter of R. P. Fessard, Aug. 2, 1863; and ARSJ, Franc., Reg., Beckx to Fessard, Dec. 13, 1862.
27. Burnichon, *La Compagnie,* IV, 479.

former, "the orators, historians, and poets of the vernacular should be treated in the same way [as the ancient authors]"; in rhetoric, "with regard to the vernacular, style should be modeled on the example of the best authors."[28]

When the *Ratio* of 1832 was published, the Society did not have the example of the old version to fall back on for the formulation of rules for classes in the vernacular, nor did it yet have any great fund of recent experience to draw on. In very short order the colleges had to provide their own rules. In fashioning the instruction and in choosing the authors in accord with the principles set down for the ancient languages, they followed not only the general directions given above but also their own inclinations. Fribourg and Brugelette had borrowed from Saint-Acheul, and they in turn, especially Brugelette, were the models for the colleges after 1850.

The study of French proceeded in the same way as the study of Latin and Greek, because "everyone agrees that in order to acquire a language, you must study (1) the *words* of which it is made up; (2) the grammar or the rules which teach correctness; (3) the turns of phrase or particular idioms. Literature which then follows is concerned with style and composition."[29] So, from the beginning of grammar study the two languages, French and Latin, found themselves linked together.

La Fontaine was always the first French author studied, from the sixth and fifth grammar classes of Brugelette in 1848–1849, to those of the plan of 1875. Fénelon was the next favorite; starting in the seventh or sixth form and going up to the third, the students pored over *Télémaque*, and also at times over selections from other of Fénelon's works. In the fourth form and third they read Racine, the *Poème de la Religion* and *Esther*, and La Bruyère and Boileau.

The second form and rhetoric inculcated, not only in Latin and Greek but also in French, the classical precepts of litera-

---

28. *Ratio*, "Regulae Professoris Supremae, Mediae et Infimae Classis Grammaticae," no. 2; and "Regulae Professoris Humanitatis et Rhetoricae," no. 1.
29. Passard, *La Pratique*, 18, 57.

ture and literary style. The compendia of such rules and the literary anthologies employed in the colleges had Jesuit editors. Among the best known and most widely used were those written by Sengler for grammar, by Boylesve and Longhaye for literature, and by Cotel for rhetoric.[30] These principles appeared in practice in the literature which was studied. This included collections of poetry, collections of the great masterpieces of oratory such as Bossuet's sermons and funeral orations, Boileau's *L'Art Poétique* (so influential in establishing the literary ideals of French classicism), and selections from the classical theater such as *Cinna, Horace,* and *Polyeucte* by Corneille, *Athalie* and *Britannicus* by Racine, *Le Misanthrope* by Molière, and *Mérope* by Voltaire. The editing and publication of such collections, anthologies, and original textbooks for history and geography was regulated in great detail by the four provincials and formalized in contracts signed with several of the larger French Catholic publishers. For example, in 1875 the four provinces divided such editorial work for all the authors used in the schools, and signed with the publishing house of Mame a contract which detailed editors, format, number of copies to be printed, exclusivity of rights and usage, royalties, discounts, and future first options for publisher and editors.[31]

30. For example, Antoine Sengler, S.J., *Grammaire latine* (Amiens, 1867); *Petite syntaxe latine pour la sixième* (Amiens, 1872); *Grammaire grecque* (Paris, 1873); Marin de Boylesve, S.J., *Principes de littérature: style, poésie, eloquence* (3 vols.; Paris, 1851–1852). The author wrote this work in 1841 and used it in duplicated form for many years before publishing it. Within a dozen years after publication it was in a sixth edition. *Principes de littérature à l'usage des jeunes personnes* (Paris, 1866); *Principes de rhétorique* (2nd ed.; Paris, 1860). Georges Longhaye, S.J., *Poésie, notes polycopies* (Brugelette, n.d.); *Théorie des belles-lettres* (Paris, 1855). A sixth edition was published as late as 1934. *Préface de "Fables de la Fontaine," suivies de quelques morceaux choisis du même auteur. Edition classique avec notes, précédée d'une notice bibliographique, d'une étude morale et littéraire* (Paris, 1870). Pierre Cotel, S.J., *De Arte Rhetorica* (Paris, 1840). A second edition appeared in 1859, a third without date, and a fourth in 1872.

31. TSJ, "Liber pro Patre Socio," 1875, and PSJ, C-13, "Enquêtes collèges secondaires, 1862–1880," "Editions des auteurs classiques," "Compte rendu de séance," Toulouse, Nov. 21, 1875.

No traditions existed for the study of "accessory subjects." At least so it sometimes seemed to the Jesuits of the era. In introducing the *Ratio* of 1832, Roothaan had explicitly spoken of the need and opportuneness of these studies, and they figured in every plan through the years. But nothing explicit was set down for them in the new *Ratio*. This was wise, because each country would have to take account of its own particular situation. This had been true also of the presuppression schools, and wherever and whenever these subjects had developed, it had been in the living context of the times, and not simply because of a set of rules. The literalism of much of the appeal of "Back to the *Ratio*" (the old *Ratio*) thus missed or falsified what the old Jesuit colleges had done. The attempted banishment of the accessory subjects is an example of such a literalist mistake. In any case, however, the time given to these subjects was quite limited. Mathematics shared with history and geography the special period reserved for accessories during the last half-hour of class in morning and afternoon, plus, often, an extra half-hour once or twice a week depending on province, school, and class.

Mathematics and the sciences usually had special teachers. History and geography often had to be content with one or the other of the surveillants, and sometimes with the regular class teacher who had to find for the preparation of these subjects some time left over after preparing his main subjects of French, Latin, and Greek. This lack of specialized teachers was frequently a subject of complaint and concern on the part of the prefects of studies.

Many parents, in their turn, did not like to have these studies called accessories, and students did not work at them diligently when they were not counted for the year-end competitive prizes, as was true for a while. The province consultors then agreed that they could be otherwise designated "given the times and circumstances," and could be counted for prizes, but it was clearly to be understood by the schools themselves that those studies were not to become "principal disciplines" and were "not to be given more time than already set down."[32]

Mathematics and the sciences could have been taught little by little and concurrently with the grammar and literary studies; this was, at the time, called the progressive method. Or, left aside almost totally until the completion or near completion of grammar and literature, they could then have been studied fully in their own right. This was called the successive method of teaching. The Jesuit colleges would frankly have liked to adopt the latter regime, for reasons previously mentioned in connection with Brugelette. Supposedly, mathematics and the sciences demanded a reasoning ability that came only in later youth, whereas literary studies took advantage of the actual intellectual and imaginative capabilities of young students. Besides, divided attention made for a less thorough study of both fields. But in practice, in the actual world of French scholastic life, a purely successive method would have been impossible, and so the colleges adopted a compromise.[33]

Mathematics was in part taught concurrently. The schools offered elementary arithmetic for four years from the sixth through the third form. In the second form or humanities came algebra and often the beginning of geometry; in rhetoric, geometry. Only after the literary studies, during the one or two years of science and philosophy, did mathematics, in the form of analytic geometry, trigonometry, and calculus, receive more time and attention. In the later years of the schools, these additional mathematics courses were often simply described in the study plans as the program for the baccalaureate in letters in the first year, and for the baccalaureate in sciences in the second. They conformed exactly to the subjects and divisions which would be required for the state examinations.

32. PSJ, "Lib. Cons.," Aug. 29, 1862. Also, for example, LSJ, "Lettres des Pères Provinciaux," Jullien, Oct. 15, 1875.

33. The state school directors had the same theories and the same resultant problems. See, for example, Falcucci, *L'Humanisme dans l'enseignement*, esp. 303–334, and Dupont-Ferrier, *Louis-le-Grand*, II, 239–240.

The natural and physical sciences began only after the completion of rhetoric. This was true, in general, in the government schools also. The courses aimed primarily to give a general knowledge of a scientific discipline. They in no sense proposed to produce students with a specialized knowledge of science. For those who chose a career in which specialization was necessary, an institution such as Sainte-Geneviève or Caousou provided a full range of courses after the baccalaureate. In those special schools the sciences were well taught and thoroughly taught, to judge by the results of the state entrance examinations for the Grandes Ecoles. As the science baccalaureate increased in importance and favor, however, the college course which prepared for it did become more specialized. Although the government schools had hesitated about whether such studies might not begin even in the years of the literary course, the same was not true of the Jesuit colleges.[34] No one questioned that science came completely after literature. Along with philosophy, it was to appear in the curriculum when reason began to reign pre-eminent.

The content of the science courses was in very general terms set down in several documents dealing with the years of philosophical studies, most notably in an Ordinatio in 1858 from Beckx, the General.[35] The studies included, in the first place, an ordinary introductory course in physics for which the General's letter gave detailed divisions. Then came a course in the general notions of chemistry, and some work in astronomy. Natural history or what might be called now natural science followed, but for none of these latter courses were there many further specifications. In the years immediately after the publication of the 1832 *Ratio,* some attempts seem to have been made to enlist the help of eminent French scientists in drawing up plans for science studies in the Jesuit

34. Dupont-Ferrier, *Louis-le-Grand,* II, 339.

35. "Ordinatio A.R.P.M. Petri Beckx pro Triennali Philosophiae Studio, ad Provincias Missa anno 1858," in *Ratio Studiorum* (Tours, 1876), 135–164.

schools. A letter of 1835, for example, reported on the submission of a plan to Ampère and to several other scientists.[36] But no one seems to have carried these contacts further, and, as the pressure of state examinations increased year by year, the program for those examinations came to be adopted more and more.

None of the specific teaching plans which were produced matched in any detail those for the grammar and literature classes. The science and mathematics teachers sometimes complained that those which were drawn up by fellow Jesuits were too arbitrary, set out by administrators in impossibly ambitious terms, and often inferior to the state plans. The state schools in turn complained about their plans which, one after another, were imposed on them, with every change making it more difficult to maintain a coherent program.[37]

The accessories in the *Ratio* of 1832 were mathematics, history, and geography. Foreign languages did not appear in that category, but right from the beginning Brugelette included them, and all the later colleges also taught them. Either English or German were available; sometimes both were presented. Since they were not official subjects in the curriculum, they were taught outside of ordinary class hours, during some of the recreation or study time and at extra cost beyond the ordinary fees. The teachers often were laymen. Through the years, the demand for these courses seems to have grown steadily, though it was always only a minority of students who took them.

This situation changed radically after 1875 with the require-

---

36. PSJ, C-11, "Plurium Animadversiones," ca. 1835, Pourelet to ?, Oct. 18, 1835.

37. For instance PSJ, C-13, "Enquêtes collèges secondaires, 1862–1880," Poulain to Chambellan, July 26, 1880, "Those men of genius who have never put their hand to a real-life science class cannot even suspect the stupidity of students, and [so] they draw up impossible programs . . . I do not ask that we accept the state programs without discussion. But, let us discuss them. And who would dare say we have done that?" See also Dupont-Ferrier, *Louis-le-Grand*, II, 339–341.

ment of a modern foreign language for the baccalaureate. All of the schools then introduced them. Lyons, for example, made German obligatory and English optional, because the former was needed for the Grandes Ecoles and helped toward learning English.[38] But at the meeting in September 1875, only a minority favored this arrangement. Most of the participants wanted both languages made obligatory, because parents seemed to prefer that. If only one was to be demanded, it ought to be English, "in view of commerce and industry and the like."[39] From this time on, "Contemporary Foreign Languages" appeared on the programs, most often "in accord with the program for the baccalaureate."

"Geography, during all of the nineteenth century, was a little like the Cinderella of history."[40] This was said of the state schools, but it was also true, though less so, of the Jesuit colleges. Both types of establishments usually attached geography to the study of history, and gave neither a great deal of time nor attention to it. But in the nineteenth century, as earlier, the Jesuit interest in foreign missionary endeavor contributed to making the subject more topical for the teachers and more vivid for the students than might have been suggested by its place in the curriculum.[41] Their own fellow Jesuits were laboring in some of the lands treated by the teachers, and textbooks came more to life when students were helping to support a child in a Chinese orphanage, or when they heard Father De Smet from the Rocky Mountain missions tell of the redskins for whom he had come to Europe to beg. These visits of missionaries were always occasions of interest to the schools.

As for the textbook subject itself, the curriculum stressed

38. LSJ, "Lettres des pères provinciaux," Jullien, "Sur les collèges," Oct. 15, 1875.

39. *Ibid.*, "Compte-rendu des séances, Sept. 1875, pour le nouveau programme d'études à établir."

40. Dupont-Ferrier, *Louis-le-Grand*, II, 303.

41. See François de Dainville, S.J., *La Géographie des humanistes* (Paris, 1940) and *La Naissance de l'humanisme moderne* (Paris, 1940).

political more than physical geography; it would be many years yet before the latter would seem as important as treaty boundary lines. In general, each year's course supplemented the history course then being taught, the geography of Palestine and the Near East with Bible history, the geography of Greece and Rome with their respective histories, the geography of the Middle Ages, modern Europe, and France in particular, turn by turn.[42]

History was by no means meant to be a Cinderella. From the very first days of the minor seminaries it loomed large in the preoccupations of the Jesuit educators. Loriquet was primarily responsible for giving "to history . . . the rank which its importance seems to assign to it," and his remark found echo in later years in Olivaint's conviction that "historical studies are no longer only important; they have become truly necessary."[43]

Several programs were drawn up for a progressive study of history, and the official study plans in general reconciled minor differences among them. The youngest students began with *Histoire sainte,* a type of Bible history, or even with a very simple Church history. Then from the sixth through third

42. See *Plan d'Études,* 1852–1853, 1868, 1875.

43. PSJ, 2220, "Annales," 819; and Clair, *Olivaint,* 263. Loriquet followed an honorable and honored precedent. The first compendium of secular and sacred history by a Jesuit was written within fifty years of the foundation of the Society, Horatio Torsellini, S.J., *Historiarum ab origine mundi usque ad annum 1598 epitome libri X,* 1598, and, apart from theology, no subject counts as many works in Sommervogel's general bibliography of all Jesuit writings. In France, in the eighteenth century, a large number of historical works were published, often due to the influence of the Jesuit teacher, Claude Buffier, at Louis-le-Grand. Voltaire was one of the beneficiaries of his experience. Buffier also wrote a manual, *Nouveaux éléments d'histoire et de géographie à l'usage des pensionnaires du collège de Louis-le-Grand,* Paris, 1718 and 1726.

Olivaint's words are at the beginning of his unpublished memoir on the study of history, drawn up at the request of Jesuit superiors. Several other Jesuits drew up memoirs of like nature. See PSJ, C-4, *Ratio* XIX–XX, "*Ratio* et Plan d'Études," by Georges Longhaye, S.J. There is a long note on the study of history inserted there. See also PSJ, C-11, "Enquêtes provinciales 1804–1848," "Notes sur l'enseignement de l'histoire," Vals, May 4, 1835 by Charles Cahier, S.J.; another copy is in PSJ, C-12, "Enquêtes provinciales, 1849–1860."

forms they studied ancient, Roman, French, and medieval history. In the humanities and rhetoric classes, modern history took over. The courses dealt with Europe and with France in particular from the fourteenth to the seventeenth century, and then from 1700 to 1815 or, later, only to 1789.[44]

The textbooks used for the history classes were, especially in the beginning, those written by Loriquet. Even before 1850 some of the Jesuits had had misgivings about the tone of his *Histoire de France*. In 1846, when there was question of reprinting it, the provincial consultors could not agree on whether it was to stay the same, or to be corrected slightly, or to be completely rewritten. The third opinion was argued for, because if there were only slight corrections, the Society would seem to approve of the rest of it and that could have greatly offended public opinion.[45] In 1847 one of the formal requests discussed by the Paris province in preparation for a meeting in Rome was "that as soon as possible the *Histoire de France* written by Father Loriquet be removed from our schools, a book which has aroused so much hatred against us, and which would arouse an even greater amount in the future." The decision was "left to the prudence of the provincial, with due regard to the esteem due to the worthy Father Loriquet."[46]

For some years the texts stood substantially unchanged, but finally several of the Jesuits wrote their own manuals and Father Gazeau did a complete revision of a good number of Loriquet's works, including the *Histoire de France* and the *Histoire Moderne*. In 1880 it was Gazeau's turn to be discussed. In the climate of the Ferry campaign, the consultors wondered whether they "should get rid of the *Histoire* by Father Gazeau in order to avoid difficulties. [One consultor] said yes, the

44. Only after 1900 did the government programs include a course that began with 1815, and during much of the nineteenth century it was considered foolhardy enough even to go up as far as that date. See Dupont-Ferrier, *Louis-le-Grand*, II, 302.

45. PSJ, "Lib. Cons.," Dec. 29, 1846.

46. PSJ, C³12, "Consultes," "Postulata Prov. Franciae," 1847, V.

others, no; and finally they thought it would be well to have a new edition emended and publicly printed."[47]

The opponents of the Jesuits often accused them of contributing to the creation of "two Frances." If by one of those Frances was meant a nation which not only embraced the revolutionary heritage (if not always the revolution itself), but also recognized as wholly fortunate its antecedents in the previous centuries and its consequences in nineteenth-century secular society, then it is true that the Jesuit schools sought to inculcate a different view of what France was and should be. In 1864 Duruy, the noted historian and then the Minister of Education, published an instruction on the teaching of history. It indicated the official viewpoint: since the fifteenth century a series of profound and fortunate revolutions, political, religious (preparing for the modern principle of tolerance), economic, artistic, philosophical (ushering in free thought), and scientific, had changed Europe drastically. Then the eighteenth and nineteenth centuries had entered onto the stage with all their new and desirable characteristics, "in such a way that from the fifteenth century to our days, one surveyed the historic cycle which had seen civilization renewing itself."[48] This was not only history, but a definite philosophy of history too; the Society's schools by no means shared in it.

To compare in several particulars Gazeau's *Histoire Moderne* with Duruy's similar textbook, *Histoire de France et des temps modernes,* is an instructive example of the differing outlooks. Duruy's book went through numerous editions and was long used in the state lycées. On Voltaire, Gazeau commented that "this apostle of falsehood never stopped preaching by his example. The avowed enemy of hypocrisy, he himself was a hypocrite right down to the most abominable sacrilege; so-called defender of an oppressed people, he compared the com-

---

47. PSJ, "Lib. Cons.," March 14, 1880.
48. "Décret relatif à l'enseignement de l'histoire dans la classe de Philosophie," Sept. 23, 1864, in Falcucci, *L'Humanisme,* 305–306.

mon people to the lowest kind of animals and asserted that they had need of a yoke, a goad and some hay! He aspired in his vanity to the title of champion of the rights of man, and he engaged in the slave trade for monetary profit, pleased with it as a good business deal."[49] For Duruy, however, the same man was a hero, and he ended his discussion of Voltaire as follows: "Social evil became as it were his personal enemy and the love of justice his most ardent passion . . . He has rightly merited the hatred of those who believe that the world ought to remain immobile, and the admiration of those who see society as obliged to work unceasingly for its material and moral betterment."[50]

Was the Civil Constitution of the Clergy brought into being by an assembly which, "finally, swept on by its hatred for the Holy See as much as by its frantic passion to do everything over, arrogated to itself the right to give a constitution to the church of Jesus Christ?" Or did it come about because, "just as it [the assembly] had established an election for everything, so it resolved to establish one for the Church, where it had existed in the beginning and where it was still found, to a degree, before the Concordat of 1516?" These are only two particular instances of the general contrast in the ways in which France's past was viewed.[51] When it came to the history of the Church itself, the viewpoints of Gazeau and Duruy differed even more widely. Finally, to appreciate the breadth of divergence in what might be taught, one has to remember that

49. François Gazeau, S.J., *Histoire moderne* (Paris, 1869), 367.

50. Victor Duruy, *Histoire de France et des temps modernes* (2nd ed.; Paris, 1859), 232–233. The French Jesuit reaction to the government's plan to celebrate officially in 1878 the centenary of Voltaire's death is summed up well in a letter from the provincial of Champagne. He spoke of the "sentiments of horror aroused in Catholic souls by the impious project," and asked that each priest offer a Mass in reparation for "this immense scandal and to turn away from France the [divine] chastisements which it will bring on" (CSJ, "Litterae Encyclicae Patrum Provincialium," Grandidier, May 24, 1878).

51. Gazeau, *Histoire moderne*, 447–448; and Duruy, *Histoire de France et des temps modernes*, 359.

neither of these two authors was the extreme representative of his respective side.

Despite the care in drawing up various programs and despite the emphasis on the subject, the history courses in the grammar classes usually had no specially trained teacher; this was often true, too, of humanities and rhetoric. Frequently, the young scholastics who were surveillants gave this course; sometimes, the professor of grammar or literature taught this subject also to his particular class. The latter situation had the advantage of making possible a continuity between this accessory and the principal subjects of study. Besides, this arrangement will seem less surprising if it is remembered that "history should be studied twice. The first study is only a preparatory work, all memory . . . but absolutely necessary for the success of the second." History was to be studied for the "second time in the years of philosophy, following the exigencies of the baccalaureate," in an "advanced course and with a special professor."[52] This second pursuit of history was to include more than just names and dates, and more than simple baccalaureate preparation. One program described it as a "project to combine in a single course the lectures on religion and the lectures on history for the students of philosophy."[53] The program concentrated its attention on two items—a section on the Old Testament as history, almost in the nineteenth-century sense of scientific history, and a section on the philosophy of history.

Although "philosophy of history" was not in itself defined, the course outline made clear what was acceptable and what wrong. It maintained that any modern philosophy of history started from two ideas which, although subject to abuse, were basically Christian. These were the ideas of the unity and the perfectibility of the human species. On these principles phi-

52. PSJ, C-4, *Ratio* XIX–XX, "Quelques observations sur la manière d'appliquer le *Ratio Studiorum*," 9, 12–13.
53. PSJ, C-12, "Enquêtes provinciales, 1849–1860," "Enseignement de l'histoire: Projet de réunir en un seul cours les conférences religieuses et les conférences historiques pour les élèves de philosophie."

losophers of history had erected diversely erroneous systems. Among those in error were "progressists" such as Vico, Turgot, Condorcet, Saint-Simon, Fourier, Cousin, and Michelet. Machiavelli, Thiers, Mignet, and Lamartine deserved to be called "fatalists." Some, such as Guizot or Châteaubriand, were at least correct in admitting the providence of God, but they were at fault in other ways. Finally, a sane philosophy of history could take as models of historical generalization men such as St. Augustine, Bossuet, Bonald, Maistre, Balmes or Donoso Cortes.

This project does not seem to have been carried out in detail in the schools. It was probably too ambitious for the time available and the students involved, and what Boylesve had said of a similar course at Brugelette in the philosophy of history applied here too: "As for that vague science . . . , it would be necessary to be a St. Augustine or a Bossuet in order to teach [it] with assurance, clarity, and fullness of reason . . . in the manner of the *Discourse on Universal History* or of the *City of God,* and one would need auditors who possessed at one and the same time history and philosophy."[54] But the spirit in which the history course was taught in the last years in college comes through in the principles expressed and in the authors recommended by the project.

In any case, the schools tried to emphasize the subject all through the years, not only in the limited time of formal history classes, but also in the religion classes, academic seances, the dramatic productions, the library, the books given as prizes, even in the dining-room reading for the students. This they did because the subject was important in itself, and also because, as report after report never ceased to emphasize, it was important for the students from an apologetic point of view when they left the colleges and faced the difficulties and dangers of the world. The books which they might then use

54. Marin de Boylesve to Rubillon, June 19, 1850 as quoted in *EJF,* I, 960. See Chapter 2, above.

often inculcated "the wrong principles." The reading of history was "the most serious and the most useful that could be advised" for the students, but "no one was ignorant of the anti-Catholic spirit that was the very soul of the best known works of this type."[55]

The Jesuits wanted the principal facts of history taught, "especially those most deformed by the enemies of the Church, . . . presenting those facts to our students in their true character and putting them in a Catholic outlook."[56] If this was the opinion in 1855 and 1858, it was even stronger twenty years later. Labrosse summed it up well: "It [the history course] is . . . of great importance, not only for the baccalaureate, but also from the religious point of view, to form the minds and hearts of our students, to give them correct ideas on essential points, even and especially on religion, too often wrongly judged by the greater number of historians. A course in history well done is almost a good course in religion."[57]

"To put the crown on all this study of history, we should have a serious course in philosophy, but alas!" The remark sums up the purpose, the hope, and the reality of the study of philosophy in the curriculum. The Jesuit tradition had been to complete the literary studies of their lay students by a training in philosophy, mathematics, and science. This tradition was carried over into the new *Ratio* too.[58] Philosophy was supposed to finish the work begun in the cultivation of the literary sensibilities; it was to engage and direct the intellect in searching out an adequate understanding of the first principles of the order of reason which existed in thought, in the external world,

55. PSJ, C-12, "Enquêtes provinciales, 1849–1860," *ibid.*, "Quaesita de Scholis, 1855," Amiens, Guidée; "Rapport de la commission des études, Sept. 1858."

56. LSJ, PSJ, TSJ, "Litterae Encyclicae Patrum Provincialium," "Rapport de la commission des études pour les trois provinces de France," Sept. 1858.

57. PSJ, C-13, "Enquêtes collèges secondaires, 1862–1880," Labrosse to Mourier, Sept. 6, 1875.

58. PSJ, C-4, *Ratio* XIX–XX, "Quelques observations sur la manière d'appliquer le *Ratio Studiorum*," 13.

and in human conduct in relation to that world. It was also to help provide a rational basis for the faith, however paradoxical that might sound, and thus, "the professor was so to teach it, that he prepared his students for the other [higher] scholarly disciplines, especially for theology, that he provided them with the weapons of truth against the errors of innovators, and especially that he encouraged them to a knowledge of their Creator."[59] As history was to be learned for itself and also for the aid that it brought to a knowledge and practice of the faith, so was it with philosophy. This was the twofold purpose of the course.

The first hope was that the colleges could fulfill such a purpose in the three-year cycle originally set down in the new *Ratio*. For a very short time in the exile colleges, such a three-year period was attempted, and once in a while a project would be drawn up to get back to it, even if only in one college of each province to which serious students could be sent. But this hope was impossible, in the real world of baccalaureate pressures, state examinations, and equally impatient youth and parents. The lycées had trouble retaining students for any philosophy at all at the times when it was not an obligatory examination subject. The Jesuit schools always had at least one year of philosophy and maintained a two-year course whenever possible.[60]

Within this two-year period the colleges hoped to combine a truly adequate science course, a philosophy course that contained at least the essentials, and the final preparation for the baccalaureate examination. In theory at least, physics and mathematics were still regarded in the schools and school man-

<hr/>

59. *Ratio,* 1832, no. 1.

60. See, for example, such a proposal from Vannes (around 1860?) in PSJ, C-12, "Enquêtes provinciales, 1849–1860," "Mémoire en faveur d'une restauration des cours complets de philosophie et de science dans les collèges de la Compagnie." See also Dupont-Ferrier, *Louis-le-Grand,* II, 281, on the philosophy classes almost "emptying themselves" at such a time (1852) in the best lycée in France.

uals as parts of philosophy, as "one of the group of scholarly disciplines which treat of the ultimate principles of all things; these disciplines are logic, ontology, cosmology, psychology, [natural] theology, physics and mathematics, and moral philosophy."[61] In practice, in the classroom the science course tended to be more and more autonomous, and increasingly taught directly in view of the baccalaureate.

Textbooks and study plans often grouped the seven tracts of the course of philosophy into three larger divisions, logic, metaphysics, and moral philosophy or ethics. Logic taught "the right use of the intellectual faculties, so that truth could be safely found," and it "examined the first principles of knowledge." This included what would now be called formal logic, which was Aristotelian in content and method, and theory of knowledge, which dealt with truth, certitude, and the ability of the mind to reach the external world. Metaphysics was "the discipline which [went] beyond nature perceptible by the senses." General metaphysics or ontology considered "things in their ultimate principles which are abstracted from objects by the operation of the mind." Special metaphysics included cosmology, which treated "of the most general and abstract principles of the corporeal world," psychology, which "dealt with the nature and faculties of the human soul" or with the principles of our intellectual and sensible life, and natural theology or theodicy, which "ascended to the first principle of all things," and "treated of God, the supreme being."[62] Ethics or moral philosophy completed the course. As both an art and

61. Salvatore Tongiorgi, S.J., *Institutiones Philosophicae in Compendium Redactae* (Annecy, 1864), I, 1–2.

62. See Pierre Fournier, S.J., *Institutiones Philosophicae ad Usum Praelectionum in Collegiis et Seminariis* (Paris, 1854), 4; CSJ, 454, Corneille, *Philosophie* (Amiens, 1873), 1; and Tongiorgi, *Institutiones*, I, 110. The material in Fournier's book was, the author said, taught at the college of Fribourg, and first put into printed form there some eighteen years previously (i.e. around 1836). Corneille's *Philosophie* was a privately printed compendium, very brief and very schematic, for use in the college at Amiens.

a science, it examined "the first principles of conduct," the former "insofar as it set forth the norms of right living," and the latter "insofar as it demonstrated or proved those norms which had been set forth."[63] Often some lectures were also given in the history of philosophy, again in accord with the state examination programs.

The several textbooks which have provided these descriptions or definitions of the courses were in general use in the colleges at the time. In their presentation and approach they are quite representative of other texts that were also used in these years, and, as far as can be determined, of private notes of individual teachers also.

According to a regulation of 1858 from the General, where a two-year course existed, there were to be two philosophy classes a day—of logic and general metaphysics in the first year, and of special metaphysics and ethics in the second. In most places this presented nothing new; such a program had existed before that date, and continued to do so later. However, where there was only a year for philosophy, the schools still attempted to squeeze into that year as much of the material as possible from all the courses. As a result, there was a proliferation of summaries.

Without question, the classes were to be taught in the scholastic method. Statement of the question, definition of terms, and presentation of the positions of adversaries preceded a syllogistic proof which was followed by the solution of the main objections to the thesis. Equally without question, Latin was to be the language of philosophical discourse.[64] In practice it was not always all that rigid. As a student recalled of the Latin of philosophy classes at Bordeaux, in the Toulouse province, the session started with it, "but the language did not correspond to the natural vivacity of the thought, so that the

63. Corneille, *Philosophie*, 1; and Tongiorgi, *Institutiones*, II, 3.
64. Some lycées still used this method too. A very large number of them employed Latin, which continued to be the regulation for Jesuit schools for a long time.

dialogue, started in Latin, almost always ended in French."[65] This exception to the rule was true of the use of syllogistic form too. But, in general, the form, the language, the large amount of matter to be covered and the restricted amount of time, the youth of the students, and the frequent conviction of the professors that they were imparting a definite and fixed body of truth, all conspired to make of many of the classes an excessive exercise in the memorization of formulae.

A few voices increasingly questioned the use of Latin, the rigid formality, and the effectiveness of the course as then taught. A strong memorandum, for example, maintained that current circumstances, the spirit of the times, and the examination pressures made Latin impossible, and that far from aiding in character formation or in preparing the students to face the world with a serious esteem and taste for the intellectual life, it was the author's "profound conviction that the current philosophy teaching was of no use to the students, that it did not inspire in them a taste for serious matters, that it, rather, bored them, and that such would always be the case insofar as that teaching was not radically changed." The author of the memorandum also remarked that if "after reading [in class] a page of M. Cousin or of M. Simon," the Jesuit professor was going to refute it in Latin, the refutation would look a lot paler than the opposition. "And if, later, our student attends in Paris, the course of Messieurs Simon and Renan, will not the superiority of its form, by an induction that is doubtless wrong but difficult to avoid, lead him to conceal from himself the basic flaw in substance?"[66] This objection hit hard at what philosophy in the colleges hoped to accomplish, but the form and the language were too traditionally fixed to be changed.

The objection hit hard because the course was meant not only to present a particular philosophical system as an ordered

65. *EJF,* I, 793.
66. PSJ, C-12, "Enquêtes provinciales 1849–1860," de Laage, S.J., "Mémoire sur l'enseignement dans nos collèges, Philosophie," 1860.

understanding of first principles, but also to prepare the students to answer, for themselves and for others, the objections to their Christian faith and to its rational presuppositions.

> For everywhere there has been a rank growth of sophists who in ordinary discourse and in their writings try in a mad rage to obliterate every notion of the true and the honorable, and to bring down every principle of faith and morals. . . . Heedless youth are often deceived by "their philosophy and empty fallacies, drawn from human tradition and from worldly principles, and not from Christ" (Colossians 2:8). Against such a terrible infection, spreading wider every day, the most effective antidote is the study of philosophy as usually taught in truly Christian schools. Experience proves that they who are versed in this subject are not easily deceived, and that, habituated to accurate rules of reasoning, they know how to detect the teachings of an adulterine philosophy, overcome the wicked enemies of religion and refute their godless systems.[67]

One of the philosophy teachers and authors wrote this in 1854, and although in the years following it would be expressed in language somewhat more temperate, the same purpose was part of the later teaching too.

This inimical philosophy was, for convenience sake, simply called the "University School," although, as Fournier admitted, "the University adhered to no system in particular, but seemed to give everyone the power to teach any doctrine at all, for it equally commended the better known philosophers, Bacon and Descartes, Locke and Malebranche, Condillac and Leibniz."[68] This was a fair judgment on the actual situation in the state system. There were, however, three schools to which one could assign the teaching in that system. The first was exemplified

67. Fournier, *Institutiones*, 3–4.
68. *Ibid.*, 626. Also see Falcucci, *L'Humanisme*, 189.

by a mild materialist such as Cabanis and by ideologues such as Volney or Destutt de Tracy, the second by those whom the Scottish philosophers had influenced—men such as Royer-Collard or Jouffroy, and the third by Victor Cousin, the eclectic par excellence.

To all of these the Jesuit colleges were opposed, and to the rationalists and deists of the eighteenth century too. Sometimes one or another of the proponents of these various philosophies would be named explicitly among the adversaries to a thesis; more often the "system" itself would be so listed. Later innovators met with even less favor. If the appearance of the positivism of Comte and the scientism and materialism of Taine and Littré appalled Cousin and his successors, this was even truer of the ordinary Jesuit philosophy teacher. Finally, socialism and communism seem not even to have entered into consideration as particular philosophies, but simply, if treated at all, as variants of atheism especially dangerous to the stability of society.[69]

The opponents of a sound philosophy could also be of the household of the faith, and they were of more concern and occupied more of the correspondence between Rome and provincials, rectors, and prefects of studies. There was little danger that the Jesuit colleges were going to teach socialism or materialism, but the dangers of ontologism and "Catholic liberalism" did fill many a letter. Ontologism continued to affect the teaching of philosophy, and the General took a firm stand against the ontologist doctrines. Indeed, he thought that even "to set out the position of the ontologists and the scholastics and to admit candidly that the peripatetic system was most generally followed . . . by no means satisfied the regulations

69. See Falcucci, *L'Humanisme*, 190–196, for the triumph of eclecticism in the state schools, and 365–369, for the change around 1880 to a purely factual, nominalist-materialist approach to philosophy. Socialism would seem to have come up more frequently in the Jesuit schools at the meetings of the congrégation or sodality, where the members, hopefully a future French Catholic elite, would be warned of its dangers to body and soul.

and the mind of the Society."[70] But here, too, there was a certain amount of inconsistency, for there is little doubt that Rothenflue's *Institutiones Philosophicae Theoreticae,* one of the textbooks which was widely used and highly praised in the French Jesuit schools, was influenced by Rosmini's positions favorable to ontologism and taught at least a mitigated version of it.[71]

To liberalism the Jesuits gave even less quarter. One could hardly accuse the Society of support for the views of Catholic liberals like Dupanloup, Falloux, Montalembert, and Lacordaire, even though on other levels these men were devoted friends of the Jesuits. Rather, the French Jesuit was known to be in the camp of Pie and Guéranger, and especially of Veuillot and *L'Univers.* Once the encyclical *Quanta Cura* and the *Syllabus of Errors* appeared in 1864, the position of the Society became even more definitely antiliberal, and continued to be so. But just as several of the editors of *Etudes,* the best known journal of the French Jesuits, were, for some at least, not zealous enough in their opposition to liberalism, so also there were quarrels about some of the teachers not wholeheartedly anathematizing that doctrine.[72] Quite typical of the many official letters from Rome was Beckx's firmness in 1871 that a particular professor of ethics at Vannes with "ultraliberal ideas . . . could not remain a teacher, neither of our [lay] students nor of our scholastics," or, in 1876, his "joy that every trace of liberalism has disappeared from among our students."[73]

It was obvious that the man who held and taught that the

70. ARSJ, Franc., Reg., Beckx to Ponlevoy, May 4, 1873. This is one of a group of letters dealing with several Jesuits said to be teaching ontologism at Vaugirard. See Chapter 1, above.

71. See Edgar Hocedez, S.J., *Histoire de la théologie au XIXe siècle* (3 vols.; Brussels, 1947–1952), II, 127.

72. There was much correspondence on this question between Rome and Paris. See the instructive article by Joseph Lecler, S.J., "Dans la crise du catholicisme libéral," *Études,* 191 (Nov. 1956), 196–211.

73. ARSJ, Franc., Reg., Beckx to Ponlevoy, April 7, 1871, and Beckx to Chauveau, Feb. 25, 1876.

Syllabus of Errors was of itself an *ex cathedra* definition and that thus it was a mortal sin not to accept it, was not a liberal. But the basic problem remained: it never really was that clear what minimum it took, in the ultramontane Society of Jesus, to make a "liberal" Jesuit. The term and the controversy, of course, extended to more fields than philosophy, but especially in that subject did it have relevance for the Jesuit colleges. For example, there was a tendency simply to repeat without examination, especially in ethics classes, theses on the relation of church and state which were even at that time showing signs of the strain of unreality. The intransigent antiliberalism of most Jesuits, the official concern in Rome, and the imprecision in the very term had the unfortunate result of simply furthering this tendency.

In general, through the years which this study covers the Jesuit schools considered themselves to be maintaining and teaching a traditional scholastic philosophy. Fournier is again interesting in describing this philosophy as adhering to no particular system, but generally admitting whatever was immediately clear to reason and whatever could be proved by ratiocination from immediately evident principles.[74] In sedulously trying to avoid the "general reason" of Lamennais and, later, traditionalism and ontologism, Jesuit philosophy was far closer to a Wolffian rationalism than they would care to have recognized. In the long run, the gravest problem that the Jesuits faced in their teaching of philosophy was their lack of basic philosophical speculation and research with but few exceptions. In the immediate present, it was the almost impossible situation of trying to teach a complete course in philosophy to students of sixteen to eighteen in two years, or increasingly in one year.

It often comes as a surprise to learn that the classes of catechism or formal religious instruction in the Jesuit schools

74. Fournier, *Institutiones*, 628.

were relatively few. Yet such was the case. In the schedule, there were only two religion periods a week—one on Saturday and the other on Sunday. The last half hour of class on Saturday afternoon was always reserved for religious instruction, but not necessarily for a formal catechism lesson, although this also could take place at times. Usually during this period each regular professor gave to his class some sort of exhortation on the Christian life. He might deal with the life of Christ himself, devotion to his person or to the Virgin Mary, the reception of the sacraments, especially confession and holy communion, a specific virtue to be practiced or a vice to be avoided, some problem in the Church, a particular moral to be drawn from the life of the class itself or from some current event. He could draw material from whatever source he wished, from the catechism or from other books, from a feast day soon to be celebrated, from the Sunday Gospels, or from his own notes and personal reflection.

On Sunday, a formal catechetical lesson or formal religious instruction always took place. In neither the boarding nor the day schools was this a problem as far as attendance went. For the boarding schools this was obvious; for the day schools, the Sunday period of Mass and religious instruction was never regarded as anything but absolutely obligatory.

Just as with history, so with the catechism, the students did the course twice over. Beginning in the sixth form, they studied in three successive years creed, code and cult, the Apostles' Creed, the Ten Commandments and particular Church precepts, and the sacraments and Christian worship. For the younger students, the class began with a simple question and answer method, with "easy explanations and especially with . . . comparisons drawn from striking objects suitable to their age."[75] Then, at the beginning of the next religion period the teacher might give a short quiz and demand recitation from memory of the matter from the previous class. On ordinary days during the week he was advised to spend a few minutes

75. Passard, *La Pratique*, 7 (Judde).

going over again the questions and answers most recently learned.

In the third form and in humanities and rhetoric, the students again saw the whole catechism for the second time, but "insofar as [they] are better instructed and more fully formed, the line of argument must be better developed, the explanations pushed further, the comparisons more suited to their intelligence, knowledge, and experience, the exhortations more insistent, and the examples used more serious and more carefully chosen."[76] During the last part of the rhetoric year and during the special religious instruction in the year or years of philosophy, the teacher was advised to complete the course by "the solution of the principal difficulties raised against religion."[77] For example, it was suggested that he treat of the historical proofs for Christianity, and of the nature of the Catholic Church itself, from the point of view of apologetics and of dogmatic theology. Usually the apologetic approach prevailed over the dogmatic. The latter involved much more philosophical background and theological sophistication than the students possessed; the former seemed more immediately useful for the young man about to face the unbelieving world. The teachers were preferably the regular professors, but other priests or scholastics had to take on these religion classes too. At times this presented difficulties, especially if the teacher was a young scholastic with many of his own studies yet to be done. As late as 1876, the general was insisting that "for the teaching of Christian doctrine in the upper classes, priests or scholastics who have already completed their philosophical studies should be assigned."[78]

76. *Ibid.*
77. TSJ, "Litterae Encyclicae Patrum Provincialium," "Sur quelques points concernant les collèges," Maillard, Oct. 13, 1853. This advice was true not only of the Toulouse province or of the early years of the colleges, but was generally applicable.
78. ARSJ, Reg., Tolos., Beckx to Blanchard, March 21, 1876. Also ARSJ, Reg., Franc., Beckx to Mourier, March 18, 1876.

As a textbook, the *Catechism* of Canisius enjoyed the greatest favor for a long time, especially in the lower forms. The influential German Jesuit of the Counter-Reformation first published this work shortly before 1554 and it continued to be published, translated, abridged, and adapted during the nineteenth century. Around it, as around Alvarez, a controversy arose in the Jesuit schools. A meeting of rectors at Paris summed up the positions briefly. Some thought it too dense, not sufficiently developed for children, containing both answers too long and lacunae too many, hard for professors to prepare and students to understand. Besides, many of the bishops and clergy would have preferred that the Jesuit schools use the particular diocesan catechisms. In answer, the proponents appealed, as often, to the venerable tradition of usage in the Jesuit schools, declared that it had not been adopted without serious examination and good reason, maintained that experience proved, for example, at Vaugirard and Poitiers and in the colleges in Lyons and Toulouse, that the book could indeed be taught even to the younger students. But they, too, added that the work could perhaps be improved by various teachers' aids. Finally all but two rectors voted to retain the text in a revised form; the holdouts remained convinced that it ought simply to be replaced.[79] In the course of the following years, as a matter of fact, the diocesan catechism did often replace Canisius.

For the upper forms, Feller's *Catéchisme philosophique* was typical of the books used.[80] The title itself gave a clue to its approach to the mysteries of the faith. In question and answer form, "if in certain places it [seemed] too simple and too ordi-

79. ARSJ, Reg., Franc., "Compte-rendu des séances des PP. Recteurs à Paris: Catéchisme du P. Canisius," Aug. 1859.

80. François-Xavier Feller, *Catéchisme philosophique, un Recueil d'observations propres à défendre la religion chrétienne contre ses ennemis* (5th ed., 3 vols.; Paris and Lyons, 1821). Feller (1735–1802) had been a Jesuit before the suppression of the Society. The first edition of the book was published in 1772 at Liège, with the author listed as Flexier de Reval, an anagram of Feller's name.

nary, it should be remembered that it was a Catechism; if in others it [seemed] too erudite, it should be recalled that it was a *philosophical* catechism." The first book dealt with proofs for the existence of God; the first chapter set out to demonstrate that atheism was impossible. From God, it went on in succeeding books to the human soul, to religion, and to Christianity, and ended with chapters on particular difficulties such as confession, the authority of the Pope, Church possessions, scholastic theology, celibacy, and superstition. Apologetic concerns dominated the approach used throughout the book. In keeping with its date of publication, it concentrated on the difficulties likely to be experienced by an eighteenth-century audience which was influenced and troubled by the arguments of the philosophers.

At the same time, the ambiguity and uncertainty of this approach for nineteenth-century students appeared in the recommendation to the teachers of such a book as Bergier's *Dictionnaire théologique*.[81] This was also an eighteenth-century work, but it was often reprinted in the early nineteenth century. It fitted in well with the religious spirit of that latter period in that, seeking carefully to guard against too great a reliance on reason, it seemed to teach at least a mildly traditionalist theology and to emphasize a universal interior sentiment as the best proof for the faith. These were probative positions that the Jesuit theologians had been combatting, but the Jesuit catechism teachers were advised to consult for background material for their classes a book which favored those very positions.

The colleges regarded religious instruction seriously, quite seriously, despite the few formal class periods devoted to it. Every province in all these years treated of it in letters, plans and conferences. It was as much the subject of worry to a

---

81. Nicholas Bergier, *Dictionnaire théologique* (Paris, 1788). In the next century, Archbishop, later Cardinal, Gousset of Reims, prepared a revision (Lille 1838), which was followed by other editions in 1852 and 1859.

superior of the Toulouse province in 1853 as it was to a teacher of the Paris province twenty years later, for, as the latter remarked, if the students in the Jesuit schools did not receive an adequate religious training, as was at times alleged, "this fact [was] of so grave a nature, so directly contrary to the very reason for the existence of our colleges, and the plan of their foundation, . . . that it was impossible to treat it lightly."[82] Superiors received urgings from higher superiors to make clear in deeds the importance of the subject, and to give adequate direction to the catechists in a detailed, obligatory program for each class, with class time really given to teaching, rather than to "pious exhortations, overabundant in our colleges, where the students are most often saturated with talks of this type." All of this was to be done so that the students might go out into the world prepared for the competition of public life.

Behind this instruction, behind this preparedness, however, there was a whole education, a whole upbringing in the faith, an interior commitment which preceded and gave force to and sustained the exterior works. There is at times a temptation to reduce an education in the faith to simple religious instruction. No Jesuit schools ever succumbed to it. However important the instruction was or ought to be, it always remained only a part of the total Christian education and life of the student. That education was to be found in part in the classroom but much more in the whole day-to-day existence of the college as a community.

82. TSJ, "Litterae Encyclicae Patrum Provincialium," "Sur quelques points concernant les collèges," Maillard, Oct. 13, 1853; PSJ, C-13, "Enquêtes collèges secondaires, 1862–1880," Georges Longhaye, S.J., "Mémoire sur l'enseignement du catéchisme," Oct. 1874.

VII

THE COLLEGE
AS A FAMILY

The community model for the nineteenth-century French Jesuit school was the family. The newer seminaries, of necessity boarding schools, had been conceived and structured in this way, partly on the model of the religious community as a family, partly in reaction to the Napoleonic model of the school as a barracks, and partly to reassure the families which had sent their sons away to the Jesuit schools at great distances and for long periods of time. The exile colleges continued the tradition of the family model. They even reinforced it by the very fact of their being outside France, and outside the reach of what were regarded as iniquitous laws which struck at the rights of a family to choose the type of education it wanted for its children.

Once it became clear that the establishments newly founded in France after 1850 had to be boarding schools, they had a tradition and a pattern ready at hand, and they all accepted it without question. So universal and so true was this, that, as Burnichon says, "to be noted, first of all is the perfect similarity from this point of view . . . of all [these] educational establishments . . . To know one is to be able to say that you know them all. A student can pass from one to another without having an impression of change. They would willingly say with an alumnus, 'We are never strangers in *our homes.*' That is, despite accidental differences, one and the same spirit animates them and gives to them all a family atmosphere."[1]

At the head of this family was the Father Rector. He was to be father not only to the members of his Jesuit religious community, but also to the students. In fact, they were not to be called *"élèves"* (students), nor *"messieurs"* (gentlemen), as in the lycées, but *"mes enfants,"* a phrase difficult to translate since it not only denoted "my children" but connoted also all the intimate relationships of a family.

If the rector was to be, par excellence, the father of this family, each of the Jesuit faculty members was also to be thus considered a father in relation to the students. Olivaint, the first prefect of studies at Vaugirard, summed up this attitude and this ambition exactly in the sermon which he gave to students and parents as the Jesuits took possession of the school in Paris in 1852. He began with a salutation from St. Paul's letter to the Galatians (4:19): "My little children, you to whom I give birth again, until Christ is formed in you." He then continued:

> Dear children, allow us to give you that name which we want to bestow on you always . . . It is, as a matter of fact, a family which gathers together today . . . The college seems to many of you, perhaps, like a sad prison. But no, thanks be to God, we are not at all jailers; we do not even come before you as masters. Even though we are charged with teaching you, the name which we seek above all,

---

1. Burnichon, *La Compagnie*, III, 457.

which we are jealous of, is the name of "Fathers." Yes, we want to be, or rather we are already for you, "Fathers."

. . . .

And you now, too, you must be for us *our children,* . . . by a free choice of your hearts . . . We desire your welfare, but *you* must *want* it also . . . Because we are your fathers, do not approach us with that fear, that mistrust, which so often in education turns the student into an enemy of the teacher, or into a slave.

Obey us, respect us, but do so as children. Admittedly, it is sometimes a little painful for you to obey, . . . and, despite all the care with which your previous upbringing was surrounded, the very air which is breathed in this century, so charged with insubordination and pride, has perhaps touched even you. Nonetheless, *you have to obey.* It is the very law of your age, of your weakness, of your inexperience. It is the condition of your progress in learning and in virtue. It is also the secret of your happiness . . . And finally, because one must obey, is it not, I ask you, more pleasant and easier to obey fathers than masters?

Have then, the respect of children; that is, in a sense, do not respect us too much. Do not attribute to us an inaccessible dignity . . . The respect of a son is balanced by a dear familiarity . . . From this moment on, we are nothing other than a family.[2]

The quotation is long, but the length is justified by the directness and clarity with which Olivaint expressed the ideal of the relations between Jesuits and students, and the basic attitudes which were to govern those relations.[3]

2. Pierre Olivaint, S.J., *L'Education chrétienne* (Vaugirard, 1852). The sermon was reprinted several times under this title. There is a copy in PSJ, C-17, Education, Brochures—XIX.

3. Of course, studies, too, occupied a great deal of Olivaint's talk, but they have been dealt with in the previous two chapters. That these were not simply Olivaint's personal attitudes is clear from other versions of the same theme through the years. See for example, Turquand's discourse on the aims and

The rector was the source of all authority in the school; he bore on his shoulders the ultimate responsibility for everything that occurred there, not only within the Jesuit community, but within the community of students also. Much of course, depended on the temperament of individual rectors. A school might have a very strong personality at its head, such as Pillon at Vannes and Lille, or it might have a man who preferred to delegate much of his responsibility for the school to subordinate officials. In any case, for help in making academic decisions the rector always had the *Ratio* itself, plus the common interprovincial policy as applied to particular provinces, and also four house consultors to whose advice he was regularly obliged to listen, if not necessarily to follow. Directly subordinate to the rector was the "Father Minister," who was charged with the day-to-day life of the religious community and with the material needs of both Jesuits and students. Then came the treasurer or procurator, a man with an unenviable job, as one might realize from the previous section of this study which dealt with finances.

The prefect of studies was the dean or master or principal. He directed the studies and discipline of the school. The ordinary principal's duties would have been enough in any case; as one prefect remarked to the general, "from morning to evening, I am completely occupied with students and parents."[4] But in addition he was responsible for the pedagogic formation of the young Jesuit scholastics or seminarians assigned to

---

methods of Jesuit education, Aug. 17, 1853, in Viansson-Ponté, *Les Jésuites à Metz*, 133, or Jenner's talk, "L'Esprit de famille dans l'éducation chrétienne," on Prize Day at Lille, August 4, 1875, in CSJ, MS 1154, Diarium Collegii St. Joseph. The latter said that this family spirit "brings about between master and student a respectful and affectionate relation called obedience, and it makes of the life of the college a prolongation of family life and a preparation for life in [civil] society. This family spirit in a college is like a mild and beneficent atmosphere. In it the chest expands, the heart rejoices, and the lips murmur, 'How good this is.'"

4. ARSJ, Tolos. 3-III, 1, Michel to Beckx, Jan. 19, 1868. Michel was prefect at this time at Sainte-Marie in Toulouse. One sometimes gets the impression that the parents, especially the mothers, were the greatest burden.

each school as "regents" during part of their training. "They [the scholastics] have to be formed in the methods of learning, of teaching, and of supervision. This formation, a point so important for the college, is the business, above all, of the prefect."[5]

The relationship of rector and prefect varied with the individuals involved, but the case of Sengler, prefect at Lille, as described by a former student, was not atypical. "He represented the rule, discipline, the daily duties . . . You felt his action much more strongly than that of the superior who, in the eyes of the students, represented above all fatherhood and leniency."[6]

For each class there was an ordinary or regular professor. He taught all that came under the heading of grammar, humanities, and rhetoric classes and, where possible, he would progress with the students from one year to the next. This ordinary professor was usually a priest. As preparation for teaching, the usual course of training in the Society, especially the juniorate or period of strongly emphasized classical studies was, certainly at first, regarded as sufficient along with private work during the summers. The baccalaureate was normal in many cases before entrance into the Society. Within a few years the provincials were prescribing that "all the young scholastics, whether students, surveillants or teachers, should prepare to take the examination for the baccalaureate in letters, or even for the one in science. It is important that our Jesuits have from now on the diploma of one, if not both, of these courses. It would even be very useful that some should have the licentiate and some the doctorate."[7] Some had these further degrees before entrance into the Society, and there were even a few, such as Olivaint, who were alumni of the Ecole Normale

5. ARSJ, Franc., Reg., Beckx to Chauveau, Feb. 28, 1879.
6. *EJF*, II, 1343.
7. TSJ, "Memorialia Visitatorum et Provincialium: Toulouse, Ste-Marie," Studer, March 7–23, 1858.

Supérieure, the Ecole Polytechnique, or of similar institutions. Philosophy and the accessory courses, particularly mathematics, had special teachers. Almost always, priests taught the philosophy courses. Scholastics often taught the history courses, and if they were especially good teachers they were sometimes also the ordinary professors for the lower forms.

The faculty, as a matter of principle and as far as possible, was all Jesuit. In some schools, the Christian Brothers and the Brothers of St. Gabriel helped with the very youngest students. The rather few laymen who were engaged usually taught modern foreign languages or some of the sciences. Almost always, too, the *arts d'agrément*, drawing, fencing, music, had laymen as masters. César Franck, for instance, taught music at Vaugirard for several years. Some of these lay teachers spent decades faithfully in particular establishments, and were a real factor in the continuity of traditions in the schools. In considering an intimation from the general that it would be good to have non-Jesuit "auxiliaries" both as teachers and as surveillants, a consultors' meeting agreed that employing more of them would release scholastics from regency sooner, which was a highly desired move as we have seen earlier. But, they countered, often these "auxiliaries" would have to live with the community and so would put restraints on a free family spirit, parents would not be happy with non-Jesuit personnel and, besides, such a program had been tried at Brugelette without too much success. This was in 1864, ten years after its closing, but Brugelette was still a potent norm.

Most often, the scholastics spent their years of regency as surveillants or prefects in one of the two or three divisions, upper, middle and lower, into which the student body was divided on the basis of age, maturity, and length of time at the school. There is little doubt that this surveillance was the most difficult, most time-consuming task in the college. Other than during actual class periods, from the moment of the students' rising, and even earlier, for the Jesuit had his religious exercises to perform first, to the indeterminate hour when they were not only abed but asleep, the regent was occupied totally with them.

For each division and its completely separate facilities, there were two or sometimes three surveillants. In any one school anywhere from six to ten or a dozen Jesuits might be fulfilling this function. The matter of fact recital which one of them gave of his duties at Metz was not at all extraordinary. In 1865 Paul Brucker began his regency as surveillant of the study hall, the recreation grounds and games, the chapel, the afternoon walks, and the dormitory for ninety students from seventh to third forms. Only the dining room was missing. In addition, he taught history in humanities class to seventy-five students, and an upper German class to forty-five others. Only the consequence was unusual, if foreseeable. "Three months after the feast of the Epiphany (January 6), I collapsed. The doctor, after examination said, 'Well he is simply at the end of his rope, this young man. Make him sleep for a week.' I slept conscientiously my whole week, and was besides relieved of my history course."[8]

In the Jesuit system the surveillant was not simply a watchman; he had a far more important task. He was "to assure the maintenance of discipline, and by this means to give to the students that formation of heart and of character [which is] an education in right conduct. It can be said that moral education is par excellence the work of the surveillant."[9] The Jesuits were convinced that the surveillant was as much a part of the total educational process as was the professor. They expected a good surveillant through day-to-day contact with a pupil to study each character in order to know its good and bad points, to

8. CSJ, MS 3252, "Curriculum Vitae-Brucker," 15. Most of this manuscript was later printed in *Lettres de Jersey*, XLII (1928–1929), 349.

9. Emmanuel Barbier, *La Discipline dans quelques écoles libres: Manuel pratique du surveillant* (Amiens, 1884), 4.

know what harmed or helped it, to know the moment to act "but as master and as father at the same time."[10] The mass of regulations, the precise details, the severity of rule, and simply the atmosphere of a large and therefore, of necessity, strictly run boarding school would utterly have stifled the students if such had been the sum total of daily activities. From all the evidence, there was much more to daily life than a series of restrictions, and some of that evidence, as we shall see later, came from witnesses such as Taine, hardly partial to the Jesuits.

The credit for making the school more than an impersonal institution was due in large part to the surveillant. He was there for the students, "to help their work, to put the finishing touches to their education, to form their character, and to enlighten and develop their religious feelings, in order to make them men faithful to God and useful to their country."[11] The strong insistence on discipline in this process could be dangerous, and sometimes it was harmful. More than once a prefect of studies or a rector or provincial or, if need be, Rome itself recalled that whatever discipline was needed was a means, not an end, and that an almost military rigor in the colleges was quite harmful to the students.

The rules for teachers and surveillants were in themselves sensible: "Do you want to have authority? You will not succeed by an air of superiority, by severity, by bluster, but by a serious, peaceful and modest air, by great exactitude in maintaining order and promptness, by a kindness which is, at one and the same time, far removed from familiarity, weakness, and despotism. Do you want to be likable? Outside of the classroom or the study hall, cease to be serious; say hello to the students; talk with them as a father and a friend; enter into their little

10. *Ibid.*, 9.
11. *Quelques avis: Principes et pratiques de surveillance* (Paris, 1910), 11–12 This was printed for Ste-Geneviève. There are copies in PSJ, C-29, "Conseils aux régents, XIX."

concerns."[12] But over and above particular rules and particular suggestions for success, the most fundamental attitudes of the surveillant were to be based on explicitly religious and apostolic motives. Every one of the rule books was clear on this; every exhortation, instruction, and, if need be, reprimand insisted on it.

In addition to teaching and prefecting there was a whole series of services to be performed in the large community of a boarding school. Although most of the schools had a considerable staff of salaried, outside help, here too, by preference, the Society tried to rely on its own members as far as possible. The lay brothers, Jesuits who had entered the order without intending to become priests, served as cooks and janitors, as infirmarians and chauffeurs, as postmen and barbers. Without the brothers, the schools could never have maintained as much of the self-sufficient atmosphere as the Society in France thought desirable. The brothers were far more necessary than was often explicitly recognized.

The students who arrived at the college at the beginning of October were to come fully outfitted for the year. With slight variations, their uniform for Sundays, for any public occasion, and for days of solemnity and celebration was a dark blue frock coat with a collar of black velvet, a dark blue pair of pants for winter and a white pair for summer, a white vest and a cravat of black silk. For ordinary days a plain and simple uniform was prescribed for the students, and neither diversity nor informality was tolerated. Their suits were never to be of unusual colors or styles, and the usual student smocks and caps were worn then as now in France.

All this was for both boarders and day students. The proportion between those who resided at a college and those who only spent the day there varied from place to place, from al-

12. LSJ, Collèges . . . en France, "Réglement . . . de Lyon, 1850," 54–55.

most nine to one at Mongré, for example, in 1864–1865 to just about three to one at Avignon in 1866–1867, or less than two to one at Saint-Etienne in the same year.[13] These figures are perhaps the extremes, but from school to school and from province to province, the boarding students were always in a very great majority. Even after 1870, when day schools were more vigorously promoted, this was only slightly less true.

Though it is not true that the Jesuits in their presuppression colleges founded the whole secondary boarding school system itself, the *"inimical* system" as Victor Laprade fiercely charged, it is true that once they adopted it of necessity after the restoration, they for long felt distinctly ill at ease with a day school population.[14] The day and boarding students followed the same courses, but "outside of classes, literary exercises, and chapel services, they [the day students] are entirely separate. Every individual contact with the boarding students is severely forbidden to them." The day student rules were almost an echo of those of Brugelette, and in a large city such as Toulouse the young men were bidden to act just as were the students in a small Belgian town. Any serious or prolonged communications with the boarders "would involve a case of expulsion." The reason for such separation lay in the overriding concern to protect the students from the "dangers of the world." If there had to be day students who faced such perils daily, that was all the more reason to protect the more fortunate boarders as far as possible from the contagion inevitably brought in from the outside. That these dangers were at the root of the concern

13. LSJ, 122[7], "Liste des élèves, Province de Lyon," Mongré: 362 interns, 43 externs; Avignon: 205 interns, 65 externs; St-Etienne: 217 interns, 120 externs.

14. See Victor Laprade, *L'Education homicide* (Paris, n.d.). Laprade was right in criticizing much of the military rigidity of nineteenth-century boarding schools, state as well as private. But rhetoric too often got the better of him, as when, in a typical instance, he spoke of "This regime of immobility, of abstinence, of physical repression and constraint of spirit, an institution as ferocious as and more harmful than the Holy Office" (26), or when he declared, "Frankly, all the old monkish pedagogy, all the moral teachings of state schools and others looks to nothing less than the destruction of the will" (168).

is clear from the rules for the externs themselves. They were to avoid "with the greatest care all bad or even suspect company, and all dangerous reading. They [were] absolutely forbidden to subscribe to circulating libraries, to frequent theaters, cafés and so forth. Any grave violation of this rule would [also] involve a case of expulsion."[15]

Because of the relatively high expenses, the clientele of the colleges came from families rather well off, though the proportion of landed proprietors seemed to have diminished gradually in favor of middle and upper bourgeoisie from the cities and small towns. Almost always, the students came from Catholic families. The Protestant was a rare exception, and his even rarer conversion to Catholicism was an event worthy both of rejoicing and of the annals. Not all the Catholic parents who sent their children practiced their faith. The distinction between *croyant* and *pratiquant* was a useful one here, and the theological and moral conditions of certain families were sometimes brought forward as arguments for boarding schools, where the children would be removed from "pernicious influences."

Why did families send their sons to the Jesuit schools? Taine, hardly a friendly witness, gave some of the reasons in his *Carnets de voyage*:

> At Metz, five hundred students at the Jesuits' [college] . . . There are other large Jesuit colleges in Paris, Vaugirard, Poitiers . . . and in several smaller cities. The old former liberals, magistrates, engineers, military personnel, send their sons there because it is the stylish fashion, because the food and the personal care [of the students] are reputed to be better, because good contacts are made there, a protection for the future, . . . because

15. TSJ, Tolos., Collège Ste-Marie, Prospectus, 1861. As at Brugelette, "the gravest motives and religion and reason conjoined" urged the observance of these rules. Of course, much of this was hardly enforceable. The acme of violation, both boarding and day, may have been perpetrated by the young Vaugirard boarder from Paris, who used his afternoons out at home to "be seduced by [his parents'] maid."

the mother of the family manages to have the boy sent there, at first for his first communion, and then manages to have him stay there afterwards, because the Fathers make themselves comrades of the students, while [in a lycée] the professor is cold and the surveillant is an enemy.

Conversation with Mme de . . . Her children are at the Jesuits. The place is doing so well that they refused seventeen [new] students this year . . . They gain the friendship of the students, become their comrades, walk around with them arm in arm on the playing fields during recreation, etc. The children love them and once grown up, they come back to see them. No obligatory piety, but nonetheless a student who would not make his Easter duty [i.e. confession and communion at Easter time] would be expelled. Very great attention to the food, the dress, the manners of the students.[16]

Motives are seldom unmixed, and what Taine said was the truth, but hardly all of it. Parents also sent their children to the Jesuit colleges because they wanted them to have a thoroughly religious training, and because they thought that even on the secular level they gave an education at least as good as, or perhaps even better than the state schools gave. For the former motive there is the same kind of testimony as that cited earlier with reference to the exile colleges, "Make my son a good Christian." For the general accuracy of the latter conviction, there were the simple facts that a baccalaureate diploma was practically necessary for the future career of the type of students in the Jesuit colleges, and that if in any significant numbers those schools had failed their students in the acquisition of that diploma, awarded incidentally not by the religious school itself but by a state board of examiners, it would not have been long before the enrollments fell drastically. On the contrary, they rose with great regularity.

16. Hippolyte Taine, *Carnets de voyage: Notes sur la province, 1863–1865* (Paris, 1897), 225–228.

The upper division in the school consisted in general of philosophers, rhetoricians, and humanists; the middle division included the grammar students from third through fifth forms; the lower division was for the sixth and seventh forms. But divisions and forms did not necessarily coincide in this way for the individual student. If he were younger, smaller, less mature, he would be in a lower division than his classroom companions. If there were only two groupings, they usually divided at the fourth form. Though rigidly separated except for class periods, all students followed the same daily order, except for somewhat more sleep for the very youngest. Here, too, in this order, the correspondence with Brugelette and even with the minor seminaries was striking.

For the smooth functioning of the school, and so that from year to year things might continue to be done in the same way, there was an extremely detailed rule book for the officials and faculty. The one prepared for the colleges of the province of Lyons was quite standard.[17] It began with preliminary philosophical and theological reflections on the importance of regulations. The first part was concerned with a general order of exercises, a schedule for ordinary days, free days, major holidays, Sundays, feast days of first and second class, and a table of exceptions, all treated in detail. Then, in the second part of the rule book, each exercise, each activity of the day, had its special dispositions, beginning with general rules on such matters as silence, subordination and respect. Yet more detail came with the particular dispositions for school uniforms, petty cash, personal correspondence, visits from parents, and such places and activities as dormitories, study halls, chapel, religious exer-

17. LSJ, Collèges . . . en France, "Règlement . . . de Lyon, 1850." A copy of this is also in PSJ, C-10, "Collèges secondaires, 1804–1860," and the rules in the other provinces differed only very slightly. There were not only rules governing relations between students and faculty. The latter were also told, for instance, to speak circumspectly to parents about their sons. "Never say that they [the sons] are without minds, without judgment, without proper upbringing, without piety, without manners, without honesty, without honor. These reproaches should be softened somewhat" (*ibid.*, 55).

cises, meals, recreation, long walks, sickness, and punishments. The rule book went so far into detail as to prescribe when paper and pen were to be distributed. Finally, there was a whole third part which dealt with "charges," a particular institution that will be discussed later in this study. The details of life in the schools presented here are drawn in part from rule books such as this, in part from daily accounts in the various community and office diaries, and in part from published and unpublished recollections of former teachers and students. In general, there was a high correlation between the printed regulation and actual practice.

Little time was given to the students on an ordinary day between rising at five o'clock and morning prayers at five fifteen, lest they get into mischief. The surveillants made their first appearance on the daily scene in routing out the sluggards from their sparsely furnished, curtained cubicles in huge dormitories. Each student had a bed, a chair, a very small bedside cabinet for personal effects, and a place to hang his clothes. From the time the boys left the dormitories in the morning until they trooped up wearily again at night, the doors were locked, and no one was permitted there under grave sanctions. The only exceptions were on walk-days when they went to change clothes, or on foot-washing days, once every two weeks, as in the lycées. On those occasions, the surveillants again were always to be present with the students.

After morning prayers came an hour and a half of study until daily Mass at seven o'clock. There might also be a special earlier Mass for those who had permission to receive Communion. Such students were often the members of the "congrégation" or sodality. Daily or even frequent Communion would have to await the changes instituted by Pope Pius X in the early twentieth century. At seven thirty, the students, quickly, in silence, and standing, took their breakfast of bread, butter, and hot milk, never coffee, rarely chocolate. Immediately after it came the first talking of the day, at a short recreation period before classes which began at eight o'clock and lasted until ten thirty.

The class schedule itself has been described in the preceding chapter. After both morning and afternoon classes there was recreation for fifteen minutes, and then at ten forty-five each division had a supervised study period in its own respective hall. During this period and those in the afternoon and evening the students prepared their lessons, and especially did their written work. Of this there was usually more than enough. A humanities or rhetoric student, for instance, in one week had to write two French compositions, one Latin composition in prose or verse, two Latin translations, one or two Greek assignments, and two English or German themes.

During dinner at noon, which was the main meal, a useful or edifying book was read while the students ate in silence, except on great feast days, examination days, some Sundays and free days, and the last three days of the school year when, it was recognized, nothing could have contained them. After the meal there was a recreation period for each division, each again in its respective yard until one thirty. Study for forty-five minutes preceded the afternoon classes which began at two fifteen. At four thirty the students had recreation and *gouter,* milk and bread, and, on special occasions, fruit and even a watered wine. They prayed the Rosary at five o'clock and then went back to study for two hours until seven fifteen. A quarter hour of spiritual reading came before supper at seven thirty. During this meal there was very seldom any talking; for reading, it was recommended that at least three times a week, according to their level of understanding, the students hear some work in dogmatic theology, for example, Gaume's *Catéchisme de persévérance* or Feller's *Catéchisme philosophique.*

After supper came a short period of recreation and night prayers in the study halls, and then immediately bed, during preparation for which the very strictest silence was to be observed. Finally, the surveillants made a last round of bed-checks,. turned down the lamps, and hoped that all were asleep or at least gave signs of being so, for their work was finished only at that point. Usually the students seemed to have given in to weariness before the surveillants did.

Such a regime can easily give the impression today of being almost monastic. It seemed less so to students and parents then, and the daily schedule of the lycées was hardly less austere.[18] In practice, there were far more holidays and half-holidays to break the routine than a school would have now. Every week, two afternoons were free for several hours for long games and for extended walks, though the latter in almost division-sized groups led by a prefect could become rather trying for the short of leg or breath. On such excursions the ingenuity of the students could not be repressed, even though the regulations catalogued wearily the things they should not do (and of course did). On a walk they were "to avoid anything that might provide the least subject of complaint, and thus they were not to do any damage to the fields, meadows, woods, haystacks, etc. They were not to climb trees, or cut anything, or buy things without permission, and most specially in hilly or mountainous areas they were not to throw anything or to start stones rolling in view of the serious accidents that could result." Even on home grounds, at school, certain precautions were necessary. At recreation, the students "were forbidden to have in their hands sharp, cutting or pointed instruments such as knives or pocketknives, or to throw stones or to light fires, etc."[19]

These promenades or outside walks were considered of great importance in getting the students out into the fresh air and

18. See Dupont-Ferrier, Louis-le-Grand, II, passim.

19. LSJ, Collèges . . . en France, "Règlement . . . de Lyon," 22. The problem of collège-lycée rivalry could arise too, especially in the cities. For instance, Guidée at Amiens remarked discreetly that Wednesday and Friday afternoons should be free, rather than Tuesday and Thursday "to avoid the many inconveniences which might arise if our hikes fell on the same days as the free days of other schools" (PSJ, C-12, "Enquêtes provinciales, 1849–1860, 1855 Report, Guidée, Amiens.) If the groups did meet, the rivalry was sometimes friendly, sometimes hardly so.

giving them at least some change from the atmosphere of the college. A *grande promenade* took place once or twice a year too, and it most certainly was a change. Though all of them were not as elaborate as the one from Vaugirard to be re-counted here, yet it is an instance which gives a good idea of the type. The minister's diary recounted the details of the excursion of July 2, 1861. Very early in the morning, after a dawn Mass and breakfast, the students all trooped off to the Gare du Nord, the youngest and the ill in a hired omnibus. From there a special train at seven forty-five took them to Chantilly. After hiking from the station to the grounds of the chateau, the excursionists immediately began several rounds of games. At ten thirty lunch was served by a special restaurateur in the former Grandes Ecuries of Condé. Student competitions of every sort filled the afternoon until the grand dinner at four thirty. On this occasion returning alumni and important guests occupied special places of honor, and the banquet was enliv-ened, as had been the games, by a hired band of twenty-nine musicians. The dinner and the speeches were barely over after several hours when the students, school banners flying, marched back through town to the train. On their return to Paris they ended the day at eight forty-five with tea and butter bread for all.[20]

In other years there were also such excursions to Enghien, Versailles, Vincennes, Saint-Germain-en-Laye, Fontainebleau, and Rambouillet, most often on the occasion of the great family feast of the year, Father Rector's Day. If the school was fortunate enough to possess a villa in the country, as Vannes for in-stance did at Penboc'h on the Gulf of Morbihan, not far from the school, then those grand feast days often took place there, with even more hours, saved from train rides, for the students to run themselves (and their masters) ragged.[21]

20. PSJ, Paris C³ 13, Vaugirard, "Diarium P. Ministri," July 2, 1861.
21. For example, see Butel, *L'Education des Jésuites,* 211–215 on Vannes and Penboc'h.

The most important recreation, however, took place every day in the game periods after classes and after meals. There the surveillant's ingenuity was regularly taxed, for he was supposed to devise, organize, promote, and encourage games in which as many students as possible, ideally all of them, took part with interest and enthusiasm. To do this day by day was not an easy task. Yet the school considered such games an important part of the whole educational process, for all had to learn to join in cooperatively. Games with only two or three were actively discouraged if not forbidden. The competition was meant to help form manly temperaments; a particular principal remarked to an officer of the army who was worriedly watching one of the more vigorous games, "General, we are not raising little girls."[22]

The more elaborate games might involve a whole division, one half pitted against the other, reds versus greens, or Carthaginians versus Romans, in a type of football or soccer, often, incredibly enough, played on stilts. There were chariot races in homemade contraptions pulled by a dozen willing combatants. The boys engaged in foot races and stilt races and volleyball and skating and every variation of any of these that imagination could construct. In later years, if imagination ran dry, one could consult the previously mentioned, sizable, illustrated volume of collected games edited by two Jesuits who had spent the better part of their religious lives as successful surveillants.[23] Again, if the college was located in the country or had its own vacation villa or the loan of such a place from a benefactor, then at the appropriate seasons the students had the opportunity for even more diversions such as swimming and sleighing.

Taine noticed, too, the place given to physical exercise. Still speaking of the Jesuit college at Metz he remarked: "Impossible

22. Burnichon, *La Compagnie,* III, 484.

23. Charles de Nadaillac, S.J., and J. Rousseau, *Les Jeux de collège* (Paris, 1875). The book was several times enlarged and reprinted.

to be more adroit in little affairs. For example, gymnastics are ordinarily neglected in other places despite the fact that they are valuable. Immediately, [the Jesuits engage] an excellent director of gymnastics, with the rigorous obligation for all the students to engage in exercise every day. In this also, their students were truly superior."[24] It is probable that he was describing what were the ordinary recreation periods. Gymnastics as such were not universally obligatory; they were an extra course available at additional expense for those who so desired them.

The "charges" were an activity, this time not play but work, in which it was hoped that all the students would at some time be engaged. These were "offices of trust" which involved many of the minor but necessary and everyday tasks that went into running a school. The appointed student incumbents had special insignia, enjoyed some few exemptions from the ordinary discipline of the school, were bound to a precise set of regulations spelled out at length in the rule book for each office, and were changed every month so that the positions could be apportioned out among as many as possible.

Such offices existed both in and outside of the classroom, and some of them even enjoyed high-sounding Latin names. In class, there were "quaestors to keep the lists of good and bad grades, collectors to gather the ordinary and the disciplinary written assignments, decurions to hear the recitations of lessons by small groups, inspectors to watch over the cleanliness of hands and uniforms."[25] Outside the classroom, the students were bellringers and sacristans, assistant librarians and external quaestors (the latter to pick up unmarked and carelessly left about items which were then redeemable only on payment of a fine, the proceeds of which went to buy game equipment). The storekeeper sold small items, but "none that were de luxe or fancy"; the table master saw to silence, order and "con-

24. Taine, *Carnets de voyage*, 227–228.
25. LSJ, Collèges . . . en France, "Règlement . . . de Lyon," 57.

sumption of some of each dish by everyone." The reading master appointed table readers; the aedile noted and reported repairs and maintenance work to be done; the lamplighter's task was obvious.

So it went, down to the equipment boys for music, drawing, painting, and games. One of the students was even "treasurer of the poor," whose very special office it was to request from the student allowances a small sum for the poor, and to gather up whatever paper and pens might be left over at the end of the week in order to give them to poor students in the public primary schools.

In the early twentieth century, some apologists thought that they saw in this whole institution of charges a beginning of student government. But that seems hardly true. At the very best, one might read into it a slight adumbration of such a system, for it would be in so many respects contrary to the whole spirit that pervaded the Jesuit schools. In a family, certainly in a nineteenth-century one, there was no sharing in government between children and father. But in such a family, there was an attempt to inculcate a sense of responsibility, and this was one of the functions of the charges. They were obviously a great help in the very running of the school itself. They were also "marks of honor and confidence."[26] But most pertinently,

> there is also another consideration which, though it might be at the moment beyond students of this age, does not lack importance, and which they will understand more fully at some other time. For since they are going to be called to varying stations in society, in order to help make move some one of the wheels of that great ensemble wherein each person is debtor of every other, it is well that the students be formed by a sort of apprenticeship . . . to sacrifice themselves for the good of others. It is important

26. Barbier, *La Discipline,* 153.

that they come to understand right from today, through the small difficulties of the running of a college, what it ordinarily costs those who are engaged in keeping society in equilibrium: that ongoing, balanced, social order which from the outside seems to function of itself, and from which a good many people draw profit without their dreaming how dearly it has been bought by care and concern.[27]

Art (*dessin*—drawing and painting), music, gymnastics and, in some places, fencing and horseback riding, were among those courses which were completely *ad-libitum*. They were not simply recreation, and so to speak of them would have seemed incongruous to the Jesuits. While more than what we would now call extracurriculars, yet they were at the same time not even on the margin of the accessory studies. Only with difficulty did such courses find a place in the colleges, and they were almost always to be taken during recreation periods alone, but then to be taken quite seriously if one had enrolled for them. Art did manage to gain a place in the annual distribution of prizes despite wondering queries from Rome, but it was a precarious foothold at the very end of the list. Rome looked with some suspicion on music too. The complaint in 1838 that certain excesses were a "serious harm to studies, a distraction, and a danger to morals," was repeated, though somewhat more mildly, in 1860 by the warning that great care was to be taken that students be not too strongly attracted to music, art, and other such subjects, with consequent detriment to studies.[28] Matters had gone farther yet by 1875 when there was discussion of operas in which the students took part. They were unanimously rejected because they "developed a taste, already too general, for music,

27. LSJ, Collèges . . . en France, "Règlement . . . de Lyon," 29.
28. ARSJ, Lugd., Reg., Roothaan to Renault, July 19, 1838, and Beckx to Gautrelet, March, 1860.

they involved no literary usefulness, and they took too much time."[29] Dramatic productions themselves occupied a very ambiguous position. They most certainly were not part of the curriculum, yet they were closely tied to the academies which were a part of the total process of Jesuit education. How they fit in, then, will be seen in the discussion of the acadamies.

Most surely a diversion for the students, and a relief for the teachers, were the home visits allowed to students at certain fixed times. Usually once a month the parents or close relatives of the boarders could take them from the school from late morning until early evening. Often, one additional outside visit every month served as a reward to those who had received more than satisfactory grades for the preceding four weeks. There was a short vacation of about ten days from Easter Monday until the Wednesday of the following week. Finally, on the great French family occasion, New Year's Day, the students could be at home from eight o'clock in the morning until eight in the evening, but this visit was introduced only reluctantly and to the distress of some of the older Jesuits who claimed that it derogated from the family spirit of the school itself. At the end of the school year came the long vacation, from prize day, usually the first part of August, until school began again in early October.

The Jesuits constantly feared what they regarded as the easygoing ways and the excessive freedom of the age, even in the Christian families that confided their sons to the school, and yet more so in the families which were lax or nonpracticing in their faith.

If family spirit and religious motives were a reality, then discipline was a reality too. Passard in *La Pratique du Ratio* simply expressed the Jesuits' agreement in quoting a non-Jesuit, Dupanloup. Discipline "protected conduct and guarded in-

---

29. PSJ, C-13, "Enquêtes collèges secondaires, 1862–1880," Compte-rendu, IV, Sept., 1875.

nocence; it was the guarantee of studies well made; it inspired proper attitudes; it preserved respect; it was the master, the dispenser, and the treasurer of time, the quickening spirit of internal regulation, and the powerful bulwark of all education."[30]

This discipline was obvious, exact, even rigorous at times. The students knew exactly where they stood if they violated the rules and, again as in the exile colleges, there was a whole series of punishments to fit the crimes. A professor or surveillant could, for instance, have the student stand in one place for a while, or give an extra written exercise, or order him to arise a quarter of an hour early, or have him kneel at the foot of his (the student's) bed, but never for more than fifteen minutes. He might lower a conduct mark for the week by one grade, or even allow the transgressor one less dish at a meal. It was carefully specified that this meant deprivation at noon of meat or vegetables or dessert, and in the evening of either of the latter two.

Reserved to the superior, and apparently to the principal, were more serious punishments such as suspension or expulsion from the sodality or the academy, public reprimands, denial of permission for parlor visits, a meal of dry bread (even if only once), fasting for more than one day, privation of walks, or kneeling publicly in the study hall, classroom, or dining room.[31] This all sounds grim enough in the abstract, and in the concrete it could be so too. No one seemed to have questioned seriously these punishments, and not only in the Jesuit colleges, for they or similar ones were in regular use in other schools too, including the state schools. The rule books for the teachers and surveillants insisted that most of the occasions for punishment could and should be avoided by the constant, firm, and discreet presence of a faculty member.

One very questionable disciplinary instrument was the

30. Passard, *La Pratique*, 12.
31. Barbier, *La Discipline*, 148–149.

signum or sign, a distinctive plaque or piece of wood given to a student involved in some transgression. At dinner or supper it had to be presented to the prefect in charge who would assign a suitable punishment. But the student who had originally received it could pass it off to any other student whom, in the course of the day, he caught in a violation of a rule, and so on through the day from one liberated culprit to the next hapless transgressor. It had to be accepted by the person who was caught, and it could not be taken by a third party on behalf of a friend.This was to turn the students into their own prosecutors, a procedure that could be nothing but detrimental to any kind of *esprit de corps,* and certainly to the family spirit that was so frequently invoked. The rule books seemed to recognize this; there was an open reluctance to use the *signum,* and it was explicitly stated that it was to be employed only as a means to cut down rapidly on the need for a large number of other punishments.[32]

Although not exactly a punishment for a particular overt fault, one other questionable practice should be noted. The Jesuits worried whether "students who had bad [conduct] notes could receive Communion without scandal." Superiors decided as a rule that students who habitually had bad or very bad notes could not participate at the general Communions.[33] It would be hard to justify this ruling today.

Striking or spanking or even touching the student in any way was not allowed. In the presuppression Society, the old *Ratio Studiorum* made provision for a paid "corrector" in each college, who was never to be a Jesuit, and who administered the punishments meted out to commoner and prince alike. The new *Ratio* officially abolished the practice. In December

32. LSJ, Collèges . . . en France, "Règlement . . . de Lyon," 27–28. Again note that this is also in PSJ, C-10, "Collèges secondaires, 1804–1860."

33. PSJ, C-13, "Enquètes collèges secondaires, 1862–1880," Compte-rendu, VI, Sept., 1875.

1868, however, the principal and vice-principal of the Jesuit college in Bordeaux were hailed into court, accused of giving whippings to three or four refractory students. The fact was true, the Jesuits were culpable, and they admitted it. The father of one of the boys brought formal complaint, although he, along with the other parents, had previously given permission for the punishments. But it was still against the rules of the Society; the rector of the school knew nothing about the particular incidents, and he had even the year before recalled the rule to the principal, apparently with reference to other such occurrences. Though the other parents had refused to join in the case, and one, a naval officer, remarked that he preferred that his son be whipped at twelve than be a rogue at thirty, the court condemned the two Jesuits to ten days of correctional detention and damages of three hundred francs to the one parent.

The repercussions ran from the Quirinal to the Tuileries, passing through the Jesuit generalate and the anticlerical clubs of Paris. "The impression produced in France has been unfortunate; it has not been any the better here [in Rome] either. The Holy Father himself has seemed affected by it painfully."[34] The Bordeaux educational officials began an inquiry into the "disorders" taking place in the Jesuit college there. It took the intervention of the archbishop of Toulouse with Marshal Niel, who in turn intervened with the Emperor, to put an end to a more generalized chase after the Jesuits for "immorality," inaugurated by some of Duruy's officials in the Ministry of Education.[35]

The General himself firmly hoped that the Jesuits "in the colleges and everywhere else, would be able to feel the real

34. ARSJ, Reg., Tolos., Beckx to Rouquayrol, Jan. 14, 1869.
35. ARSJ, Franc., Laurençot to Beckx, April 30, 1869, as described in Burnichon, *La Compagnie*, III, 496–497. The general sent Laurençot especially to France at this time. "Educational immorality" meant nonfulfillment of certain legal requirements set down by the ministry.

need of the rules [of the Society] and of obedience. To it alone is the blessing of heaven attached."[36] The provincial of Champagne, in concert with the other provincials recalled again to the Jesuits that corporal punishment had been abolished, that "absolutely forbidden was every and any kind of ill-treatment against the students of our colleges, even at the express request of parents," and that one might well question some of the punishments then allowable, "the fastings, too frequent and too prolonged, the privations of sleep, and the excessive retention [in class]."[37]

For the adversaries of the Society, the case was an opportunity not to be missed. Pillon quoted a complaint, officially appended to the indictment, which summed up their position quite well. It asked that the two Jesuits be punished if they had been acting outside their Rule. But, if it was judged "that they obeyed instructions . . . or orders given to them, that they were the blind instruments of an evil Rule, then they will have the right to your indulgence . . . In that case let your judgment be brought to bear on that Rule which can, doubtless, as has been attributed to it, form docile, submissive, and respectful pupils, but which will not produce proud and free citizens."[38]

No one, of course, had asked the opinions of the students, but to judge from the previous eighteen or nineteen years of experience in the colleges, they had not been anywhere so passive as the indictment suggested. Matter of fact reports and discussions speak of almost every one of the usual school boy misdeeds. They were always out of order, despite the fact that "no one was at any moment of the day to separate himself from the group without permission." They fought with fellow students; they threw sticks and stones, used bad language, and

36. ARSJ, Reg., Tolos., Beckx to Rouquayrol, Jan. 14, 1869.
37. CSJ, "Litterae Encyclicae Patrum Provincialium," Pillon, Jan. 5, 1869.
38. *Ibid.*, quoting *Journal judiciaire*. Ponlevoy, the Paris provincial, protested to Baroche, the minister of justice, against the tone of the indictment.

made off with food from the dining room. They wrote on the walls, "a shameful thing for them and for us," and they mocked and made fun of their fellow classmates and "indeed even of certain of our Jesuits."[39] Finally, more than once the consultors of a house had to decide what to do with a Jesuit, useful, pious, and dedicated, but who, for all that, was totally incapable of controlling a class of these supposedly "docile, submissive, and respectful pupils."

The Society was not unaware of the dangers inherent in strict discipline. In 1855 the meeting of rectors and prefects warning against adopting "the cold rigor of the state schools; in that case, piety, conduct, and studies are harmed. Also to be feared is the relegation of studies to a place after purely external order, under the pretext of a mathematical discipline."[40] Rome recalled, too, that discipline was a means, not an end, and that an almost military rigor in the colleges was harmful. Twenty years later, the four provinces were still cautioning against "too great a severity on the part of some in punishing . . . a severity which smacks of a lord and master and not of a father and a religious with apostolic zeal."[41] All in all, as the years went on the external norms did become less rigorous than they had been in the minor seminaries and during the first years of the new colleges. At the same time, the Jesuits thought that in general over these years there had been a definite improvement in the character and conduct of the students.

Along with discipline, the colleges sought to inculcate good manners and good breeding. Undoubtedly, the Jesuits would have thought a formal course in such a subject an incredible

39. LSJ, Collèges . . . en France, "Règlement . . . de Lyon," 20, 27–28; TSJ, "Memorialia Visitatorum et Provincialium: Toulouse, Ste-Marie," Studer, June 4–20, 1862, and June 15–28, 1859.

40. PSJ, C-12, "Enquêtes provinciales, 1849–1860," "Quaesita de scholis," 1855, Metz.

41. TSJ, "Lib. Cons.," Feb. 5–7, 1877.

usurpation of class time, but there was a "very great care for . . . neatness in dress and for manners," and politeness was simply expected without question from the very first day.[42] These manners even extended to speaking clearly and to writing legibly and correctly, "without making mistakes which would bring a blush to a child of the poor, educated by the Christian Brothers." Such good manners were not only useful but necessary, for without them "knowledge, talent, literary success, even virtue, are not enough always to crown the forehead of the youthful student with that luminous aureole which foretells a brilliant future."[43] Again, the atmosphere of a strict family, in which children were respectful to their parents and to those who took the place of parents, contributed much to this training.

The military air of the schools was also influential here, and such an air was certainly common. At Toulouse, for example, the spirit was very strong. There, "with what evident satisfaction the Father Minister of the house mentioned in his diary the upper-echelon officers present at such or such a great dinner; a general, six or seven colonels . . . A general would come to the college to pass in revue the young amateur soldiers who marched and drilled impeccably before him."[44] Such a spirit may not have been as ardent elsewhere as it was at Toulouse, but in the north, too, it was not a great exception when, at Lille in 1874, General de Martray and the Prefect of the North, Baron Le Guay, assisted at a feast day, and the general "at dessert [proposed] a most eloquent toast to the honor of the Society, recalling the close relations of St. Ignatius and the Society with the military life."[45] All of this, to be sure, was in keeping with the military attitude of much of the Church in nineteenth-century France, where a Cardinal Bonnechose could

---

42. Taine, *Carnets de voyage*, 228.
43. LSJ, "Litterae Encyclicae Patrum Provincialium," Gautrelet, Oct. 15, 1860.
44. TSJ, "Les Maisons SJ de Toulouse: 12-Collège Ste-Marie." Part of this manuscript became the article on Ste-Marie in *EJF*, IV, 1375–1379.
45. CSJ, MSS. 3203: Collège St-Joseph, "Diarium P. Ministri," July 8, 1874.

say in the Senate, apropos of the hierarchy and the religious orders: "There is not a general in this place who would submit to the reproach of not knowing how to make himself obeyed by his soldiers . . . Each of us also has a regiment to command . . . and it is on the march!"[46] The Jesuits had more than a sufficient share of this military attitude.

Such an attitude existed in easy harmony with a spirit even more fundamental in the Jesuit educational policy. This was the spirit of emulation and rivalry which the colleges strongly and universally encouraged.[47] In every class, in every subject, and at every level, competition was the rule. This competition was supposed to engage the personal activity and initiative of the student, and to stimulate him to work under the spur of individual and class rivalry.

For instance, every student was, ideally to have an antagonist or opponent. A class would be divided into groups of ten students headed by a "decurion," the pupil with the highest class marks of the group. "Romans" and "Carthaginians" were pitted against each other in an oral review of all the class matter of the week or a month. To the victors went the spoils in the form of battle flags and, more appreciated, exemptions from certain assignments. Written themes, too, were matter for competition. For the poorest of them defenders were appointed in order to show how indefensible their horrendous errors really were. There was also a lazy man's bench where once in a while the indolent suffered the indignity of having to listen to explanations of their own class material by students of a lower form.

Each week, every student received a class ranking for his written compositions and a publicly announced grade for ap-

46. *Journal Officiel: Sénat,* March 11, 1865, as quoted in Orhand, *Pillon,* 214–215. The cardinal himself recognized that this was going rather far, and three days later publicly regretted the brusk and rather uncanonical sentiments.
47. This competitive rivalry need not have had military overtones, and, as a matter of fact, did not have them to the same extent in the presuppression schools.

plication and diligence. Once a month, in a school gathering open to the public, the students meriting top grades received decorations in the form of ribbons with palms of silver or gold for diligence and for excellence.[48] At the end of the year, in a solemn ceremony on prize day there was almost a flood of recompense, publicly proclaimed. In the first place of honor came the "Prix de Sagesse," the testimony of a year of exemplary conduct voted to one student by his peers. Then there were prizes in every class, for religious instruction, for general accomplishment, for effort, for composition, for translation, for poetry, followed by enough honorable mentions to grace a good part of the student body.[49]

These recompenses included not only the public proclamation of names, and ribbons, decorations, and even classical victors' wreaths, but also books, one for each prize gained. A list of the volumes bestowed is itself an interesting commentary on the schools. Among those typically suggested in the 1870's were histories, lives of saints, and missionary accounts. Some particular prizes were: Beauchesne, *Louis XVII, sa vie, son agonie, sa mort;* Bossuet, *Histoire universelle;* Cobbett, *Lettres sur la réforme protestante;* Cyr, *La Franc-maçonnerie;* several works of de Maistre and of Louis Veuillot; la Rochejacquelin, *Mémoires;* de Smet, *Missions de l'Oregon et aux Montagnes Rocheuses;* and Tapparelli, *Essai historique de droit naturel.*[50]

48. LSJ, Collèges . . . en France, "Règlement . . . de Lyon," *passim*. Also in PSJ, C-10, "Collèges secondaires, 1804–1860," and in PSJ, C-29, "Conseils aux régents, XIX, Notes d'élèves." Apparently the level of what one could expect from the students had risen in the years since Brugelette. In the 1870's, the lowest grades signified that the students were doing rather poorly or poorly or very poorly, while earlier they had indicated such judgments as "Frequent faults," "after several warnings one fears for his expulsion," "expresses the *last* warnings of Superiors." PSJ, Brug. 3:2253, "Coutumier," 52.

49. This traditional practice dated back to the early days of the Jesuit colleges. The first General Congregation of the Society in 1558 sanctioned the practice, in granting a request that "small gifts, usually called prizes, be offered and awarded to the . . . students in order to incite them to literary studies." *Institutum Societatis Jesu* (Florence, 1893), vol. 2, no. 184.

50. PSJ, C-20, Collèges, 1880, "Catalogue des livres . . . en prix." See also

Holding first place among all the tokens of esteem for excellence in studies was membership in the academy. This was "a select group of students, outstanding in talent and religious practice, chosen from the whole student body, who meet under a Jesuit moderator to engage in certain special exercises which pertain to studies."[51] Not only was this organization supposed to provide a stimulus to excellence in class work by holding out the hope of membership; it was also in itself to furnish an occasion for further intellectual formation. In addition, the academies, along with the sodalities, which will be discussed later in this chapter, came to be the centers of religious and academic training outside the classroom and chapel.

The academy met every week in private session. At the meetings, either the moderator gave a talk or, more often, the students themselves presented brief papers on principles of rhetoric or literature, on classic Latin, Greek or French authors, or on philosophy, or they read their own compositions, poems, orations, essays. Once a month there might be a more general session. Once or twice a year each academy also undertook a public session, a presentation of declamations, poetry, debates, tableaux, essays and drama, "with some external formality before a gathering of distinguished guests," usually parents, friends, clergy, and civil and military authorities.[52]

In 1879, with the purpose of helping new and inexperienced moderators, Antoine Sengler published a collection of the programs given by the academies of all the Jesuit schools from 1815 to 1878.[53] As has been quite correctly remarked, "no work has yet offered a more authentic nor a truer witness to the spirit which animated, during all the nineteenth century, the teaching

---

Raoul de Scorraille, S.J., "Les distributions des prix dans les collèges," *Études*, 41 (1879), 269–282 and 354–378.

51. *Ratio*, "Regulae Academiae," no. 1.

52. LSJ, Collèges . . . en France, "Règlement . . . de Lyon," 43–47, *passim*, and *Ratio*, "Regulae Academiae Rhetorum et Humanistarum," no. 3.

53. Antoine Sengler, S.J., *Souvenirs d'Académie: Séances littéraires et dramatiques données dans les collèges de la Compagnie de Jésus en France de 1815 à 1878* (Lille and Paris, 1879).

of the colleges of the Jesuits in France."[54] Province by province, school by school, year by year, academy by academy, the individual programs of the séances were detailed. Out of the mass of detail, certain patterns clearly emerge. Philosophy, religion, literature and history were, in ascending order, the subjects most frequently treated, and history led all the others combined in number of distinct titles and number of individual presentations.

The philosophy sessions often defended in syllogistic form selected theses from scholasticism. For instance, in theodicy the young men at Toulouse in 1867 argued that "the existence of God is proved by metaphysical, physical and moral argument," or that "Pantheism involves every absurdity and leads to the most evil consequences."[55] In religion, the subjects included such topics as pilgrimages or "The Church and Her Contemporary Struggles," or "Faith and Genius in the Nineteenth Century."[56] More often, they dealt with Jesus Christ and with the Virgin Mary. The favorite subjects were a series of homages to Mary, and accounts of the shrines dedicated to her, at Chartres, for instance, or Loretto, or Lourdes. The presentations in literature dealt with that topic in general, or with eloquence, poetry, and grammar as might be expected, or with literary history. Sometimes the treatments were quite original and provocative as, for instance, "A literary gathering at Chateaubriand's home on an evening in 1802, discussing Corneille's *Polyeucte*."[57] Eloquence was described and lauded over and over again. Literary history presented almost every great figure of antiquity, praised the French classics, especially the works of Corneille, and gave short shrift to the Romanticists.

History was the great predilection of the academies. While

54. *EJF*, II, 1344.

55. *Ibid.*, 677. The Tolosans seem to have been the most disputatious of the academicians.

56. *Ibid.*, 347. The men of "Faith and genius" here included de Maistre, General de Lamoricière, Garcia Moreno, and Daniel O'Connell.

57. PSJ, Paris: Vaugirard, "Diarium Ministri," Feb. 9, 1879.

in the old Jesuit colleges the preference for biblical history had been marked, in the nineteenth-century schools the choice of Church history and national history was equally striking. More than two hundred and fifty different titles appeared in these two lists, and one hundred of these dealt with the history of France alone. The most frequently presented theme from Church history was the First Crusade and the characters connected with it. For France, Joan of Arc, though not yet a saint, was most popular. Charlemagne, the ancient Gauls, St. Louis, and the Hundred Years' War came next. There were many themes, too, that dealt with France at the service of the Church, the mission of France, the destiny of France, the hopes of France, and God protecting France.[58] When one school prepared a good program, schools in other regions used it also.

Several scientific sessions took place, for instance on physics or mathematics or, "to a full house" at Vaugirard in 1880, on "Physics and Electricity," in which "all the experiments actually worked."[59] Finally, there were occasional pieces, on the order of "Fragments of a Poem on Industry at St. Etienne," with verses dedicated to the discovery of coal and the manufacture of steam engines, or "Rail Transportation," which included a historical survey, a debate on the merits of diligences and trains, narrative poetry, and an imitative choir of the railroads.

At times, these public presentations got out of hand when directors took too great a part in the composition of what was supposed to be students' work. The General complained more than once that while they should have helped "to the progress of letters, they rather hindered it, for in preparing participants, music and decorations, much time [was] lost, and the minds of the young were distracted and turned from serious studies."[60] But by and large, and within the context of an acceptance of

---

58. Sengler, *Souvenirs*, 861. This concern for France made especially galling to the Jesuits the often-repeated charge by their opponents that they and their schools were not concerned with producing French patriots.

59. PSJ, Paris: Vaugirard, "Diarium Ministri," Feb. 22, 1880.

60. ARSJ, Reg., Franc., Beckx to Mourier, March 18, 1876.

a classic and fixed set of literary rules, the academy fulfilled its purposes well. It gave the better students an opportunity to work together and to benefit from one another's criticisms; it habituated the members to fairly frequent public appearances; it helped provide an intellectual *esprit de corps* for the college; finally, it was a public witness on the part of the Jesuits to the importance of scholastic excellence.

Theatrical productions took place most often in the context of these academic séances, and at first they were staged more as declamatory pieces with an absolute minimum of decoration and costume. Gradually the productions became more elaborate, and this elaboration was regularly a cause of concern to superiors. The themes were much the same as those presented in other sessions of the academies. For tragedy, religious and historical subjects were predominant. Comedies were not officially held in great favor, but they made their appearance regularly. A large number of both types of plays presented were written by Jesuits, either in the presuppression Society or for a current occasion in the nineteenth-century colleges.

The reluctance of superiors to sanction the theater in the minor seminaries and the exile colleges has been mentioned earlier. Finally Brugelette received permission to present two plays a year. For the later colleges, the same reluctance and almost the same regulations finally obtained. Some details will profitably illustrate the sharp change from the enthusiastic commitment to the theater of the presuppression Society to the suspicion of it by the nineteenth-century Jesuits. They will also serve as a particular illustration of the tendency finally to face up to the realities of a situation, but to do so exceedingly slowly.

A consultation in Paris in 1853 decided that "plays written in French are generally disapproved of for the colleges . . . An express authorization would be necessary to produce even a single one of them. Plays in Latin, written by our professors, are allowed under the following conditions: 1. There will be no more than one a year, at least without special permission.

2. The costumes and sets should remain within the limits of simplicity. 3. However, there is no obligation to put on even this one Latin play."[61]

The schools tried to hold to these rules, but it was a losing battle in the face of a number of realities. Stumpf, the rector at Metz, in answering a request of the provincial to explain the presentation at the college of a play in French expressed some of them very well. After remarking that the production, about a Roman boy martyr, St. Felix, "was worth more than a Lenten preaching course or a series of sermons," and that the celebration of the Rector's Day should have a certain brilliance, for the honor and influence of the house and of the Society, the rector went on to describe the audience:

> We have succeeded in attracting here the elite of society and the authorities [of the city], but we cannot disguise the fact that they come through good will and to show their sympathy for our work rather than through taste or pleasure. We have been told more than once that they must like the Fathers very much to move their dinner hour and change their domestic schedule, and all that to come to listen for two or three hours to Latin which they think quite classical and of which they understand nothing. . . . Is it not proper to offer to your invited guests a show which interests, instructs and edifies them, and not a performance which bores and humiliates them? I use the word *humiliate*, because it has often been distressing to some of the men present, to some colonels, for example, not to be able to answer a word to their wives or to those sitting next to them when they would be asked for an explanation of a scene that had just finished. . . . Why then, on a day of rejoicing, impose a sacrifice and an obligatory boredom?[62]

61. PSJ, C-12, "Enquêtes provinciales, 1849–1860," "Consulte sur les études," April 22, 1853.

62. *Ibid.*, "Emploi du latin dans les classes, les drames, etc., 1860—." Stumpf to Fessard, June 23, 1862.

The next year, 1863, with the divided counsel of the province consultors, the Paris provincial gave limited permission for drama in the vernacular, especially since other provinces were already acting thus.

By 1875 the general rule was that only twice a year were there to be dramatic pieces. If the play were a tragedy, the college could perform it in French, though Latin was still preferred. As for comedies, there was to be only one a year, and in it "nothing shallow or trivial, nothing which could offend a religious audience, but only [what was] full of propriety and good taste." This was to "conform . . . to Father General's letter, in which he lamented that 'the themes were chosen not from sacred antiquity but from modern, not to say unseemly, shallowness.' "[63] Most seriously, meetings of the academies were even sometimes used to introduce "wholly modern theatrical pieces of the present day" in which small changes in title or story "hardly kept our poor young students, already so exposed to peril during vacation periods and holidays, from being strongly tempted to go to see these productions put on at the Opera or in the theaters of our larger cities, productions so full of obscenities and impieties of every kind."[64] The question of actors from the Théâtre Français even came up. In 1867, and again in 1876, Rome wanted to know if the unheard of event were true, that outside actors, performing and singing, had presented selections or scenes from their repertoire for the students. "Though they are not the ordinary type of actors but, as they say, *artists*, this event arouses wonder even among our Jesuits in France; how much more would it arouse in Rome if the affair should be known there. Such actors therefore should not be invited any more." This time too, with divided counsel, the provincial attempted to point out that the

63. LSJ, "Litterae Encyclicae Patrum Provincialium," Jullien, Oct. 15, 1875, and PSJ, C-13, "Enquêtes collèges secondaires, 1862–1880: Compte-rendu des séances des recteurs . . . Sept., 1875."

64. ARSJ, Camp.: 2-XII, 11, Sengler to Rubillon, Jan. 31, 1876.

presence of the actors did not involve the "serious difficulties that it was said to have."[65]

In truth, the really serious inconvenience which drama did involve was the great amount of time and energy it consumed in preparations on the part of students and teachers. Besides, any attempt to introduce into the schools outside productions had to take account of the rather dubious reputation which the theater generally still had among nineteenth-century Catholics, and certainly among the higher superiors of religious orders. These scholastic exigencies and the persistent hostility or reluctance of Jesuit superiors and administrators were the main factors in the very slow progress of any serious interest in the theater in the colleges. This was a condition far different from that which had obtained in France under the presuppression Society, when the Jesuit theater had flourished greatly and had been a truly formative influence on French secular drama. The whole situation was, finally, an important and illuminating example of the attitude with which the Jesuit colleges approached many secular values.

Religious values held first place in the schools; nothing could be allowed to disrupt their specifically religious program. "Piety was the characteristic of these colleges; such in fact was the idea which the public had of them."[66] Though the particular religious exercises were by no means many in number for the schools of the time, a strong religious orientation was an intimate part of the life of each and every day. The colleges existed "to make of the young men confided to us Christians enlightened as to their religious duties and solidly grounded

65. *Ibid.*, Beckx to Ponlevoy, Sept. 24, 1867; Beckx to Mourier, March 18, 1876, and PSJ, "Lib. Cons.," April 4, 1876.
66. Burnichon, *La Compagnie*, III, 477. A dissertation on the spiritual life of Catholics in France during the Second Empire is being prepared by Claude Savart. See his article, "Vie spirituelle et liturgique au XIXe siècle," *Maison Dieu* (1962), 67–77.

in the practice of virtue, to make of them men deeply instructed and capable of filling with distinction the positions to which they are destined."[67]

The formal instructional part of the religious program has been described in the previous chapter. The solid grounding in virtue and in religious duties would, it was hoped, take place through the exercises of piety common to all the colleges and through the general atmosphere of the place. Each day there was for everyone a short period of morning and evening prayer, attendance at Mass, recitation of a part of the rosary, and a brief period of public spiritual reading in the afternoon study hall. This was the sum total of the daily exercises of piety, other than short prayers before and after classes, study periods and meals. On Sunday a sermon was preached at the student Mass, or an instruction was given by the spiritual director of the students, and in the afternoon they recited vespers and attended benediction.[68]

Special occasions called for special observances. A sung Mass was celebrated for such great days as Christmas, Easter, Pentecost, the Sacred Heart, and the great feast days of St. Ignatius Loyola, the founder of the Jesuits, and St. Aloysius Gonzaga, the patron of youth. The month of May was special, too, in the extra devotional practices, prayers and spiritual reading which dealt with the Blessed Virgin Mary, as was the month of June for the Sacred Heart of Jesus.

The colleges endowed two occasions with the greatest solemnity, the first reception of the Eucharist and the annual retreat. Both were important in themselves, and in their use as a visible reminder of the two most emphasized religious practices in the colleges, the regular reception of the sacraments and the regular personal examination of one's own conscience in its relationship to God.

67. LSJ, "Litterae Encyclicae Patrum Provincialium," Gautrelet, Oct. 15, 1860.
68. For these details and for an illustration of the fact that there were no substantial changes over the years, see for example, PSJ, C-12, "Enquêtes provinciales, 1849–1860," "Quaesita de scholis, 1855," Amiens, Guidée, and CSJ, MSS. 3203: "Diarium Ministri Collegii Sti. Josephi," Lille, 1873.

For six months before the first reception of Communion, the twelve year olds followed special catechism classes until the great day in May. To the Communion Mass were invited parents, relatives, and friends. The chapel was decorated, the preacher was chosen with special care, the Mass was offered by the rector, and a twofold family celebration followed, for the student's own family and for the family of the college.[69]

The annual retreat of three or four days took place near the beginning of the school year. Frequently a Jesuit from another college was invited to give this retreat which followed the pattern laid down in the *Spiritual Exercises* of St. Ignatius. It opened with considerations of the purpose of creation and the end of man, went on to treat of sin and judgment and death and hell, of penitence and conversion. (It is to be feared that this section of the retreat, on sin and its wages, resembled at times the scene of the hell and damnation sermon from James Joyce's *Portrait of the Artist as a Young Man.*) But the Kingdom of God was portrayed too, and the generous service of the Lord was urged upon the students. Then they meditated and prayed over the mysteries of the life of Jesus, of his passion, death and resurrection, of the love of God and of the beatitude of the saved.[70]

All of this was designed to dispose the student to a lasting devotion to Christ, expressed in service in and to the church. One could serve thus only if one knew oneself, and both dur-

69. So much did the families of the students want this special preparation for Communion by the Jesuit colleges that a delicate problem arose in the early 1870s when there was briefly a question in some places of allowing First Communion in parish churches only. At Dijon, for example, the college arranged with the diocese that boarders and half-boarders could continue the practice at the school. "Immediately all the families enrolled their [day student] sons as half-boarders." Burnichon, *La Compagnie,* IV, 468, quoting Stumpf to ?, March 4, 1874. Incidents such as this were not calculated to make the Jesuits popular with the parochial clergy.

70. See any complete edition of the Spiritual Exercises for details of the material used and its manner of presentation during a retreat. For example, *The Text of the Spiritual Exercises of St. Ignatius Loyola,* translated from the original Spanish by John Morris, S.J. (Westminster, Maryland, 1943). Of course, the individual retreat director adapted this material to the particular retreat which he was giving.

ing and after the retreats, the students were urged to examine their consciences daily and to go to confession frequently for forgiveness of their sins and for preparation for the reception of the Eucharist.

Thus the retreat and the self-knowledge attained therein joined to reinforce the emphasis put on penance and the Eucharist. The reception of the sacraments was everywhere encouraged, and part of the success of the schools in inculcating the faith was measured in the regularity and frequency of these practices. So strong was this insistence that as school began in the autumn each year the prefects would even "collect the vacation confession slips (signed by confessor or parents)," attesting that the young man had received the sacrament of penance during that time.[71]

The congrégation, or sodality as it is usually called in English, was the special organization dedicated to deepening and broadening this religious spirit. It concentrated on an elite group of students and it hoped, through this elite group, to influence the whole atmosphere of the college. The sodality was usually the first organization set up in a newly founded school. One relevant indication of how seriously the Jesuits regarded the sodality was that despite the usual worries about finances, the colleges regularly established a special chapel for the sodality in addition to the common college chapel in each of the institutions. The sodality was placed under the patronage of the Virgin Mary, and Marian devotion always occupied a large place in its life. Often there were at least two sodalities in a school, corresponding to the separate divisions. Almost always there was also a particular sodality for the day students, because the separation from the boarders applied even here.[72]

71. CSJ, MSS. 458: "Diarium Praefecti," Dijon, 1877.
72. In PSJ, C-12, "Enquêtes provinciales, 1849–1860" there is a report by Guidée on the sodality which he founded in 1851 within six months of the opening of the college at Amiens. See also *EJF*, I, 229–231 for further development of this material. The practices described in the report were almost identical with those set down in the handbooks for directors written twenty years

Students could request membership or they were invited by the director to join. They were to be young men of "energy, common sense, fine character or at least such that they can be made so, good personalities who were aware of how to make themselves acceptable to their fellow pupils, students who were successful in their studies, at least relatively."[73] After a probation period of several months, occupied with learning and practicing the rules of the organization, the candidates entered fully into the life of the sodality by an act of consecration at a ceremony designed to impress all the students with its solemnity.

Within the sodality there were special academic programs too, which often reflected the religious concerns of the day. The diary of the sodality at Vaugirard presented typical examples. In July 1867, for example, there was the "reading of a letter from a member of our sodality now defending the Supreme Pontiff." Another letter sometime later recounted the experiences of "a certain godless adolescent who later returned to religion."[74] As the anticlerical campaigns after 1875 mounted in intensity, the sodalities reflected the tensions. The academic sessions of the sodality now frequently dealt with the combats and triumphs of the faith all over the world and the patience of the Pope, while the progress of the Catholic religion in Protestant England was a source of consolation. Through 1878 the tempo of the meetings was stepped up. They treated, for instance, the love of one's country, Catholic liberalism, an epistolary controversy between Montalembert and Döllinger, Catholic liberalism again and especially its view of liberty of the press, modern principles such as universal suffrage, "nonintervention" and acceptance of a political *fait accompli,* and

later, such as the one by Charles Franchet, S.J., *Directoire des congrégations dans les collèges* (Lyons, 1875).

73. Franchet, *Directoire*, 30.

74. PSJ, Vaugirard, "Cong. BVM, Diarium Congregationis," July, 1867, and May, 1868.

Christian duties in civic life. In 1880, one month after Ferry's attempt to push through anti-Jesuit legislation, the topic was "Persecutions," and in June, before the young men went out into the world, it was the "Index of Prohibited Books."[75]

But all was not simply chapel devotions or meeting room discussions. Among its projects, the sodality had its own retreat each year. It assumed the responsibility for welcoming new students and for making them feel at home. It maintained a special library for its members and sent books to the French troops serving in the Papal states. It actively promoted and helped support financially the foreign missions. Most important, it undertook visits to and help for the poor, the sick, and the imprisoned. What was said of the sodality at Bordeaux, for example, was true everywhere, that though the young men often came from rich families, the schools consistently tried to teach them to love the poor.[76] In later years some of the most faithful members of the St. Vincent de Paul Society, an association of laymen working for the poor, founded by the Catholic liberal Ozanam, were to be found among the Jesuit college alumni who had been sodalists.

Such a selective organization, of course, presented some problems. The directors' handbooks recognized them well. Some students might join the sodality simply for human motives. This was especially true because the Jesuits made sodality membership a condition for membership in such other activities as the ordinary scholastic academies. There was the danger of jealousy and envy on the part of others, of complacency and pride on the part of the sodalists. "Particular friendships," for which the teachers and surveillants were always, and perhaps

75. *Ibid.*, Oct., 1875; Jan., Feb., May, 1878; April and June, 1880. In 1882, when Jesuits were no longer officially teachers in their own schools but when they were still directors of the sodalities, two typical meetings dealt with "what was to be done in these days since the Church is everywhere under assault," and "Freemasonry," (*ibid.*, June 1 and 22, 1882).

76. *EJF*, I, 791. See also Franchet, *Directoire*, 103, for care of the poor as an important apostolate outside the school, and PSJ, Vaugirard, "Cong. BVM, Diarium Congregationis," 1861–1863, for concrete instances of this.

excessively, on the watch, might arise.[77] And since the "school-boy spirit," which saw the master as an enemy, was always in existence, fellow students might often suspect sodalists of being informers. In fact, once in a while they were, even though the handbooks warned that never was this to be tolerated, for nothing could have been more detrimental, since "all the good which [the] colleges [could] do was founded on the mutual affection of master and student."[78]

The religious tone of these schools had another characteristic too. "The military spirit gave in many instances a special color to the piety. Among the [students in the] middle forms the 'Militia of the Pope' was in honor; the older students had gone off or were preparing to go to the support of Pius IX."[79] This was said of the college in Toulouse, but it was true in other places also. Because of the sodalities, because of the tradition of St. Ignatius as a soldier saint, because of the family and personal backgrounds of some of the influential Jesuits after the restoration of the Society, and because of the concern to root the teaching and the practices of the schools in the Christian traditions of France, the piety of the Jesuit colleges was "Marian, military, and historical."[80] That combination was admirably summed up and symbolized in the public processions and pilgrimages of the colleges which were in their own way a part of the great pilgrimages and thronged processions of nineteenth-century France to shrines such as Lourdes and Paray-le-

77. Safeguarding the chastity of the students greatly preoccupied the colleges, and purity was frequently and strongly stressed in the retreats. The historian of one of the colleges even went so far as to remark that a hidden but most efficacious reason for the physically salubrious condition of that school was the purity of the students. See L. Viansson-Ponté, *Les Jésuites à Metz,* 169.

78. Franchet, *Directoire,* 56 and *passim,* especially 39, 41, 43–44, 53, 55.

79. TSJ, Tolos., "Les Maisons SJ de Toulouse, Collège Ste-Marie." In the "Militia of the Pope" the students rose in military rank by exemplary classroom conduct and by prayers and sacrifices offered for the Holy Father in his struggles of the day.

80. CSJ, 2364-4: Lille, "Cortège de l'Immaculée Conception aux fêtes du couronnement de N.D. de la Treille, 21 juin, 1874." This was also published as a brochure by Antoine Sengler, S.J. (Lille, 1874).

Monial, where religion and political ideology were often, if only half-consciously, intertwined. In one procession in 1874 at the college in Lille the students memorialized the Merovingian epoch, Philip of Burgundy and the Knights of the Golden Fleece, Louis XIV's consecration of the city to the Virgin, and modern devotion to the Immaculate Conception.

Faith and fatherland were closely linked. Burnichon summed it up with pride: "Only with the Jesuits the love of country [was] never separated from attachment to religion and the Church. An alumnus put it proudly . . . 'Others can call themselves Catholics and French; but we will never grant that they can say that they are more Catholic and more French than we.' Besides, this alliance between a patriotic faith and a religious faith is the only one there recognized." As under the Second Empire, so under the Third Republic the attempt by the state "to produce Frenchmen without qualification," was going to bode ill for the colleges. The Jesuits were convinced that this attempt was but one more and the most violent attack by "those who took it upon themselves to dechristianize France."[81]

81. Burnichon, *La Compagnie,* III, 474–475.

VIII

NEW BEGINNINGS
AND FINAL DAYS

Between 1870 and 1878 the French Jesuits opened thirteen colleges, twelve of them between 1870 and 1874. The first two, at Le Mans and Boulogne, involved the acceptance of schools which had recently been in other hands; the one in Algiers revived a previous halfhearted attempt at a foundation. The other new schools, at Brest, Lille, Tours, Lyons, Marseilles, Dijon, Reims, Paris, and Montpellier, were all newly opened during the first decade of the Third Republic.

At Le Mans in 1868 the bishop had asked the Paris province to take over a college previously staffed by the Congregation of the Holy Cross. Ponlevoy refused, for reasons by now abundantly clear. "All these boarding schools are a burden, almost the ruination of the province. The surveillance especially is overwhelming us . . . Already, at the present moment, more than fifty of our young men are in that bottomless pit. We have a rather well-founded hope of soon setting on foot day-schools.

Would it not be more worthwhile to keep ourselves ready for that eventuality?"[1]

The bishop, however, was persistent, not only with the provincial, but with the Superior General, the Pope, and with the government in Paris. He even found a benefactor willing to put up the money. Meanwhile, the imperial government, in the persons of Pierre-Jules Baroche, the Minister of Justice, and Victor Duruy, the Minister of Education, was adamantly against another Jesuit college.

The elections of May 1869 were harbingers of the liberal empire. The ministers who replaced Baroche and Duruy confirmed the governmental opposition, but only as a formality, and they were not as doctrinairely anti-Jesuit as their predecessors. In August 1869 the bishop persuaded Pius IX and Beckx to take the college, and in September he decided, with the agreement of the provincial, to ignore the unpublished privy council decision of 1859 and, relying on the public law of 1850, to go ahead with the college. The original benefactors had lost heart, and the bishop had to work desperately to find gifts and loans to purchase the property. In the spring of 1870 the Jesuits took possession of the bare buildings of the old College of the Holy Cross, without bothering to reply to the pro forma protestations of the imperial government. When the school opened in October 1870, soldiers had already arrived before students; the empire was in ruins; France was going under; and the armies of Germany were on the route to Le Mans, their farthest point of penetration.

The last Jesuit college founded under the Second Empire had encountered the same difficulties to which the first one had been subject—lack of men and money, reluctance to take on the burdens of a boarding school, improvisation of the material resources needed in a college, and, finally, governmental hostility. In 1850 the benefits hoped for from the colleges had been a strong enough incentive to overcome those obstacles. The

1. PSJ, Reg., Ponlevoy to Beckx, Aug. 1, 1868.

conviction that those benefits had been realized during the last twenty years was an even stronger incentive in the eyes of many Catholics to urge the foundation of yet more schools in the years after 1870.

During the Franco-Prussian war itself, many of the colleges, besides attempting to stay open as schools, became hospitals for wounded soldiers and homes for refugees displaced by the combat. In the province of Champagne, most of the Jesuit residences housed first the French wounded and then the German, as the Prussian armies overran the north and east of France. At Amiens and Metz especially the colleges served both sides.

At Le Mans, several hundred French, former members of the pontifical army now dismissed after the taking of Rome by the Piedmontese in September 1870, used the newly opened college for regroupment and became, along with recruits from nearby, the Volunteers of the West. After the wounded and diseased came the Prussians, who took Le Mans in January 1871. A house journal described their advent: "This evening they [the Prussian troops] overran the college; 500 artillery horses in the classrooms, the study halls, the dining room, the parlors, the cloister of the church and the chapter house."[2] To the more than twenty thousand men lodged at the college during eight months most of the Jesuits had acted as chaplains. All of them had taken ill and two had died. But in the midst of this, a small group of students continued their classes, so determined were the Jesuits that the college would survive as such. When the last of the German troops and the last of the wounded had left in March 1871, the place was a shambles.

With the fall of the empire and the formation of the Government of National Defense, the unrest and uncertainty in many parts of the country often took an anticlerical turn. At Lyons and Marseilles revolutionary groups invaded and sacked the Society's residences, profaned its churches, and threw the

2. PSJ, Le Mans, Journal, Jan. 13, 1871.

Jesuits in prison—in some cases for periods of several months. At Dôle, Garibaldi and his troops expelled the Jesuits and wrecked their house. The colleges of Saint-Etienne, Mongré, and Avignon were requisitioned more or less illegally for various military groups. At Poitiers, at the seminary of Périgueux, at Bordeaux, the disturbances ranged from crowds smashing windows or breaking into the church to sing the *Marseillaise,* to mobs roaming the corridors of the buildings and stealing or destroying whatever they could.

At Paris, when the war started, the Society turned the college at Vaugirard and the preparatory school of Sainte-Geneviève into hospitals, and the Jesuits served as chaplains and nurses while trying to keep classes in session. During the Prussian siege, Olivaint, superior of the main residence on the rue de Sèvres, sent out news by balloon to the provincial. Though life was difficult for all, the Jesuits rejoiced that under the press of adversity the Parisians had recovered much of their religious fervor; the city seemed "constantly disposed to stick it out. There has been a movement of grace in many souls. Our fathers are working hard." At Vaugirard classes went on as usual, even though in January "the bombardment doubtlessly causes some uneasiness in our regard. But Providence protects us. The [school on] rue des Postes and the [residence on] rue de Sèvres took several hits . . . At Vaugirard, there was a regular rain of shells; I don't know how the buildings escaped it."[3] Most difficult for the Parisian Jesuits was the isolation from all news of their brethren in the rest of France. After the city capitulated on January 28, they wondered whether in other parts of the country there was the same "hatred of God among a truly dreadful minority."[4]

With the advent of the Commune in March 1871, the peril became great. Olivaint called his community together on

3. PSJ, Olivaint, Olivaint to Ponlevoy, Dec. 20, 1870, and Jan. 10, 1871.
4. PSJ, Sainte-Geneviève, Ducoudray to Hubin, Jan. 28, 1871. Ducoudray was the rector at Ste.-Geneviève, Hubin the superior at Brest.

March 28, and said frankly that they "should perhaps count on being victims, that some at least among their number would have to pay with their lives. He recommended to all prudence and zeal, courage always and confidence *even so, even in spite of everything*. Finally to each he gave a little money and assigned a place of refuge."[5]

In the early morning of April 4, a battalion of *gardes nationaux* took over Sainte-Geneviève, and transported to prison the community of eight Jesuit priests and four brothers together with seven of the lay workers at the school. That same evening the militia came with two official envoys of the Commune to the rue de Sèvres, ransacked the house and took to prison the only two Jesuits still there, one of whom was Olivaint. The Commune in a few days released all but five of the Jesuits—Ducoudray, the rector of Sainte-Geneviève, Alexis Clerc, Bengy, Olivaint, and Caubert. By April 14 they were all in the prison of Mazas near the Gare de Lyon. For most of the time that they were there, the hostages, for that is what the Commune intended that they be, could send letters out, and by various means of concealment the Eucharist was introduced into the prison for their communion and consolation.[6]

As the troops of Thiers breached the ramparts near Issy[7] and entered Paris on May 20, the last desperate days of the Commune began, during which the massacre of the hostages took place. On May 22, the communards transferred their prisoners in box cars from Mazas to the more formidable La Roquette, where they finally numbered somewhat more than two hun-

5. Armand de Ponlevoy, S.J., ed., *Actes de la captivité et de la mort des RR. PP. Olivaint, Ducoudray, Caubert, Alexis Clerc et de Bengy, de la Compagnie de Jésus* (17th ed.; Paris, n.d.), 25. This is a collection of the remembrances and testimony of those, especially their fellow members of the Society, who were participants in any way in the events leading up to the execution of the five Jesuits by the communards.

6. Their letters are in the *Actes* cited above.

7. It was exactly near here, close to the Porte de Versailles, that the college of Vaugirard was located. In April the whole community of two hundred persons there had fled first to the country house at Issy-les-Moulineaux, then to Versailles, and then to Sainte-Germain-en-Laye (*EJF*, III, 1378–1379).

dred. The first executions took place in the evening of May 24; six prisoners were shot, including Archbishop Darboy, Bonjean, the eminent jurist, two diocesan priests, and two of the Jesuits, Ducoudray and Alexis Clerc. " 'It was a magnificent sight,' wrote an eyewitness; 'these traitors stretched on the ground . . . the deadly enemies of civilization, auxiliaries of all the monarchies and propagators of ignorance in every generation.' " By a certain irony, "Bonjean who, as befitted an eminent Gallican lawyer, had been strongly opposed to the Jesuits, made his peace with the Society in the face of death, receiving the last sacraments from a Jesuit hostage." Two days later, and two days before the end of the Commune, Olivaint, Caubert and Bengy were at the head of forty-seven more prisoners taken from La Roquette, paraded through the working-class quarters of Menilmontant and Belleville, and finally shoved into a courtyard of the rue Haxo where a mob composed of National Guards, street ruffians, and a drunken crowd of both sexes, by now lusting for blood, massacred them with rifle, revolver, bayonet, sword, and knife. "One body, it was later noted, had seventy-two bayonet wounds in it." This was the body of one of the Jesuits.[8]

The members of the Society in France during the next decade, and even beyond, never did, indeed never could, forget what had happened to them during the Commune, and the importance to them of the experience has justified recounting it at this length. Some of the survivors of the original arrest later came to hold important posts in the Society in France, and by that very fact they helped influence attitudes and policies. In addition, the very family spirit fostered in the Society helped to maintain a sense of identity with the slain victims of the Paris revolt, who themselves, in death, were also symbols of the other acts of violence perpetrated on the Society in various parts of France in the months after the defeat of 1870.

8. D. W. Brogan, *The Development of Modern France, 1870–1939* (London: Hamish Hamilton, 1940), 71–72.

There was no need now to dispute the merits of one form of government over another. It was clear and simple to the Jesuits that the men who had called for a republic or for socialism before 1870 were usually the very men who had inveighed against the Church and the Jesuits in the same breath. But with republic and socialism had come disorder, blasphemy, and carnage. Most of the Jesuits, despite their reputation to the contrary, were quite politically unsophisticated, and were in no condition to make nice distinctions between one republic and another. Communards might dominate one and dukes the other, but the latter was acceptable to them only because it was an interim solution to the problem of a truly authentic government for France—a Christian kingdom of justice and order. Such was the usual judgment on these terrible experiences of 1870–1871, and in the years before 1880 the advocates of the republic, with their almost ritually regular and increasingly vocal attacks on the Church and the Society did as little as possible to modify that judgment.

Burnichon forty years later expressed the opinion of almost two generations of Jesuits: "Over the souls of Frenchmen passed a breath of Christian regeneration which gave warrant to the finest hopes for France's future. The anticlerical virus, congenital, it seems, to a republican regime, would unfortunately soon have to unchain again religious persecution and throw the country into those discords and strifes to which . . . we still see no end. But the beginning of this decade of 1871–1880 . . . was for the Church of France a moment of happy liberty, in between the uncertain and unfriendly alliance with the government of the day before and the violent hostility which the government of tomorrow was brewing."[9]

But action, not speculation, was in 1871 the order of the day. Little as the new government was loved, its guarantee of liberty of education was a blessing of which fullest advantage was to be taken. In 1871 the Society took on the direction of

9. Burnichon, *La Compagnie*, IV, 407–408.

two colleges, in 1872 three more, in 1873 another four, in 1874 an additional two, after which there was a surcease until 1878 when one last school was launched in the very teeth of the rising gale of anticlericalism. These twelve schools had to face many of the same internal problems as had beset the earlier colleges—problems of finances, personnel, physical facilities, and a marked preference for boarding schools. The programs of study and the daily life of the students too, although modified in some accidental details, were substantially the same ones that had served the colleges from 1850 to 1870.

The two schools founded in 1871 were located in the northwest of the Champagne province at Boulogne-sur-Mer and in the southeast of the Lyons province at Lyons. For both establishments the questions of a boarding versus a day school arose immediately. Boulogne had a boarding school from the start, but at Lyons the provincial, Gaillard, was determined to cut this Gordian knot of boarding schools and to make a new day college there the exemplar for the other schools of his province. Thus, the College of St. Joseph at Lyons began as the first purely day school founded since the restoration of the Jesuits in France in 1814. The great step was taken.

Unfortunately, it had been taken too early. Difficulties arose everywhere, most seriously at Saint-Etienne, which was also to be turned into a simple day school in 1871. Six days before classes were to start there, only fifty day students were enrolled, and certain ruin loomed ahead. Gaillard had to back down; Saint-Etienne again welcomed boarders. When a new provincial, Jullien, took office in 1874, he was within weeks sending to Rome a bleakly pessimistic picture of the Lyons venture: "the complaints against a day school . . . alone and the desires for a half-boarding school continue to be obvious among our Jesuits and among the very great majority of families. Our Jesuits complain of having very little influence on the students; the spiritual ministrations are cut down to little of anything . . . The parents say that they cannot get their children to work at home. Some have been placed as half-boarders with secular masters; but these establishments have their dangers and impose expensive terms on the families . . . Finally, the [financial] returns of this plain day school are quite incapable of meeting its expenses and debts."[10]

The next year, the rector, Gautrelet, added his warning cries to those of the provincial. The debt was rising; the gulf of insolvency loomed larger; the parents were unanimously in favor of a half-boarding school; the other French provinces thought a pure day school impossible of success. In the fall of 1876 the Superior General gave permission to take half-boarders.

The attempt to excise completely in one province a root cause of many of the difficulties of the Society in France in manpower and in adequate academic preparation had failed before the more deeply rooted habits of teachers and, especially, of parents. Within a year the college in Lyons, now day and boarding, was flourishing with three hundred in attendance. From now on, though day students in large numbers went to several of the colleges, yet all of them were mixed establishments, except Mongré which was exclusively a full boarding school.

Brest, Tours and Lille were the next sites for new colleges, with all three founded in 1872. As with Le Mans in 1870, the first two of these colleges belonged to the Paris province. Brest and Tours both had Jesuit residences. Both cities had received refusals to earlier requests for Jesuit colleges. But in the fall of 1871 more importunate demands were made as usual, and by the autumn of the next year both Brest and Tours had their Jesuit colleges in operation, despite enormous problems.[11] As usual, schools had their debts. At Brest, despite the enthusiasm of the initial benefactors, by 1874 the college had to

<hr/>

10. ARSJ, Lugd., Jullien to Beckx, Dec. 12, 1874.
11. PSJ, "Lib. Cons.," Nov. 23, 1871. The consultors' secretary summed up the sense of a meeting on Brest in a Virgilian line: *Hic labor, hic nova et inextricabilis difficultas.*

borrow up to 350,000 francs. Tours was somewhat more fortunate in having as a consistently generous friend Alfred Mame, the head of one of the most important Catholic publishing houses in France. The college bought property for new buildings, partly on the site of the presuppression Jesuit church. The location had the disadvantage of a theater on one side and a funeral establishment on the other; from this, however, the teachers supposedly could illustrate for heedless youth the words of Scripture, "Sorrow marches on the heels of joy."[12]

In Lille too the Society had previously had a college, in this instance from the very early year of 1592. The Paris province had established a residence there in 1843, and after the closure of Brugelette the usual petitions went to Rome for a college in Lille.

In 1870 Pillon urged the General to accept a college there, since Lille was "the city of our province with the brightest future ahead of it," and since it would be "a new proof of your . . . solicitude for this poor province of Champagne which always tends to regard itself as disinherited." But the superior of the residence had a word of caution: "Yes, undoubtedly Lille has a population of 150,000, but 100,000 of them are workers. Limited to 50,000, the bourgeoisie [already] has for the education of its children first, the lycée and then the church institution supported by the archbishop."[13]

Cardinal Regnier was eager to have the Jesuits open a college, and so the already existing day school of St. Joseph was ceded to the Society, where it would be "the concern of the Fathers . . . to bring about a flourishing state of piety and work by the same methods as [had been used] at Brugelette."[14] Despite the strong editorial hostility of several journals of the city, supporters of the college even started to lay plans for one

12. Burnichon, *La Compagnie*, IV, 422–423, quoting Prov. 14:13.
13. ARSJ, Camp., Pillon to Beckx, May 22, 1870, and Douillet to Beckx, June 1, 1870.
14. *EJF*, II, 1333.

of the new Catholic universities after the law of 1875 which granted liberty in higher education.[15] Five such institutions, begun before a later law after 1880 stopped such foundations, managed to survive the tempests of 1880 and 1901–1905.

The colleges were now to extend not only from one end of France to the other, but even beyond, into North Africa again. In 1873 the province of Lyons started a college at Marseilles and reactivated a former school in Algiers, while Champagne compensated for the loss of Metz by establishing a college in Dijon. Earlier petitions for a college at Marseilles had been refused, even when, in 1864, the non-Catholic financier, Péreire, in opening a new quarter of the city for development, and thinking that a Jesuit college would give it the tone he desired, offered to build the place at his own expense. But in 1873 the provincial wrote that he "thought that after the letter of the bishop and in the state of public opinion in our regard, a refusal would be morally impossible and that the Society owed it to itself to respond to this eager initiative of the Marseilles families . . . We would not have wanted to proceed so quickly, but we have had our hand forced by circumstances."[16]

The persistent influence of earlier Jesuit colleges was illustrated in the letter of support from the president of the lay corporation set up to prepare for the new school. M. Rostand d'Ancezun recalled to the General that he, "the author of this note, . . . [was] an alumnus of Fribourg where he had passed ten years of his childhood and youth and he thus knew perfectly what a college of the Fathers of the Society was like

15. Matters became so bad that in 1874 the Jesuits instituted a suit for defamation against two papers, *Progrès du Nord* and *L'Echo du Nord*. It was very seldom and with great reluctance that the Society engaged in this sort of contest in France; it dreaded any involvement with the courts. In this instance, the Jesuits, joined by the Dominicans, won their case and also saw it sustained on appeal. See CSJ, MSS. 3203: "Diarium Ministri Sancti Joseph," 137 and 161.

16. ARSJ, Lugd., "Messieurs de Marseille" to Beckx, Feb. 8, 1873, and Gaillard to Beckx, Sept. 2, 1873.

[and] he knew equally well what a day school was since Fribourg had had as many day students as boarders."[17]

As at Oran so at Algiers, immediately after the passage of the Falloux Law the province of Lyons had received the offer of a college. In 1853 a small beginning was attempted, but the school was never really organized officially and the colonists were still rather halfhearted about such an educational venture, so that in 1858 it closed down.[18] Fifteen years later, when Lavigerie became bishop of Algiers, he encouraged the establishment of a day school, but it always remained too small a college to justify the men and money expended on it, and the regrets were not excessive when, in 1880, the Ferry decrees forced its closure.

At Dijon the Society thought that the city was "still much imbued with the old gallican traditions of the *parlements*. Except for families whose heads had been students in the minor seminaries . . . or a little later at Brugelette and Fribourg, the Jesuits were known only from the press campaigns which . . . had never stopped disparaging and caricaturing them to the point of making them legendary beings."[19]

This, coupled with the rivalry between the Jesuit provinces of Lyons and Champagne over the inclusion of Burgundy in their respective jurisdictions militated against the establishment of a college at Dijon. The General categorically refused permission to move there the boarding college and preparatory school which the new German masters of Metz had recently closed, but he did allow the Champagne province to accept an unexpected invitation from the bishop in May 1873 for a day college at the Jesuit residence. Such a school, without competing with the boarding establishment at Dôle, would fulfill a need ever growing as the "alarm [grew] at the progress of evil

17. ARSJ, Lugd., Rostand d'Ancezun to Beckx, July 28, 1874.
18. *EJF*, I, 155.
19. *Ibid.*, II, 113.

schooling."[20] The municipal council of Dijon showed its attitude toward the whole venture by renaming the street on which the new buildings of the Jesuit school were situated "Boulevard Voltaire."[21]

In the four years since 1870 Lyons had taken on three new schools, Champagne four, and Paris three, while Toulouse had been content with the five it already had after it had given up the college at Mende in 1864. At that time, the imperial government had forced the Society out by refusing to sanction the renewal of the contract between the commune and the Jesuits without imposing its own control on the school. The Toulouse provincial had then withdrawn from the college because, he said, "it would oblige us to accept for an acknowledgedly private institution . . . an organization of courses, and programs, methods and textbooks which would no longer be of our own choice; despite all the good will on our part, this position is unacceptable."[22] The list of schools for Lyons was now filled, while Champagne and Paris each took on one more institution, and Toulouse accepted its sole post-imperial foundation.

The relocation at Reims of the college of Metz was proposed, but since the lycée and a college of the Christian Brothers "shared about equally the student clientele of the upper and lower bourgeoisie," the Jesuit day school opened only in 1874.[23] Among the boys were a good number of sons of army officers; as a result, there was great enthusiasm at academic séances when the subject of patriotism or "revanche" came up.

The Paris province still lacked a day school in the capital. Vaugirard was a boarding college and it intended so to remain. An earlier attempt, in 1858–1859, to found a day school had come to nought for lack of men, but in September 1874,

20. ARSJ, Camp., Stumpf to Beckx, April 8, 1873.
21. Burnichon, *La Compagnie*, IV, 438.
22. TSJ, Reg., Rouquayrol to "M. le Maire de Mende," Feb. 1, 1864. See Chapter III for the original contractual arrangement.
23. *EJF*, IV, 326.

the College of St. Ignatius, so named in memory of the Jesuit founder's stay in Paris, began classes in the town house of the Mignon family, generous benefactors of the Society. By 1878 there were seven hundred students in new buildings which, after the expulsions of 1901, became the National Conservatory of Music. There was no compromise with the nonboarding character of this school, even as a temporary measure for those students whose parents left Paris early in the summer for their country houses.[24]

Montpellier was the last college to be founded before the troubled days of 1880. In October 1878 the Toulouse Jesuits formally opened a day school there, but the life of this school before 1880 was too short to be particularly noteworthy, and its day-to-day existence was identical with that of the twenty-six other French Jesuit colleges.

There would have been many more schools if petitioners had had their way. In the archives of the several provinces there are, for example, requests from and correspondence with Evreux, Limoges, Angers, Nevers, Saint-Pol, Besançon, Chambéry, Annecy, Grenoble, and Arles, to name only several of the cities, and the letters often began with a statement such as, "Here now it is the third time that I have presented this request."[25]

The internal life of all of these new schools was much the same as that of the older foundations, and in the relations of all these colleges, old and new, with the secular world, one basic problem loomed just as large as it had previously; indeed, it loomed even larger and more menacing every year. What was to be the situation of the Jesuit schools in the mind of the government, especially a government which seemed to be growing, if not increasingly anti-Catholic, which it regularly denied, at least increasingly anticlerical, which it proudly

24. PSJ, Reg., Mourier to Beckx, June 5, 1874; "Lib. Cons.," July 2 and 17, and Aug. 15, 1874, Oct. 20, 1877 and Feb. 19, 1878.
25. LSJ, 12:1081, Callies to Gaillard, March 29, 1874.

affirmed? By the elections of 1876 the Jesuits were becoming quite worried. An overwhelmingly republican chamber was not their concern; it was rather that eighty of those three hundred republicans were of the left, and that openly anticlerical leaders such as Gambetta, Ferry, Grévy and Paul Bert were more important and more vocal every day. As interpreted by such men, the "Principles of '89" and the "Revolution" were impieties from beginning to end for the French Jesuits. As one Jesuit proclaimed on prize day at Le Mans in 1876: "The Church and the Revolution, necessarily enemies, eternally at war, as the good and evil which they personify, are centering their conflict at this moment on the ground of education . . . , a combat without any doubt decisive for the salvation or for the ruin of our country . . . The Revolution is a work of social demolition; the principles with which it has been inspired since its beginning, the means which it has used for this task, all tend to the single goal which it proposes, the overthrow and the ruin of everything which bears the mark of Christianity."[26]

The protagonists of the other side agreed that the opposition was ineluctable. Jules Ferry, who was as convinced a republican as he was a secularist in his educational policies, had been sure in 1872 that "the republic . . . has only one formidable enemy, the clergy. But the nonsense of Lourdes shows clearly the latter's irremediable decadence. This shifting, decomposing body will never triumph over a living society whose entire progress is absolutely laic . . . separating it more and more from the old worship and the old idols."[27] Paul Bert was frank about the goals envisaged. "We shall make war on the good Lord, and we shall succeed. We must laicise France. Among ourselves, Voltaire's great peals of laughter have long

---

26. Charles Clair, S.J., *Que devons-nous à l'église et à la révolution en fait d'éducation publique* (Le Mans, 1876), 5, 25.

27. Jules Ferry, *Lettres* (Paris, 1914), 167, to his brother in 1872, as quoted in Evelyn M. Acomb, *The French Laic Laws, 1879–1889* (New York: Columbia University Press, 1941), 36–37.

ago swept away superstition. Our religion will be . . . a patriotism that is ardent, intransigent, capable of every daring deed, ready for every sacrifice. This is worth a lot more than Capuchin mummeries and Jesuit deceit. Science lights our path and guides us; love of our fatherland inspires us; we shall be the victors."[28]

From 1876 on the four provincials of France consulted together about their legal situation in the light of detailed studies by several lawyers. They thought they had nothing to fear on the basis of the legislation then in force, but "in case of a revolutionary law nothing could guarantee [the situation] effectively."[29] In 1877 the provincial of Champagne wrote to superiors about the official responses to be given to governmental inquiries on unauthorized religious congregations.[30] After MacMahon's dismissal of the Chamber on May 16, 1877, and the new election of a large majority for the left, the Society felt that danger was yet more imminent. The Paris provincial even began looking into the possibilities of an exile college and approached the English provincial about the matter.

In letters to and from Rome, the specter of dissolution hovered over future plans. As the General remarked to Mourier about a particular project: "Since you are in danger of seeing the college closed and even worse, how can I authorize you to build without delay?" In 1878 the consultors at Toulouse remarked that in the usual questions from the school inspectors

28. Paul Bert to von Bulow, in Bernhard von Bulow, *Memoirs*, trans. by G. Dunlap and F. Voigt (Boston, 1932), IV, 347. In *The Doctrine of the Jesuits* (trans. from the thirteenth French edition but translator not given) (Boston, 1880), Bert wrote a horrified protest against what he depicted as the theological teachings of the Society of Jesus especially in matters pertaining to sexual morality. Also included in the book are several of his speeches on Ferry's proposed educational laws. The Jesuits would hardly be led to expect from his hand any more than from Ferry's any tender mercies when he became minister of education.

29. TSJ, "Quatre Provinces—Compte-rendu," Grandidier (Champagne) to ?, Sept. 25, 1876.

30. CSJ, "Litterae Encyclicae Patrum Provincialium," Grandidier, April 16, 1877.

"there seem to be some new problems both in the way they are asked and in the intentions of the inquisitors." Superiors feared the worst and their letters contained typical phrases such as "dreading a revolution at any instant" or "financial ramparts . . . very feeble in stopping a revolutionary rapacity."[31]

The detailed story of the early years of the first anticlerical campaign of the Third French Republic, has been well told in Acomb's work, and it need not be repeated in such detail here. Suffice it to say that the laws concerning higher and secondary education formed an initial and important part of that campaign. With a republican majority in the Senate added, in January 1879, to that of the Chamber, and with the advent of Jules Ferry to the post of Minister of Education in the Waddington cabinet, the campaign got down to legislative specifics. On March 15, 1879 Ferry introduced in the Chamber two education bills. The first secularized the Conseil Supérieur de l'Education Publique. The other, on "freedom of independent education," enforced everywhere the same rules in regard to registration and study programs and allowed state faculties alone to give examinations and confer degrees. No independent institution of higher education, in reality the four or five new Catholic establishments, could style itself a "university."

Most controversial was "Article Seven" of the second bill, which declared that "no one [was] to be allowed to teach in state or private schools nor to direct a teaching establishment of any kind whatsoever if he belongs to a non-authorized religious congregation."[32] The article was not exactly germane to the rest of the bill, but it accomplished its purpose. It struck not only the Jesuits, of course, but also most of the other religious orders of men. The Society, however, was the main

---

31. ARSJ, Reg., Franc., Beckx to Mourier, Nov. 2, 1877; TSJ, "Lib. Cons.," May 14, 1878; and ARSJ, Franc., Chauveau to Beckx, Jan. 31, 1879.

32. *Journal Officiel, Chambre,* April 1, 1879, as detailed in Acomb, *Laic Laws,* 136–142.

target of Ferry and his supporters as was obvious from the whole tenor of the debate which raged in the Chamber for weeks. The arguments of the 1820's, of the 1840's, and of 1850 were brought up again by both sides. In the Chamber, in the journals, in pamphlets and books and speeches, if the heat was greater than before, the light was no brighter, and if it was familiar to hear the Society dubbed "the militia of the counterrevolution," it was at least novel to be told that if freedom were given to the Jesuits, it would have to be given to the Communists too.[33]

Ferry was open enough to remark, "If the republic does not act at this time, when it is all powerful, if it does not profit by this maximum force which belongs to every new government to put itself in a state of defense, when will it do so?"[34] The republic did act. The Chamber passed the law on July 9, 1879 by 347 votes to 143, and "Article Seven" specifically by 333 to 164. But the Senate refused to be hurried, despite Ferry's urgings. The Toulouse Jesuit consultors recognized, as did all their brethren, that "the affair was completely lost in the Chamber," but they thought that "this is not the case with the senators who do not seem to give support to these calumnies and injustices."[35] Only in February 1880 did the bill come up for discussion in the Senate, after having been discussed all over France during the summer, fall, and winter. Even Jules Simon, ardent left republican though he was, had declared against the article: "The religion of the state oppresses the conscience, and the education of the state, thus understood, suppresses it . . . Freedom of thought is not the abstract right to have an opinion to oneself in the secret of his conscience . . . It is freedom spread abroad by word and by book."[36] The opposition to the article was well organized by senators such as

33. *Journal Officiel, Chambre,* June 12 and 27–28, 1879, quoted in Acomb, *Laic Laws,* 139.

34. Ferry, *Discours,* III, 59, quoted in Acomb, *Laic Laws,* 123.

35. TSJ, "Lib. Cons.," July 12, 1879.

36. *Journal Officiel, Sénat,* Dec. 27, 1879, quoted in Acomb, *Laic Laws,* 141.

Chesnelong, Broglie, and Dufaure, and on March 9, 1880 the Senate rejected it by 149 votes to 132.

The Jesuit houses rejoiced. At the college in Bordeaux, for example, a telegram brought the news that night. The students were overjoyed early the next morning at a totally unexpected free day, and at a grand party that evening in the largest hall in the school the provincial of Toulouse, then at the college, received the congratulations of the community and offered prayers of thanksgiving.[37]

When the government failed by legislative means to exclude the unauthorized orders from the schools, it achieved the same end in another way. On March 29, 1880 the *Journal Officiel* published two executive decrees based, according to their text, on already existing laws. By one, all unauthorized orders except the Society of Jesus had, within three months, to request governmental authorization or to face the possibility of dissolution. By the other, the Jesuit order was to be dissolved in France within three months, with a special extension until the end of the school year in August for its colleges. Among the laws cited as foundations for this decree were *arrêts* of the *parlement* of Paris in 1762 and 1767, royal edicts of 1764 and 1777, laws of the revolutionary governments of 1790 and 1792, and articles of the concordat and sections of the penal code.

Charles de Freycinet, who was now premier, in his memoirs attributed the responsibility for the decrees to Gambetta and not to Ferry, and he said that Grévy thought them unnecessary and provocative.[38] Whatever the source, this act was more than enough to seal the opinion of the Jesuits on the republic, especially when more than four hundred magistrates resigned rather than enforce the decrees,[39] and when almost two thou-

---

37. TSJ, "Diarium Provinciae," March 9–10, 1880. Even the scholastics in the early years of their Jesuit training heard of the victory from newspaper accounts read to them in the community, a rare occurrence then for young seminarians (TSJ, "Diaire de juvenat, June 1877–Dec. 1883," March 11, 1880).

38. Freycinet, *Souvenirs, 1878–1893*, 143–147, quoted in Acomb, *Laic Laws*, 144.

39. However, as D. W. Brogan remarked in *The Development of Modern*

sand lawyers concurred in a brief prepared by several eminent jurists "that the unauthorized orders had a legal right to live a common life, hold property and be free, and could be dissolved only by court action, not by decree."[40]

In any case, on June 30, 1880, the first Jesuit expulsions took place. The government had to pick the locks and break the chains on the doors of the Jesuit residences because the Society had decided to reserve what it felt were all its legal rights by not yielding except to force. At the main residence on the rue de Sèvres in Paris, the Jesuits waited to be pushed out of their rooms and then walked out of the house, "on the arms of distinguished pupils," often members of the Senate who had led the opposition.[41] Even Louis Andrieux, the prefect of police who directed the expulsions, worried about their rather unfavorable reception by the working classes and by foreigners in Paris.[42] As for the colleges, between June and the end of August the government engaged in a series of petty harassments against them, while the Jesuits worked carefully to make their legal positions as impregnable as possible.

All the provinces consulted on how best to keep the colleges open even if Jesuits could not live in them nor direct them. One of the most important decisions to be made dealt with forced expulsion, as had happened in the residences, versus voluntary withdrawal before the date set for execution of the decrees. Another involved the composition of the legal entities set up to hold the property of the colleges.[43] The government, radical and anticlerical as it might be, was still in 1880 com-

---

France (London, 1959), 150–151, the government did not really mind this opportunity "to republicanize the legal system even further." He also mentioned that among those who resigned was "Pierre de la Gorce, who thus found the leisure to turn historian."

40. Acomb, *Laic Laws*, 144. See also Lecanuet, *Les Premières Années du Pontificat de Léon XIII*, 54–56.

41. Brogan, *Modern France*, 150.

42. Acomb, *Laic Laws*, 144.

43. E.g., CSJ, "Lib. Cons.," "St. Joseph, Lille," July 14, 1880; TSJ, "Lib. Cons.," April 22 and 26, May 23, 1880.

posed of men far too bourgeois to have anything but the most profound respect for private property, so that as a result, even though more than five thousand male religious were expelled and, in all, two hundred and sixty-one of their establishments were closed, the property itself was not expropriated.[44] Only at the next expulsion in the early twentieth century did the government also confiscate to its own benefit the holdings of the religious orders.

The arrangements made for Vaugirard exemplified with minor changes those put into effect at the other colleges too. A layman friend of the Jesuits became president of the Société Civile, which owned the property and buildings of the college. Another corporate body, the Société Anonyme des Ecoles Secondaires Libres, was set up to "lease [the] college and do undertake to operate it as such at a profit."[45] The board of directors of this corporation chose a superior, professors, and surveillants for their college. To be completely safe, the superior was usually not a Jesuit but, as for example at Vaugirard, a former auxiliary bishop of Rennes, Monsignor de Forges. Former students or young diocesan priests became the resident surveillants. The principal, his assistant, and a number of other Jesuits, in addition to laymen and secular priests, were engaged as teachers by the corporation; the spiritual direction and counseling of the students remained exclusively in the hands of members of the Society who came to the school for these purposes.

In most instances the Jesuit community quietly dispersed before the deadline, so that as far as possible the college could avoid any danger to its continued functioning. Jesuit priests in small groups of three, four or five rented apartments or lived in parts of private homes loaned to them by their lay friends. Usually a very few Jesuit lay brothers stayed at the

---

44. Dietz, "Jules Ferry et les traditions républicaines," *Revue politique et parlementaire,* 160 (1934), 509–512, as detailed in Acomb, *Laic Laws,* 146.
45. ARSJ, Franc., Chauveau to Beckx, Aug. 7, 1880.

colleges to oversee the property; the government seldom bothered these nonteaching members of the Society.

At Vaugirard, to use it again as a typical example, most of the community dispersed on August 26, 1880.[46] Three days later the bishop arrived. On August 30, the last of the Jesuit residents left the school. On the morning of September 1, the execution of the Ferry decrees began with the appearance of the commissioner of police. He met de Forges and the board of directors, publicly read the text of the decree, found everything quite juridically correct, gave a copy to the board for verification, and set seals on the external doors of the chapel lest the general public make use of the spiritual ministrations of an unauthorized congregation. Then the commissioner left. But he must have had some scruples about the thorough performance of his duties, for he immediately notified the school that he would return at three o'clock in the afternoon. At that time, each of the directors had to read for himself the declaration of the government; then the commissioner "ascertained that there were no Jesuits in the house," and drew up an official report of the proceedings, all in perfect courtesy. "No unpleasant or disagreeable incident occurred. There was no one out on the street."[47] In general, the same situation prevailed elsewhere, except perhaps at Poitiers where there were crowds in the streets to witness the expulsion of the Jesuits.

When questions arose about hiring members of the Society for the schools, the new directors replied that since the order was legally dissolved in France, these individual priests were obviously under the jurisdiction of the superior of the college and of the bishop of the diocese as far as the law was concerned. Their private adherence to any group was a matter of personal conscience into which the directors had absolutely no business inquiring since it was an inalienable right of every

46. PSJ, Vaugirard, "Diarium P. Ministri," Aug. 26–Sept. 2, 1880 and PSJ, Paris, C-32, passim, for these details.
47. PSJ, Vaugirard, "Diarium P. Ministri," Sept. 1, 1880.

Frenchman. For a month or so the Jesuits thought that they were legally unassailable in this manner and that the government would "harass us a lot, but let us live perhaps all this year."[48] The illusion was not to be long lasting. On October 14, 1880 at Toulouse began what some of the Jesuits called "the siege of Sainte-Marie." "To our great surprise, and contrary to general expectations, our college of Sainte-Marie was surrounded this morning at about eight o'clock by soldiers. A good number of police searched the inside and chased out all the teachers, surveillants, chaplains, and the principal, who were all pointed out as having been members of the Society of Jesus."[49] For several days the siege of the college continued, just to be sure that no Jesuit slipped back through the lines into the school.

In one version or another, the same kind of incident occurred at other colleges, with an exception here or there due to the friendliness of a particular state official. By a crowning irony, the government in its chase after the Jesuits used a provision of the Falloux Law itself which declared that "the director of a private secondary school can for misconduct or immorality be arraigned before the Council of Public Instruction and be forbidden the exercise of his profession permanently or temporarily."[50] With this weapon in hand the government could cite for immorality the legal non-Jesuit directors who presumed to employ any Jesuits in their colleges. Local councils closed some schools for several months; the higher council sustained the verdicts, and a sword thus hung over the former Jesuit colleges, automatically unsheathed at the employment of any members of the Society, and used at the arbitrary pleasure of the government.

So serious was the problem in 1880 and early 1881 that there was even for a time question of purely and simply clos-

48. LSJ, Reg., Monnot to ?, Oct. 9, 1880.
49. TSJ, Reg., Blanchard to Beckx (?), Oct. 14, 1880.
50. Loi Falloux, art. 68.

ing the schools. For several years, however, they struggled on in this way, still bearing their old names but directed by others. They employed quietly what members of the Society they could, without those Jesuits being able to determine finally the policies of the schools. After 1887 tensions relaxed somewhat, but details of that still uncertain period up to the final expulsion early in this century is outside both the present availability of archives and the scope of this study.

In 1814, at the restoration of the Society of Jesus, there was still alive in France only one Jesuit who had gone through the full formation of the Society. In 1850, at the enactment of the Falloux Law, one Jesuit school existed in France, founded at Avignon the year before. In 1880, when the Ferry decrees took effect, twenty-seven colleges, then educating more than ten thousand students, became illegal precisely because they were Jesuit establishments. A revived system of Jesuit education in France, its dreams and hopes, its thirty-five years in the penumbra of legality, as well as its thirty-year public attempt at realization, existed no longer.

IX

THE PROBLEMS

OF PRINCIPLES

Were these nineteenth-century Jesuit colleges in France both securely rooted in the traditional pedagogy of the Society and also adaptable to contemporary circumstances? Any answer to such a question can be nothing other than complex. First, as to the traditional pedagogy, the *Ratio Studiorum* was too often taken in its every particular as an immutable body of clearly enunciated prescriptions upon the exact implementation of which the whole success of a school depended and by which it was to be measured. The colleges seldom saw in the *Ratio* the combination of broad and permanent principles joined to specific precepts fully applicable only in a particular historical situation, most especially in the pedagogical, intellectual, and social situation of the seventeenth and eighteenth centuries. The revision of 1832, however well intentioned it was, only served to perpetuate an unduly simplified view of the *Ratio,* because those who were most adamant in maintaining every jot and tittle of the law could point to what looked like a current edition of that law.

When it came to the intellectual ideals proposed to the students, the identification of Christian humanism with the study of the Greek and Roman classics was presented to boys and young men between the ages of ten and seventeen in a drastically narrowed version that was heavily slanted toward grammar. The problem took on additional complications when this Christian humanism was presumed to set before the students a so-called body of truths perennially accessible to man's own reason and in incontrovertible accord with the teachings of Christianity. Could the study of the classics and of the Christian heritage really be taken seriously in the situation in which the schools functioned? They were surely said to be so, but could they be, given the stage of intellectual development of the students, the fact that for most of them there was to be no further higher education to broaden and deepen their understanding of those subjects, and given also the very restricted opportunities for scholarship available to the teachers? Of course, the same questions could be asked of the state secondary schools too, which equally prided themselves on imparting such a humanistic, if not specifically Christian, education to students of the same age range, and which experienced almost the same obstacles to it. Both types of colleges never solved, indeed probably never really faced, this problem.

The Jesuits always maintained that the education which they gave had to be not only traditional, but also properly contemporary, in accord with their founder's ideals of adaptability and timeliness. It was contemporary in the restricted sense of conforming to official curriculum changes and of introducing some specific courses to meet obvious and specific needs. The programs of studies and the success in governmental examinations bear witness to that. But in the broader sense of an education "directed to informing pupils with those ideas and to creating for them those capacities which [would] enable them to appreciate the current thought of their epoch," the contemporaneity of these colleges is open to some question.[1] Perhaps the Jesuits would have been proud of such a judgment. While they undoubtedly wanted to prepare their students for their way in the world and certainly not for a universal monasticism, yet they openly rejected much of the "current thought of their epoch" and were happy to do so. "Appreciation" need not imply acceptance, of course, and one of the functions of an educational institution and certainly of a religiously committed one is to judge the society in which it exists. But judgment and/or rejection must first involve an understanding and, if possible, a sympathetic understanding, of what is being judged. Among the Jesuit colleges there was surely no sympathy for the way the world was going, and the understanding of that world on its own terms was at the best minimal and often nonexistent.

An example may help to show why. When the question arose of what journals were to be received regularly in the colleges, for the Jesuits but not for the students, the replies of the Toulouse provincial and consultors portrayed all too general an attitude. In 1858, the provincial thought that at Toulouse *L'Ami de la Religion* and *L'Univers* were enough, plus the local paper but without the serial story or commentary [*feuilleton*]. No *revues* were to be allowed except perhaps one of a scholarly sort for those engaged in such work.[2] A year later the same decision was reached in another case, but the consultors disagreed on such items as the *Revue des deux mondes,* really a rather moderate and serious periodical, or the *Revue contemporaine.* One thought preachers should read them "in order to know and refute adversaries of the faith." Two were in doubt. The last was against allowing this type

1. Alfred North Whitehead, *The Aims of Education and Other Essays* (New York: Macmillan Company, 1929), 116.

2. TSJ, Sainte-Marie: "Memoriale Visitatorum et Provincialium," Studer, March 7–23, 1858.

of publication, "asserting that the Holy Scriptures, the Fathers of the Church and the theologians and serious books supplied satisfactory weapons, especially since *L'Univers* was available."[3] This was not simply a temporary or isolated decision. Even in 1882 the provincial stated that "we should not read, no matter what our age, the journals which do not have ideas which are completely sound, and certainly the *Constitutionnel* does not have them."[4] To see the world that one was ineluctably involved with only through the eyes of "completely sound" journals such as *L'Univers* was to be completely cut off from any possibility of a sympathetic presentation of the complex of variant ideas in that world. Yet, to refer again to a judicious remark of Whitehead, "There is no such thing as a successful system of education . . . which is divorced from immediate contact with the existing intellectual atmosphere."[5]

When it came to the actual structuring of the schools, their daily order and their emotional and social climate as distinct from course work and intellectual ideals, another root problem appeared. The minor seminaries through the exile colleges had provided the patterns of existence and the sources of what were taken to be authentic traditions. This was a great misfortune, because the minor seminaries were *not* really in the direct line of succession as genuine heirs either to the instructional or to the more broadly educative traditions of the old Society of Jesus. Those first schools after the restoration had been far too hurriedly founded, in too great numbers, in quite precarious circumstances, by men of undoubted good will but of rigid principles of conduct and of minimal acquaintance with the former practices of the Society. Yet to those schools, to institutions such as Saint-Acheul and Brugelette, the colleges looked for their examples.

But in one way, at least, those minor seminaries were true

3. TSJ, "Lib. Cons.," Jan. 11, 1859. However, it should be recognized that some of the house libraries *do* have remarkably complete back collections of the *Revue des deux mondes*.

4. TSJ, Reg., Carrère to (superior?) at Arcahon, Dec. 10, 1882.

5. Whitehead, *Aims of Education*, 117.

ancestors of the new colleges. In both cases, the circumstances of their foundation and of their daily existence help explain many of the features which one can, in the light of history, validly question. The siege mentality of European Catholicism in the nineteenth century was pervasive. The real, frequent, and official hostility of empire and republic, and the exigencies of the state educational bureaucracy obviously reinforced such a mentality and made more justifiable to the Jesuits their cautious and defensive mentality. Then too, the whole Catholic educational system of which the Jesuit colleges were a part was regarded by friends and enemies alike, always and everywhere, as an inevitable rival to the state system. This attitude on both sides was hardly the matrix of cordiality, much less of cooperation with anyone or anything in the opposite camp. Finally, the conviction and at times the imputation of bad faith on both sides could only harden whatever positions had been taken and sustained. If one maintained that the term of serious philosophical investigation by any man of good will was at least the threshold of the Catholic church, what else could one do but be convinced of the malice in those who not only did not arrive at that threshold, but who in passing it by or before deliberately turning their backs on it took great care that they spat on it?[6] Certainly the Jesuits sincerely thought their opponents, the vigorously anticlerical politicians, educators, and writers of those years, in such bad faith.

As for those opponents themselves, one need not go to a Gambetta or a Ferry or a Bert or a Spuller or a Victor Hugo for an example of such a judgment on the Jesuits. Even a conservative, thoroughly nonegalitarian, bourgeois critic such as Edmond Scherer, a learned man, later quite disconcerted by the naturalism of an author such as Zola, could in all sincerity describe a Jesuit in the following terms in 1879:

> When a person has at an early age renounced the opportunity to think for himself, when he has grown up in the

6. See, for example, Chapter II and Chapter VI.

habits of a passive obedience, when he has learned to sti-
fle in his soul all the voices of nature, all the demands of
his dignity as a person, even all the revulsions of his conscience, then he is in no condition to bring to mature
growth men who merit the name of men and citizens of
the kind that the state requires today. The picture of that
religious order is henceforth complete. We have seen pass
before us in successive review the fanatic, the hypocrite,
and the eunuch. And it is this kind of character who aspires to be the teacher and the guide of our children. This
is the model on which he seeks to fashion man and society.[7]

How could such a person, and there were all too many like
him, regard the Jesuits as anything but monstrous aberrations
and their colleges as anything but cancers in the political and
moral body of France?

To the defensiveness and conservatism engendered by such
a situation, a further factor must be added. Any institution,
precisely because it is a thing of the past, is adapted to past
circumstances and never situated in full accord with present
needs. By that very fact, of course, it is a conservative social
force. By that fact too, if it is to function with optimum effectiveness, it must have as much freedom as possible to readjust
to new circumstances. It must have room to maneuver.

This room to maneuver is precisely what the Jesuit colleges
did not have. They lacked it externally by reason of all the
problems that were ever present to their schools: manpower,
money, boarding-school complications, and the pressures of a
conservative middle and upper class clientele. Even more, they
lacked this maneuverability internally by reason of their remembered heritage of arbitrary suppression, their pejorative
estimate of the world in which they functioned, and their

7. Edmond Scherer, "Ce que c'est qu'un jésuite," *Revue politique et littéraire*
(July, 1879), quoted in *Lettres de Fourvière*, II (3rd ser., Lyons, 1936), 353.

almost inevitably defensive psychological reaction to the pressures of that world. Their capacity for growth in and adaptation to contemporary society was inhibited by the near impossibility of an ordered and fruitful exposure to the dominant forces of their environment. The Society and its colleges in France led essentially too sheltered a life, no matter how accidentally they were exposed to the hubbub of daily affairs.

On the other hand, it is striking that when the French Jesuits left France or entered educational work other than at colleges they were imaginative and inventive. At the same time that important business interests in Bordeaux, for example, proposed a commercial course in the college and were rejected by the Jesuits because it was "not in accord with our teaching apostolate," the preparatory school of Sainte-Geneviève, precisely because it was not a college, could and did employ the latest techniques and imparted the very best of current scientific and mathematical knowledge in preparing young men for the Grandes Ecoles and thus for careers in governmental and, especially, military service. At the very time that there were worried consultations in France on how to maintain in their pristine integrity classical colleges and classical colleges alone, French Jesuits in mission posts such as Egypt or Indochina or the Middle East were opening and staffing with their own members medical schools, agricultural colleges, and institutes for the natural sciences. While trying to fulfill what they said was their basic aim, to educate Christian leaders for a contemporary world, the French Jesuit colleges were themselves unable to engage in an untroubled apostolate in that world or to render about it a serene judgment.

That was the pity of it. For despite all the factors that inhibited or vitiated their work, despite the frequent inability to confront the nineteenth century in meaningful terms, those schools did have a deep-seated awareness of many of the values which were needed by that century and which would be increasingly needed by the next. The French Jesuit colleges did stand in principle for the values of a humane education, for the primacy of the spirit over a material prosperity, for the existence and freedom of diverse institutions in the face of an omnipotent state, for the seriousness and importance of genuine philosophizing, for man in his relation to his God, to the society he lived in, and to his own inmost self.

APPENDIX   BIBLIOGRAPHY   INDEX

APPENDIX

Jesuit Colleges in France, 1878– 1879[a]

Province and school	Boarders	Half board	All day	Day	Apostolic school[b]	College Total	Priests
Champagne							
Amiens	360	50	77	52	55	594	47
Boulogne	291	47	6	14		358	30
Dijon		95	45	46		186	20
Lille		155	214	140		509	30
Reims	173	78	6	12		269	24
Total	824	425	348	264	55	1916	151
Lyons							
Algiers		30	50	27		107	14
Avignon	227	9	69	38	72	415	28
Dôle	276		64	64	19	423	29
Saint-Etienne	190	40	51			281	24
Lyons		110	67	171		348	24
Mongré	311					311	26
Marseille		122	58	38		218	17
Oran	47	28	57	31		163	14
Yseure (MS)[c]	390	39	21	30		480	28
Total	1441	378	437	399	91	2746	204
Paris							
Brest	45	27	55	103		230	25
Le Mans	316	40	40	91		487	36
Paris (St. Ign.)		449	112	114		675	38
Paris (Vaugirard)	552			129		681	42
Poitiers	271	12	30	58	35	406	37
Tours		47	62	124		233	20
Vannes	290			186		476	38
Total	1474	575	299	805	35	3188	236

Toulouse

Bordeaux	317	154	32	24	51	578	37
Montauban (MS)	348	24	98	6		476	26
Montpellier		119	59	39		217	11
Sarlat (MS)	274	7		23		304	24
Saint-Affrique	217	10		59		286	25
Toulouse	297	92	113	22		524	32
Total	1453	406	302	173	51	2385	155
Grand Total	5192	1784	1386	1641	232	10235	746

Sources: *Catalogi Provinciarum Galliae* and PSJ, C-13, *"Enquêtes collèges secondaires, 1862–1880."*

[a] Not included in this list, because not strictly colleges, were the two special schools, Sainte-Geneviève at Paris and Caousou at Toulouse, preparatory for the Grandes Ecoles of the state. Sainte-Geneviève had 403 boarders and was staffed by 41 Jesuits. At Caousou there were 184 boarders and 28 Jesuits.

The Society also supplied teachers at times for the Major Seminaries at Aire, Blois, Chambéry, Mende, Montauban, Perigueux and Valence, in all of which in 1878–1879 there was a total of 569 students.

The number of scholastics employed in the schools does not figure in this table because the province catalogues do not supply satisfactorily controllable statistics.

[b] The Apostolic School was a special residence for students who were contemplating the possibility of a priestly vocation for the foreign missions. These students attended regular classes in the college, but lived completely apart from the other boarders.

[c] MS = Minor Seminary.

Jesuit Major Superiors in France

May 19, 1814	Pierre de Clorivière (Sup. Gen.)
January 28, 1818	Louis Simpson (Sup. Gen.)

Province of France (Provincia Galliae)

January 19, 1820	Louis Simpson
June 25, 1820	Jean Rozaven (Vice-Prov.)
February 20, 1821	Didier Richardot
February 20, 1824	Nicolas Godinot
January 2, 1830	Julien Druilhet
April 25, 1833	François Renault

Province of Paris (Provincia Franciae)

August 15, 1836	Achille Guidée
February 4, 1842	Clement Boulanger
March 16, 1845	Ambroise Rubillon
March 19, 1851	Frédéric Studer
April 25, 1857	Michel Fessard
November 30, 1864	Armand de Ponlevoy
August 15, 1873	Emmanuel Mourier
September 21, 1879	Henri Chambellan

Province of Lyons (Provincia Lugdunensis)

August 15, 1836	François Renault
August 18, 1839	Louis Maillard
October 4, 1846	Julien Jordan
September 8, 1849	Louis Maillard (II)
September 1, 1852	Joseph Bon
December 25, 1852	Joseph de Jocas
April 28, 1857	François-Xavier Gautrelet
November 17, 1861	Lazare Reynaud
October 10, 1867	Sebastien Gaillard
October 7, 1874	Michel Jullien
December 16, 1877	Ambroise Monnot

Province of Toulouse (Provincia Tolosana)

August 7, 1852	Louis Maillard (see Lyons)
May 10, 1855	Maurice Ogerdias
February 6, 1858	Frédéric Studer (see Paris)
October 18, 1863	Jean-Baptiste Rouquayrol
August 15, 1869	Jules Servières
August 17, 1875	Guillaume Blanchard

Province of Champagne (Provincia Campaniae)

December 8, 1863	Victor Mertian
December 17, 1866	Adolphe Pillon
August 4, 1872	François Grandidier
July 2, 1878	Edouard Dorr
September 8, 1880	François Grandidier (II)

Selected and Annotated Bibliography

ARCHIVAL MATERIAL

Because this study deals principally with the internal life of the French Jesuit schools, the primary source material for the greater part of it is found in the official archives of the Society of Jesus, both in those of the four French Jesuit provinces of the nineteenth century, and in the general archives of the Society in Rome. The manuscript material includes, for example, the records of the monthly or semimonthly meetings of provincial and house consultors, the official house diaries, the records of principals and prefects, the constant and detailed correspondence between rectors, provincials, and superiors general, especially the official letters which all superiors and consultors were obliged to write at set intervals to Rome, the correspondence of ordinary, nonoffice-holding Jesuits with superiors at all levels, and the provincial registers in which were kept detailed summaries of all letters of any official nature written by those superiors, the *Litterae Annuae* (accounts of the more significant and newsworthy happenings of each house forwarded annually to Rome), and finally class and lecture notes.

The two most directly important individual archival documents for the early nineteenth-century French Jesuit schools (and indirectly important for the schools after 1850 in the influence they continued to exert and the continuing conditions they depicted) are the "Annales du petit-séminaire de Saint-Acheul," and the "Plan d'études et Reglement de St. Acheul." Both are by Nicolas Loriquet, S.J. The former, in the archives of the Paris Province (PSJ), is an eight hundred page handwritten account of the college life of Saint-Acheul, interspersed with edifying biographies of deceased students and teachers. It gives quite detailed information on the daily life of a Jesuit post-Restoration minor seminary. The latter, in the archives of the Champagne province (CSJ), is the daily order, rule, and curriculum devised by Loriquet for such schools, the model upon which the colleges later drew up their own curricula and regulations.

Among the more useful printed archival materials are the annual province catalogs which list the residence, status, and occupation of each member of the province, the provincial newsletters, official curricula and study plans, prospectuses, textbooks, and devotional manuals.

Archives Nationales (AN), Paris. See F^{17} and especially F^{19}, which is the most useful section for research on religious questions and on education under religious auspices.

Archivum Romanum Societatis Jesu (ARSJ), Rome. General archives of the Society of Jesus.

Archivum Provinciae Parisiensis Societatis Jesu (PSJ). Archives of the Paris province, Chantilly (Oise), France.

Archivum Provinciae Lugdunensis Societatis Jesu (LSJ). Archives of the Lyons province, Paray-le-Monial (Saône-et-Loire), France.

Archivum Provinciae Tolosanae Societatis Jesu (TSJ). Archives of the Toulouse province, Toulouse (Haute-Garonne), France.

Archivum Provinciae Campaniae Societatis Jesu (CSJ). Archives of the Champagne province, Lille (Nord), France.

BOOKS AND PUBLISHED DOCUMENTS

L'Ami de la religion: journal ecclésiastique, politique et littéraire. Paris, 1814–1862.

Barbier, Emmanuel. *La Discipline dans quelques écoles libres: Manuel pratique du surveillant.* Paris, 1888.

Beauchamp, A. de. *Recueil des lois et règlements sur l'enseignement secondaire.* Paris, 1881.

Bellemare, Jean-François. *Le Collège de mon fils.* Paris, 1827.

Bergier, Nicholas. *Dictionnaire théologique.* Paris, 1788. A compilation much used in the nineteenth century. Recommended for Jesuit teachers of religion. Antirationalist.

Beugneot, Auguste-Arthur. *Rapport au comité de l'enseignement libre sur l'exécution et les effets de la loi organique du 15 mars, 1850, par une commission spéciale.* Paris, 1852. Many details on the practical carrying out of the Falloux Law. Sympathetic to the law and its consequences.

Bonald, Cardinal Louis de. *Lettre pastorale du 2 mars, 1848*. Lyons, 1848.

Boutmy, Emile. *Le Baccalauréat et l'enseignement secondaire*. Paris, 1899.

Boylesve, Marin de, S.J. *Appel à la jeunesse catholique contre l'esprit du siècle*. Paris, 1851.

——— *Principes de littérature à l'usage des jeunes personnes*. Paris, 1866.

——— *Principes de littérature: style, poésie, eloquence*. 3 vols. Paris, 1851–1852. The author wrote this work in 1841 and used it in duplicated form for many years before publishing it. Within a dozen years after publication it was in a sixth edition.

——— *Principes de rhétorique*. 2nd ed. Paris, 1860.

Brugelette: Souvenirs de l'enseignement chez les jésuites, par un de leurs élèves. Toulouse, 1879. Anonymous author, "Ch. de ˣˣˣ," was Charles de Raymond-Cahusac. Detailed account of life at Brugelette.

Buffier, Claude, S.J. *Nouveaux éléments d'histoire et de géographie à l'usage des pensionnaires du collège de Louis-le-Grand*. Paris, 1718, 1726.

——— *Traité des premières vérités et de la source de nos jugements . . . Ouvrage qui contient le développement primitif de l'autorité générale adopté par M. de Lamennais comme l'unique fondement de la certitude: Pour servir d'Appendice au t. II de l'Essai*. Avignon, 1822. A re-editing and adaptation of Buffier's famous treatise of 1724 to fit the current needs of the "Mennaisien doctrine." The latter part of the title called the attention of the reader to this use.

Cahen, Léon, and Albert Mathiez. *Les Lois françaises de 1815 à nos jours, accompagnées des documents politiques les plus importants*. 4th ed. Paris, 1933.

Cahour, Arsene, S.J. *Des Études classiques et des études professionnelles*. Paris, 1852.

Captier, François-Eugène. *Le Collège chrétien devant la société moderne*. Paris, 1864. Brief treatment of prize day ceremonies. Mirrors thinking of clergy.

Champeaux, G. de. *Loi sur l'enseignement avec un commentaire.* Paris, 1850. By a lawyer in the Cour d'Appel de Paris.

Chauveau, Emile, S.J. *Souvenirs de l'école Sainte-Geneviève.* 3 vols. 5th ed. Paris, 1880.

Chipon, Maurice. *Notices historiques sur le collège ténu par les pères jésuites à Dôle-du-Jura.* Besançon, 1885.

Collegium Brugelettense et convictus . . . coutumier. Brugelette, n.d. In PSJ and CSJ.

Combalot, Théodore. *Lettre à Mgr. Dupanloup, évêque d'Orléans.* Paris, n.d.

———— *Mémoire aux évêques de France et aux pères de famille sur la guerre faite à l'Église et à la Société par le Monopole Universitaire.* Paris, 1843.

Comment les jésuites ouvrent un collège. Le Mans [?], 1880.

La Commission extraparlementaire de 1849: Texte integral inédit des procès-verbaux. Introduction by Georges Chenesseau. Paris, 1937. Most useful.

Controverse sur le projet de loi présenté par M. de Falloux. Paris, 1849. A compilation of favorable articles from *L'Ami de la religion* on the Falloux Law.

Corneille, R. P., S.J. *Philosophie.* Amiens, 1872. Brief and schematic textbook for college class at Amiens. Good example of the genre.

Cotel, Pierre, S.J. *De Arte rhetorica.* Paris, 1840. Used regularly in the colleges; by 1872 there was a fourth edition.

Cournot, Antoine. *Des Institutions d'instruction publique en France.* Paris, 1864.

Damas, Amadée de, S.J. *Le Surveillant dans un collège catholique.* Paris, 1857.

Daniel, Charles, S.J. *Des Études classiques dans la société chrétienne.* Paris, 1853. An answer to the attacks of the "Gaume crisis."

Decaunes, Luc. *Réformes et projets de réforme de l'enseignement français de la Révolution à nos jours, 1789–1960.* Paris, 1962.

Delattre, Pierre, S.J., ed. *Les Établissements des jésuites en France depuis quatre siècles: repertoire topo-bibliographique.* 5 vols. Enghien, 1949–1957. An absolutely essential cooperative work of all the French Jesuit provinces, with the collaboration of lay specialists in history and in archival work. Cited in text as *EJF*.

Deschamps, Nicholas, S.J. *Le Monopole universitaire destructeur de la religion et des lois, ou la Charte et la liberté d'enseignement.* Lyons, 1841. Originally published under name of author as "Desgarets." Violently antiuniversity and antigovernment.

———— *Du Paganisme dans l'éducation, ou Défense des écoles catholiques des quatre derniers siècles contre les attaques de nos jours.* Paris, 1852.

Didierjean, R. P., S.J. *Souvenirs des collèges de la Compagnie de Jésus en France (1850–1880).* 2 vols. Paris, 1882. Biographical sketches of alumni of the colleges.

———— *Souvenirs de Metz: l'École St. Clément, ses élèves, ses derniers jours.* 2 vols. Paris, 1875.

Dion, L. *Recueil complet de la législation de l'enseignement secondaire.* Paris, 1922.

Documents sur l'Histoire religieuse de la France pendant la Restauration (1814–1830), edited by the Ministry of Public Education. Paris, n.d.

Dupanloup, Félix-Antoine-Philibert. *Conseils aux jeunes gens sur l'étude de l'histoire.* Paris, 1872.

———— *Lettre de Mgr. l'évêque d'Orléans à MM. les Supérieurs, directeurs et professeurs de ses petits-séminaires et autres ecclésiastiques chargés dans son diocèse de l'éducation de la jeunesse par l'emploi des auteurs profanes grecs et latins dans l'enseignement classique.* Orléans, 1852.

Duruy, Albert. *L'Article Sept. et la liberté d'enseignement devant le Sénat.* Paris, 1880. Polemics for the state schools and against the Jesuits.

———— *L'Instruction publique et la démocratie.* Paris, 1886.

———— *L'Instruction publique et la révolution.* Paris, 1882.

Duruy, Victor. *Histoire de France, du moyen age et des temps modernes, du XVIe au XVIIe siècle . . . pour la classe de seconde.* 2nd ed. Paris, 1852.

Duvergier, J. *Collection complète des lois . . . formant ainsi la table générale de la législation française depuis 1788 jusqu'à 1889 inclusivement.* 4 vols. Paris, 1890.

Ecoles libres de Sainte-Marie et de l'Immaculée-Conception (Caousou) de Toulouse: Annuaire général des anciens élèves (1850–1888). Toulouse, 1888.

Elèves du collège Nôtre Dame de Mongré, 1851–1892: Liste générale. Lyons, 1892.

Epistolae et Encyclicae Visitatorum et Provincialium Provinciae Franciae. Vol. I: 1820–1886. Paris, 1892. Source material of decisions by major Jesuit superiors in Paris province.

Epitome Instituti Societatis Jesu. Rome, 1949. Collection of prescriptions and directives pertaining to the Society of Jesus, excerpted from Church law, from the Jesuit *Constitutions,* from the decrees of the General Congregations, and from the decisions of the Fathers General.

Les Établissements des Jésuites en France depuis quatre siècles: Répertoire topo-bibliographique, ed. Pierre Delattre, S.J. 5 vols. Enghien, Bel., 1949–1957.

Eucologe romain à l'usage des collèges de la Compagnie de Jésus. 9th ed. Paris, 1871. Prayer book for Jesuit college students used throughout the nineteenth and into the twentieth century with very slight modifications.

Fabre, Jules. *Réponse aux lettres d'un sensualiste contre l'ontologisme.* Paris, 1864. By a former Jesuit, an ardent supporter of ontologism.

Falloux, Alfred, Comte de. *Mémoires d'un royaliste.* 2 vols. Paris, 1888.

―――― *Le Parti catholique, ce qu'il a été, ce qu'il est devenu.* Paris, 1856.

Feller, François-Xavier de, S.J. *Catéchisme philosophique, ou Recueil d'observations propres à défendre la religion chrétienne contre ses ennemis.* 5th ed. 3 vols. Paris, 1821. Used in nineteenth-century Jesuit colleges; originally written in the eighteenth century.

Fournier, Pierre, S.J. *Institutiones philosophicae ad usum praelectionum in collegiis et seminariis.* Paris, 1854. An example of Catholic philosophy textbooks.

Franchet, Charles, S.J. *Directoire des congrégations dans les collèges.* Lyons, 1875. How a sodality should be run.

Gaume, Théodore. *Lettres à Mgr. Dupanloup, évêque d'Orléans, sur le paganisme dans l'éducation.* Paris, 1852.

―――― *Le Ver rongeur des sociétés modernes ou le Paganisme dans l'éducation.* Paris, 1851.

Gazeau, François, S.J. *Histoire moderne.* Paris, 1869. Textbook for Jesuit colleges. Contrast with Duruy's text for state schools.

Gréard, O. *Education et instruction.* 4 vols. Paris, 1889.

Hamy, Alfred, S.J. *Chronologie biographique de la Compagnie de Jésus.* 1ʳᵉ *série: Province de Lyon 1582–1762: noms, prénoms, lieu d'origine, dates de naissance, d'entrée, de degré, lieu et date de mort de tous les jésuites demeurés fidèles à leurs voeux jusqu'à la fin.* Paris, 1900.

———— *Documents pour servir à l'histoire des domiciles de la Compagnie de Jésus dans le monde entier, de 1540 à 1773, collationnés par le P. Alfred Hamy.* Paris, 1892.

———— *Galerie illustrée de la Compagnie de Jésus, Album de 400 portraits choisis . . .* Paris, 1893.

Hyacinthe, M. *Coup d'oeil dans l'intérieur de Saint-Acheul, ou de l'éducation que donnent les jésuites modernes à la jeunesse française.* Paris, 1826. A good example of the usual anti-Jesuit production.

Institutum Societatis Jesu. 3 vols. Florence, 1893.

Les Jésuites du collège Ste. Marie à Fribourg en Suisse. 2 vols. Lausanne, 1834.

Journal officiel de la république française. Paris, 1869–1880. Parliamentary debates published with documents in daily newspapers. After 1880 the debates were published in separate volumes for each year. *Chambre* and *Sénat* are in separate volumes. The *JO* took the place of the *Moniteur universel* after 1869.

Lacombe, H. de. *Les Débats de la commission de 1849: Procès-verbaux.* Paris, 1879. Not strictly *procès-verbaux,* but from notes of Dupanloup. Later editions correct the title.

Lamennais, Félicité de. *Défense de l'Essai sur l'indifférence en matière de religion.* Paris, 1821.

Lettres de l'épiscopat français à propos des Projets Ferry. Paris, 1879.

Lettres de Fourvière. Lyons, 1936. This is a periodical for "private circulation only," dealing with the history, spirituality, theology, and current problems of the French Jesuits.

Lettres de Jersey. Wetteren, Bel., 1936. The same remarks apply to this as to the *Lettres de Fourvière.*

Le Livre d'Or des élèves du pensionnat de Fribourg en Suisse. Paris, 1889.

Le Livre d'Or du centenaire de l'école St. Joseph, Sarlat, 1850–1950. Sarlat, 1950.

Longhaye, Georges, S.J. *Dix-neuvième siècle: Esquisses littéraires et morales.* Paris, 1900. The works of Longhaye were a mirror of and influence on the appreciation of literature by French Jesuits of the late nineteenth and early twentieth centuries.

———— *Histoire de la littérature française au dix-septième siècle.* 3 vols. Paris, 1895.

———— *Poésie, notes polycopies.* Brugelette, n.d.

———— *Préface de "Fables de la Fontaine," suivies de quelques morceaux choisis du même auteur. Edition classique avec notes, précédée d'une notice bibliographique, d'une étude morale et littéraire.* Paris, 1870.

———— *Théâtre chrétien.* Paris, n.d.

———— *Théorie des belles-lettres.* Paris, 1885. A sixth edition of this work was published as recently as 1934.

Loyola, Ignatius. *The Text of the Spiritual Exercises of St. Ignatius Loyola.* Trans. by John Morris, S.J. Westminster, Maryland, 1943.

Maillaguet, Abbé. *Le Miroir des ordres et instituts religieux de France.* 2 vols. Avignon, 1865–1866.

Manuel des jeunes professeurs. Paris, 1842. Details of the attitudes and practices of the ideal teacher in a Catholic school of the time.

Masson, A. *Le Miroir des collèges, ou les vices effrayants de l'éducation universitaire.* Paris, 1847. Typical polemic against the state schools.

La Milice du Pape. 1874. Booklet detailing purpose and rules of this Jesuit college student organization for prayers and "good works" for Pius IX.

Le Moniteur universel. Paris, 1814–1869. Official journal of the French government from 1799 to 1869, when its place was taken by the *Journal officiel.* The *Moniteur* had been founded in 1789 by the book dealer Panckoucke.

Montlosier, François-Dominique de Reynaud, Comte de. *Les Jésuites, les congrégations et le parti prêtre, en 1827, mémoire à M. le Comte de Villèle*. Paris, 1827. Passionate exhortation to drive the Jesuits out of France.

———— *Mémoire à consulter sur un système religieux et politique tendant à renverser la religion, la société et le trône*. Paris, 1826. The most anti-Jesuit work of the Restoration, by a convinced monarchist and Gallican.

Nadaillac, Charles de, S.J., and J. Rousseau, S.J. *Les Jeux de collège*. Paris, 1875. Collection of games, contests and sporting events for use of students. Authors were long-time surveillants in Jesuit colleges. Many editions.

Correspondance de Napoléon Ier, publiée par ordre de l'Empereur Napoléon III. 32 vols. Paris, 1858–1869. Vol. X used for comments on Jesuits.

Olivaint, Pierre, S.J. *L'Education chrétienne*. Paris, 1852. A sermon given at the opening of classes by the Jesuits at Vaugirard, later reprinted in brochure form.

———— *Conseils . . . aux jeunes gens*. Paris and Lille, 1897. Collection of sermons, lectures, and articles from published sources and from unpublished notes of Olivaint, intended especially for young men who had just finished their secondary education or who were about to do so, and who would soon go into "the world."

Parisis, Pierre-Louis. *La Démocratie devant l'enseignement catholique, cas de conscience: Seconde série*. Paris, 1849. One of a famous "series" of liberal pronouncements, subsequently embarrassing to the author who was bishop of Langres, later of Arras, and a member of National Assembly.

Ponlevoy, Armand de, S.J. *Actes de la capitivité et de la mort des RR. PP. P. Olivaint, L. Du Coudrey, J. Caubert, A. Clerc, A. de Bengy*. Paris, 1871. Widely popular account of the "Jesuit Martyrs of the Commune." By 1907 it had gone into its seventeenth edition. It includes remembrances and testimony of those, especially fellow Jesuits, who were participants in the events leading up to the execution of the five Jesuits by the Communards.

Pradié, Pierre. *La Question religieuse en 1682, 1790, 1802, et 1848, et . . . les travaux du comité des cultes de l'assemblée constituante de 1848*. Paris, 1849. Much useful information from a secretary of this committee.

Prampain, Edouard, S.J. *Souvenirs de Vaugirard, mon journal pendant le siège et pendant la Commune, 1870–1871*. Paris, 1887.

———— *Précis d'histoire contemporaine de 1789 à 1889. Cahiers et tableaux d'histoire de France, par F. Gazeau, complétés, refondus et rédigés, conformément aux programmes officiels de 1890*. Amiens, 1891. Example of Jesuit textbook for rhetoric and philosophy classes.

Quelques avis: Principes et pratiques de surveillance. Paris, 1910. Originally printed for Sainte-Geneviève and later distributed for use in other Catholic schools.

Ratio atque Institutio Studiorum Societatis Jesu. Rome, 1832. Original 1832 edition, with Roothaan's letter at beginning.

Ravignan, Xavier de, S.J. *De l'Existence et de l'Institut des jésuites*. 7th ed. Paris, 1855. The book that caused needless worry to Jesuit superiors, for it was received enthusiastically in late 1840's despite current anti-Jesuitism.

Rochemonteix, Camille de, S.J. *Souvenirs de Nôtre-Dame de Sainte-Croix du Mans*. Le Mans, 1883.

Saint-Nexant, Charles. *Examen du projet de loi sur la liberté de l'enseignement secondaire*. Paris, 1848. Strongly Gallican and *universitaire*. A very typical example of this viewpoint.

Sengler, Antoine, S.J. *Grammaire grecque*. Paris, 1873. This and the following are examples of the college textbooks written by Jesuit teachers and administrators.

———— *Grammaire latine*. Amiens, 1867.

———— *Petite syntaxe latine pour la sixième*. Amiens, 1872.

———— *Souvenirs d'académie, séances littéraires et dramatiques données dans les collèges de la Compagnie de Jésus en France de 1815 à 1878*. Lille and Paris, 1879. A collection of all the programs given by academies through all these years. Very important. The most authentic witness to the spirit which animated the teaching in the nineteenth-century French Jesuit colleges.

Simon, Jules. *L'Education*. Paris, 1850.

Societatis Jesu Constitutiones et Epitome Instituti. Rome, 1949.

Souvenir du 10 mai, 1876. Vannes, 1876. Typical laudatory address at Jesuit college function.

Souvenirs du collège Saint-François-Xavier. Vannes, 1887.

Souvenirs de l'enseignement chez les jésuites, par un de leurs élèves. Toulouse, 1879. Anonymous and affectionate work about Brugelette. Author later identified as Charles de Raymond-Cahusac.

Taine, Hippolyte. *Carnets de voyage: Notes sur la province, 1863–1865.* Paris, 1897. Informative comments by an observer who is usually rather astute.

Tongiorgi, Salvatore, S.J. *Institutiones philosophicae in compendium redactae.* Annecy, 1864. Textbook by an Italian Jesuit, frequently used in the French colleges.

L'Univers. Paris, 1839–1860, 1867–1914.

Vasco, Enrico, S.J. *Il Ratio Studiorum adattato ai tempi presenti ossia Esposizione Ragionata.* 4 vols. Rome, 1851. Preliminary attempt at adaptation of the *Ratio,* encouraged by Roothaan but never put into practice anywhere on a sustained basis.

Vivier, Alexandre, S.J. *Catalogi Sociorum et Officiorum, 1819–1836.* Paris, 1894. Reconstruction of catalogs of early years of restored Society of Jesus.

——— *Status Assistentiae Galliae Societatis Jesu, 1762–1768.* Paris, 1899. Reconstruction of catalogs of turbulent last years of French Jesuit assistancy during and after suppression.

Secondary Sources

This part of the bibliography includes only works which dealt directly with the problems herein investigated and those items which helped especially to illuminate for the author the social, political and religious context within which the subject of the study was situated.

Acomb, Evelyn M. *The French Laic Laws (1879–1889).* New York, 1941.

Aulard, Alphonse. *Napoléon Ier et le monopole universitaire.* Paris, 1911.

Bagge, Dominique. *Les Idées politiques en France sous la restauration.* Paris, 1952.

Barbier, Emmanuel. *Histoire du catholicisme libéral et du catho-*

licisme social en France . . . (1870–1914). 5 vols. Bordeaux, 1924. Very antiliberal, or inclined to view modern movements with alarm.

———— *L'Initiative au collège*. Paris, 1899.

Baunard, Louis. *Un Siècle de l'église de France, 1800–1900*. Paris, 1901. Interesting remarks on the military mentality of French church.

Beau de Loménie, Emmanuel. *Les Responsabilités des dynasties bourgeoises*. Vol. I: *De Bonaparte à MacMahon*. Vol. II: *De MacMahon à Poincaré*. Paris, 1943, 1947.

Bellesort, André. *La Société française sous Napoléon III*. Paris, 1932.

Bert, Paul. *Le Cléricalisme*. Paris, 1900.

Bertier de Sauvigny, Guillaume de. *Le Comte Ferdinand de Bertier (1782–1864) et l'énigme de la congrégation*. Paris, 1948. An excellent work, very complete, carefully distinguishing the several meanings and realities of the *congrégation*.

———— *La Restauration*. Paris, 1955. Fine work of synthesis, generally sympathetic to work of the Restoration.

Bertrand, L. *Histoire des séminaires de Bordeaux et de Bazas*. 2 vols. Bordeaux, 1894.

Blanchard, Marcel. *Le Second empire*. Paris, 1950.

Bliard, Pierre, S.J. *Le Père Loriquet: la légende et l'histoire*. Paris, 1922. Only full length treatment of one of most important French Jesuits of the early post-Restoration years.

Bourgeois, Emile. *La Liberté d'enseignement, histoire et doctrine*. Paris, 1902.

Bourgin, Georges. *Les Sources manuscrites de l'histoire religieuse de la France moderne*. Paris, 1925. Part of "Bibliothèque d'histoire ecclésiastique de la France." Author was an archivist at Archives Nationales.

Bournand, François. *Le Clergé sous la troisième république*. Paris, 1890. Proclerical. Gives a good insight into mind of French clergy of the time.

Boutard, Charles. *Lamennais: sa vie et ses doctrines*. 2 vols. Paris, 1905.

Brogan, D. W. *The Development of Modern France, 1870–1939*. London, 1940.

Brucker, Joseph, S.J. *La Compagnie de Jésus.* Paris, 1919.

Brugerette, Joseph. *Le Comte de Montlosier et son temps (1775–1838).* Aurillac, 1931.

——— *Le Prêtre français et la société contemporaine.* 3 vols. Paris, 1933–1938.

Buisson, Ferdinand. *La Foi laïque.* Paris, 1913. Typical explanation of such a faith by one of its convinced adherents.

Buisson, Ferdinand, and Frederic E. Farrington. *French Educational Ideals of Today.* New York, 1919. An anthology of writings by the molders of French educational thought from Edgar Quinet to Paul Painlevé.

——— *La Lutte scolaire en France au dix-neuvième siècle.* Paris, 1912. A series of essays, very laicist orientated.

Buisson, Ferdinand. *Un Moraliste laïque.* Paris, 1933.

Burnand, Robert. *La Vie quotidienne en France de 1870 à 1900.* Paris, 1947.

Burnichon, Joseph, S.J. *La Compagnie de Jésus en France: Histoire d'un siècle, 1814–1914.* 4 vols. Paris, 1914–1922. A fifth volume exists in manuscript form at Chantilly, taking the story from 1880 on; it has never been published.

——— *Un Jésuite, Amadée de Damas.* Paris, 1908.

Butel, Fernand. *L'Education des jésuites.* Paris, 1890. Deals with the college at Vannes; details of everyday life.

——— *La Vie de collège chez les jésuites.* Paris, 1882.

Campbell, Thomas, S.J. *The Jesuits, 1534–1921.* 2 vols. New York, 1921.

Canron, Augustin. *Les Jésuites à Avignon.* Avignon, 1875.

Capéran, Louis. *Histoire contemporain de la laïcité française: La crise de seize mai et la revanche républicaine.* Paris, 1957. An excellent work, essential to a study of this question on a national scale.

——— *Histoire contemporaine de la laïcite française: La révolution scolaire.* Paris, 1960. Also excellent. Bibliographical indications good, as in previous volume.

——— *Histoire de la laïcite republicaine: La laïcité en marche.* Paris, 1961.

Caron, Pierre, and Henri Stein. *Répertoire bibliographique de l'histoire de France.* 6 vols. Paris, 1923–1938.

Carrez, Louis, S.J. *Atlas Geographicus Societatis Jesu.* Paris, 1900.

Charléty, Sebastien. *La Restauration (1815–1830)*, and *La Monarchie du juillet (1830–1848)*. Vols. 4 and 5 of *Histoire de France contemporaine, depuis la Révolution jusqu'à la paix de 1919*, ed. Ernest Lavisse. Paris, 1921.

Charmot, François, S.J. *La Pédagogie des jésuites: ses principes, son actualité.* Paris, 1943. A mine of information, especially on the presuppression Society, although it tends to idealize conditions.

Chastenet, Jacques. *Histoire de la troisième république.* 6 vols. Paris, 1952–1960.

Chastonay, P. de. *Les Constitutiones de l'ordre des jésuites.* Paris, 1941.

Chateau, J. *Les grands pédagogues.* Paris, 1956.

Chaumu, Pierre. *Eugène Sue et la seconde république.* Paris, 1948.

Chazournes, Léon de. *Vie du R. P. Joseph Barrelle.* 2 vols. Paris, 1858.

Chesnelong, Charles. *Discours: la liberté de l'enseignement.* Paris, 1910.

Chossat, Marcel, S.J. *Les Jésuites et leurs oeuvres à Avignon, 1553–1768.* Avignon, 1896.

Clair, Charles, S.J. *La Congrégation de la très sainte vierge à Saint-Acheul, 1815–1828.* Paris, 1897. Helps show the continuity and similarity of sodalities from minor seminary to college.

——— *Pierre Olivaint.* Paris, 1878. Detailed biography, but too uncritical at times.

——— *Que devons-nous à l'église et à la révolution en fait d'éducation publique.* Le Mans, 1876. Prize-day discourse, hardly sympathetic to the republic.

Cogniot, Georges. *La Question scolaire et la loi Falloux en 1848.* Paris, 1948.

Le Collège des jésuites à Avignon: 1565–1950. Avignon, 1950. Commemorative booklet put out by college for 1850–1950 anniversary. Carefully done.

Collins, Irene. *The Government and the Newspaper Press in France, 1814–1881.* New York, 1959.

Collins, Ross William. *Catholicism and the Second French Republic, 1848–1852.* New York, 1923.

Compayré, Gabriel. *Histoire critique des doctrines de l'éducation en France depuis le seizième siècle.* 2 vols. Paris, 1885. An aging, but still major reference. Very inaccurate in some of its material on the Jesuits.

Cretineau-Joly, J. *Histoire religieuse, politique et littéraire de la compagnie de Jésus.* 6 vols. 2nd ed. Paris-Lyons, 1846. Most detailed complete history to its time. Careful factual information but very pro-Jesuit in interpretation.

Curley, Frédéric de. *Les Congrégations de la très-Sainte-Vierge à Avignon, de 1572 à 1880.* Avignon, 1880.

Dainville, Françoise de, S.J. *La Géographie des humanistes.* Paris, 1940. This and the next volume are essential to an understanding of presuppression Jesuit pedagogy.

———— *La Naissance de l'humanisme moderne.* Paris, 1940.

Damas d'Anlezy, Comte de. "L'Education du duc de Bordeaux," *Revue des deux mondes,* 11 (1902), 612–622.

Daniel, Charles, S.J. *Des Jésuites instituteurs de la jeunesse française au XVIIᵉ et au XVIIIᵉ siècle.* Paris, 1880. Attempts to rectify some of the inaccuracies of Compayré.

Daniel-Lacombe, H. *Souvenirs et espérances.* Poitiers, 1881. Prize-day discourse after the Ferry Decrees.

Daniel-Rops, Henri. *L'Eglise des révolutions.* Paris, 1962. Excellent general work of high level popularization.

Dansette, Adrien, *Destin du catholicisme français, 1926–1956.* Paris, 1957.

———— *Histoire religieuse de la France contemporaine.* 2 vols. Paris, 1948–1952. One of the best short religious histories of modern France available.

Darbon, Michel. *Le Conflit entre la droite et la gauche dans le catholicisme français, 1830–1953.* Toulouse, 1953.

Debidour, Antonin. *L'Eglise catholique et l'état sous la troisième république, 1870–1906.* 3 vols. Paris, 1906–1909. Rather hard on the church.

———— *Histoire des rapports de l'église et de l'état en France de 1789 à 1870.* Paris, 1898.

Delfour, L. Clodomir. *Catholicisme et romantisme.* Paris, 1905.

Denzinger, Henricus, S.J., and Adolphus Schönmetzer, S.J. *Enchiridion Symbolorum, Definitionum et Declarationum de*

Rebus Fidei et Morum. 32nd ed. Freiburg, 1962. Handbook of Catholic dogmatic decrees, declarations, and decisions, taken from creeds, councils, papal letters, and so on.

Deslandres, Maurice C. *Histoire constitutionelle de la France de 1789 à 1870.* 2 vols. Paris, 1932.

Dictionnaire de biographie française, ed. Michel Prévost, *et al.* 8 vols. Paris, 1933–1956.

D'Irsay, Stephen. *Histoire des universités françaises et étrangères des origines à nos jours.* Paris, 1933–1935.

Douarche, Aristide. *L'Université de Paris et les jésuites.* Paris, 1888. Concerned with the colleges and controversies of the sixteenth and seventeenth centuries.

Du Lac, Stanislas, S.J. *Jésuites.* Paris, 1901. Author was chief agent of the Society in the campaign in 1881 against the Ferry decrees. At one time rector of Sainte-Geneviève, he was also involved in the Dreyfus case.

Dupont-Ferrier, Gustave. *Du collège de Clermont au lycée Louis-le-Grand.* 3 vols. Paris, 1921–1925. Invaluable study of this great school. A lifetime labor of love and scholarship. Helpful in contrasting the nineteenth-century lycée and the Jesuit college.

Durkheim, Emile. *L'Evolution pédagogique en France.* 2 vols. Paris, 1938.

Duruy, Victor. *L'Administration de l'instruction publique de 1863 à 1869.* Paris, n.d.

────── *Histoire de France et des temps modernes.* 2nd ed. Paris, 1859.

Duveau, Georges. *Les Instituteurs.* Paris, 1957. Semipopular, interesting illustrated booklet on French teaching profession since 1789.

Elwell, Clarence E. *The Influence of the Enlightenment on Religious Education in France, 1750–1850.* Cambridge, Mass., 1944.

Estaunié, Edouard. *L'Empreinte.* Paris, 1896. Anti-Jesuit novel which gives a good indication of how a Jesuit college was regarded and depicted by an adversary. The author was a member of the Académie Française.

Falcucci, Clement. *L'Humanisme dans l'enseignement secondaire en France au XIXe siècle.* Toulouse–Paris, 1939. Very useful though rather diffuse study. Good for showing similarities and contrasts of lycées and Jesuit colleges.

Farrell, Allan, S.J. *The Jesuit Code of Liberal Education.* Milwaukee, 1938. Development and scope of the *Ratio Studiorum,* especially in the presuppression Society of Jesus.

Farrington, Frederick E. *French Secondary Schools.* New York, 1910. Account of the origin, development, and organization of secondary education in France.

Fernessole, Pierre. *Témoins de la pensée catholique en France sous la troisième république.* Paris, 1940.

Ferté, H. *Programme et règlement des études de la Société de Jésus.* Paris, 1892. Translation of *Ratio Studiorum,* though with several inexactitudes.

Fitzpatrick, Edward. *St. Ignatius and the Ratio Studiorum.* New York, 1933.

Foucher, Louis. *La Philosophie catholique en France au XIXe siècle—Avant la renaissance thomiste et dans ses rapports avec elle, 1810–1880.* Paris, 1955. Enlightening study of authoritarian current in Catholic philosophy in France.

Fouqueray, J., S.J. *Histoire de la Compagnie de Jésus en France.* 5 vols. Paris, 1910–1925.

Ganss, George E., S.J. "The Fourth Part of St. Ignatius' Constitutions and the Spirit of the *Ratio Studiorum,*" *Analecta Gregoriana,* 70 (1955), 163–180.

——— *Saint Ignatius' Idea of a Jesuit University.* Milwaukee, 1954. Argues for Ignatius' idea of adaptability to times as one of central concepts of his educational philosophy. A carefully done and controversial work.

Garnier, Adrien. *Frayssinous, son rôle dans l'université sous la restauration, 1822–1828.* Paris, 1925.

——— *Les Ordonnances du 16 juin d'après des documents inédits.* Paris, 1929.

Gerbod, Paul. *La Condition universitaire en France au XIXe siècle.* Paris, 1965.

——— *La Vie quotidienne dans les lycées et collèges au XIXe siècle.* Paris, 1968.

Germiny, Eugène de. *Mémoire sur le progrès de l'esprit antireligieux dans l'instruction publique.* Paris, 1872.

Grandidier, François, S.J. *Vie du R. P. Achille Guidée, S.J.* Amiens, 1877.

Grandmaison, Geoffroy de. *La Congrégation, 1801–1830.* Paris,

1890. The best book on the Congrégation until that of Bertier de Sauvigny; still valuable.

Gréard, Octave. *Education et instruction: enseignement secondaire.* 2nd ed. 2 vols. Paris, 1889. Useful especially for reforms of Third Republic.

Grimaud, Louis. *Histoire de la liberté d'enseignement en France.* 6 vols. Grenoble, Paris, 1944–1954. By far the most detailed work on the subject to 1847.

———— *Histoire de la liberté d'enseignement en France, depuis la chute de l'ancien régime jusqu'à nos jours.* Paris, 1898. Apparently the author's original work on the subject, after which each part was developed into a separate volume over the next fifty or so years.

Guerard, Albert. *Napoleon III.* New York, 1955.

Guihaire, P. *Lacordaire et Ozanam.* Paris, 1939.

Guillemin, Henri. *Histoire des catholiques français au XIXe siècle (1815–1905).* Paris, 1947. Good summary history by a Catholic sympathetic to liberal movements.

Halévy, Daniel. *La Fin des notables.* Paris, 1930.

———— *La République des ducs.* Paris, 1937.

Halphen, Louis. *L'Histoire en France depuis cent ans.* Paris, 1914.

Herman, J. B., S.J. *La Pédagogie des jésuites au XVIe siècle: ses sources, ses caracteristiques.* Paris, 1914. Good study, excellent for comparison with later practices and ideals.

Hocedez, Edgar, S.J. *Histoire de la théologie au XIXe siècle.* 3 vols. Brussels, 1947–1952. Indispensable for Catholic theology of the period, but much work is yet to be done on particulars.

Hoog, Georges. *Histoire du Catholicisme social en France, 1871–1931.* Paris, 1946.

Hudson, Nora E. *Ultra-royalism and the French Restoration.* Cambridge, Eng., 1936.

Israel, Alexandre. *L'École de la république: la grande oeuvre de Jules Ferry.* Paris, 1931.

Ker, Paul. *En Pénitence chez les jésuites.* Paris, 1910. Genial portrayal of life in a Jesuit institution.

———— *Nos Doctrines classiques traditionelles.* Paris, 1921. Defense of classicism as understood by French Jesuits.

Kothen, Robert. *La Pensée et l'action sociales des catholiques, 1789–1944.* Louvain, 1945.

Langlois, Charles V., and Henri Stein. *Les Archives de l'histoire de France.* Paris, 1891–1893.

Laprade, Victor. *L'Éducation homicide.* Paris, n.d.

Latreille, André, and André Siegfried. *Les Forces religieuses et la vie politique: le catholicisme et le protestantisme.* Paris, 1951.

Latreille, André, et al. *Histoire du catholicisme en France.* 3 vols. Paris, 1962. Vol. II: *La Période contemporaine* is excellent in every way except that it has no index. Moderately liberal outlook.

Lecanuet, Edouard. *Les Dernières années du pontificat de Pie IX, 1870–1878.* Paris, 1931.

———— *L'Église de France sous la troisième république.* 4 vols. Paris, 1930–1931. A basic work.

———— *Montalembert.* 3 vols. Paris, 1895–1902. Vols. 2 and 3 treat extensively the battle for liberty of teaching and the Church in the Second Empire. Archival citations are frequent and accurate as to sense, but sometimes they are not absolutely exact transcriptions.

———— *Les Premières années du pontificat de Léon XIII, 1878–1894.* Paris, 1931.

Lecler, Joseph, S.J. "Dans la crise du catholicisme libéral," *Études,* 291 (November 1956), 196–211.

Leflon, Jean. *La Crise révolutionnaire, 1789–1846.* "Remarkably free from bias," as Cobban remarks. This is vol. 20 of *Histoire de l'église depuis les origines jusqu'à nos jours,* ed. Augustin Fliche and Victor Martin. Paris, 1949.

———— *L'Eglise de France et la révolution de 1848.* Paris, 1948.

Legrand, Louis. *L'Influence de positivisme dans l'oeuvre scolaire de Jules Ferry: Les origines de laïcité.* Paris, 1961.

Le Poil, Constant. *Les Jésuites sous la troisième république.* Paris, 1880. Very favorable apology for the Jesuits. Interesting collection of citations.

Leroy-Beaulieu, Anatole. *Les Catholiques libéraux: l'Église et le libéralisme de 1830 à nos jours.* Paris, 1885.

Lhande, Pierre, S.J. *Un Maître humaniste, le Père Longhaye.* Paris, 1923.

Liard, Louis. *L'Enseignement supérieur en France, 1789–1889*. 2 vols. Paris, 1888–1894.

———— *La Science positive et la métaphysique*. 5th ed. Paris, 1905. Includes an interesting treatment of *morale civique* and *morale laïque* in the latter part of the nineteenth century.

Liber Saecularis Historiae Societatis Jesu, ab anno 1814 ad annum 1914. Rome, 1914. Large commemorative book on the first hundred years of the restored Society of Jesus.

Littré, Emile. *De l'Etablissement de la troisième république*. Paris, 1880.

Lucas-Dubreton, Jean. *Louis-Philippe*. Paris, 1938.

Malo, Henri. *Thiers, 1797–1877*. Paris, 1932.

Maurain, Jean. *Un Bourgeois français au XIXᵉ siècle: Baroche, ministre de Napoléon III d'après ses papiers inédits*. Paris, 1936.

———— *La Politique écclésiastique du Second Empire, de 1852 à 1869*. Paris, 1930. The great work on the subject, indispensable, contains a very full index. Maintains that the Society of Jesus tried carefully not to meddle in politics but that it sometimes failed.

———— *Le Saint-Siège et la France, de décembre 1851 à avril 1853: Documents inédits*. Paris, 1930. Archival study of texts.

Mellon, Stanley. *The Political Uses of History: A Study of Historians in the French Restoration*. Stanford, 1958.

Menorval, E. de. *Les Jésuites de la rue St. Antoine, l'église St. Paul–St. Louis, et le lycée Charlemagne*. Paris, 1872. The lycée Charlemagne of the nineteenth century was housed in the old main residence of the presuppression Society of Jesus, and the church of St. Paul–St. Louis was the former chapel of this "professed house."

Meuriot, Paul. *Le Baccalauréat: son évolution historique et statistique des origines à nos jours*. Nancy, 1919.

Michel, Henry. *La Loi Falloux: 4 janvier, 1849–15 mars, 1850*. Paris, 1906. A careful following through of the whole process, plus appendices, the projects elaborated by the extra-parliamentary commission, and the texts of the law as presented and as voted, in parallel columns.

Mourret, Fernand. *Le Mouvement catholique en France de 1830 à 1850*. Paris, 1917. General view of the Church, account of the campaign of *L'Avenir*, the encyclical *Mirari Vos*, the fight for liberty of teaching.

Murray, John Courtney, S.J. "On the Future of Humanistic Education," *The Critic*, 22 (February–March 1964), 37–43.

Nourrisson, Paul. *Histoire légale des congrégations religieuses en France depuis 1789*. 2 vols. Paris, 1928. Useful history and documents compiled by lawyer of the *cour d'appel*.

——— *Trois précurseurs de la liberté d'enseignement: Berryer, Montalembert, Lamartine*. Paris, 1922.

Ollivier, Emile. *L'Eglise et l'état au Concile du Vatican*. Paris, 1879. The author was a Protestant former premier of France. In many ways he had one of the best understandings of Pius IX and the situations which that Pope faced.

Orhand, R. P., S.J. *Le Père Pillon et les collèges de Brugelette, Vannes, Sainte-Geneviève, Versailles et Lille*. Lille, 1888. Biography of one of the most influential Jesuit superiors and administrators of the period. Frequently too uncritical.

Ozouf, Mona. *L'Ecole, l'église et la République*. Paris, 1963.

Pariset, G. *Le Consulat et l'empire (1799–1815)*. Vol. 3 of *Histoire de France contemporaine, depuis la Révolution jusqu'à la paix de 1919*, ed. Ernest Lavisse. Paris, 1921.

Passard, François-Xavier, S.J. *La Pratique de Ratio Studiorum pour les collèges*. Paris, 1896. Excellent first-hand testimony of the way the *Ratio Studiorum* was regarded and how it was applied.

Pernoud, Régine. *Histoire de la bourgeoisie en France: les temps modernes*. Paris, 1962.

Pidoux de la Maduère, A. *La Compagnie de Jésus à Dôle (1579–1850)*. Dôle, n.d.

Piobetta, Jean B. *Le Baccalauréat de l'enseignement secondaire*. Paris, 1937.

——— *Les Institutions universitaires en France*. Paris, 1951. Short sketch of administrative and pedagogical organization of French state schools.

Ponlevoy, Armand de, S.J. *Vie du R. P. Xavier de Ravignan, S.J.* 2 vols. 10th ed. Paris, 1876.

Ponteil, Félix. *Histoire de l'enseignement en France: les grandes étapes, 1789–1964*. Sirey, 1966.

Poupard, P. *L'Abbé Louis Bautain: Un essai de philosophie chrétienne au XIXe siècle.* Tournai, 1963. Good account of Bautain and of the intellectual milieu of fideism and traditionalism.

Pouthas, Charles. *L'Église et les questions religieuses sous la monarchie constitutionelle (1814–1848).* Paris, n.d. Lecture and seminar notes based on archival researches by an eminent modern historian of nineteenth-century France.

———— *L'Église et les questions religieuses (1848–1877).* Paris, n.d.

Powers, Richard. *Edgar Quinet: A Study in French Patriotism.* Dallas, 1957. Quinet's nationalism emerges as a curious blend of humanitarianism, liberalism, and intolerance toward the Catholic Church, which supposedly thwarts the mission of France.

Prévost, Marcel. *Le Scorpion.* 2nd ed. Paris, 1887. A novel about the Jesuits.

Quicherat, Jules. *Histoire de Sainte-Barbe, collège, communauté, institution.* 3 vols. Paris, 1860–1864.

Rambaud, Alfred. *Jules Ferry.* Paris, 1903.

Ravelet, Armand. *Les Jésuites et les associations religieuses devant les lois prochaines.* Paris, 1870.

Reclus, Maurice. *Une Grande époque: la troisième république de 1870 à 1918.* Paris, 1945.

———— *Grandeur de "la Troisième" de Gambetta à Poincaré.* Paris, 1948.

———— *Jules Ferry.* Paris, 1947.

———— *Le Peguy que j'ai connu. Avec 100 lettres de Charles Peguy.* Paris, 1951.

Reisner, E. *Nationalism and Education since 1789: A Social and Political History of Modern Education.* New York, 1922.

Rémond, René. *La Droite en France de 1815 à nos jours.* Paris, 1954.

Renan, Ernest. *Souvenirs d'enfance et de jeunesse.* Paris, 1883.

Ribot, Alexandre. *La Réforme de l'enseignement secondaire.* Paris, 1900.

Ricard, Antoine. *L'Abbé Combalot . . . l'action catholique de 1820 à 1870.* Paris, 1891. An account of the combative *abbé.*

Rimbault, P. *Histoire politique des congrégations religieuses en France, 1790–1914*. Paris, 1926.

Rivet, J. *Les oeuvres de charité et les établissements d'enseignement libre de 1789 à 1945*. Lyons, 1945.

Rochemonteix, Camille de, S.J. *Un Collège des jésuites au XVIIe et XVIIIe siècles: le collège Henri IV de la Flèche*. 4 vols. le Mans, 1889. Extensive treatment of one of the greatest of old French Jesuit colleges; provides interesting contrasts with nineteenth-century schools.

———— *Les Congrégations religieuses non-reconnues en France, 1789–1881*. 2 vols. Cairo, 1901.

Rollet, Henri. *L'Action sociale des catholiques en France (1871–1901)*. Paris, n.d. Invaluable for the study of slow but steady growth of this type of Catholic involvement.

———— *Sur le chantier social*. Lyons, 1955. Condenses material of previous work and carries forward the story to 1940.

Rosette, A. *La Compagnie de Jésus a Dôle après son rétablissement: Un siècle de labeur, 1823–1920*. Paris, 1945. Good for a view of ensemble and also for results in priesthood, army, and other careers.

Rouzic, L. *La Jeunesse catholique française au XIXe siècle*. Paris, 1908. Rather eulogistic account of various movements, from the group around Lamennais through the education battle and the pontifical zouaves to the "Catholic Associations."

Sagnac, Philippe. *La Formation de la société française moderne*. 2 vols. Paris, 1945–1946.

Schimberg, André. *L'Éducation morale dans les collèges de la Compagnie de Jésus en France sous l'ancien régime (XVIe, XVIIe, et XVIIIe siècles) avec des notes et pièces justificatives*. Paris, 1913. Detailed and thorough examination of this particular aspect of Jesuit education.

Schmidt, Charles. *Les Sources de l'histoire de France depuis 1789 aux Archives Nationales*. Paris, 1907.

Seignobos, Charles. *La Révolution de 1848, le Second Empire (1848–1859), Le Déclin de l'empire et l'établissement de la troisième république (1859–1875)*, and *L'Evolution de la troisième république (1859–1875)*. Vols. 6, 7, and 8 of *Histoire de France contemporaine, depuis la Révolution jusqu'à la paix de 1919,* ed. Ernest Lavisse. Paris, 1920, 1921, 1922.

Sevrin, Ernest. *Les Missions religieuses en France sous la Restauration.* 2 vols. Paris, 1948, 1959. Basic work on the subject. Unfortunately never completed by the promised third volume.

Simon, W. M. *European Positivism in the Nineteenth Century.* Ithaca, N. Y., 1963.

Simpson, Frederick A. *Louis Napoleon and the Recovery of France, 1848–1856.* 3rd ed. New York, 1951.

Soltau, Raymond. *French Parties and Politics, 1871–1930.* London, 1930.

Sommervogel, Charles, S.J., and Augustin Backer, S.J. *Bibliothèque des écrivains de la Compagnie de Jésus.* Liège and Paris, 1869. Basic bibliographical reference work for all Jesuit authors and writings.

Spencer, Philip. *Politics of Belief in Nineteenth-Century France.* New York, 1954. Basically, a study of Lacordaire, Michon, Veuillot.

Terrien, Jacques, S.J. *Histoire du R. P. de Clorivière de la Compagnie de Jésus.* Paris, 1891.

Thomas, Alexandre. *Note à consulter sur l'état présent de l'Université.* Paris, 1848. *Anti-universitaire* work by former history teacher in state school at Dijon.

Thompson, James M. *Louis Napoleon and the Second Empire.* Oxford, 1954.

Thureau-Dangin, Paul. *Histoire de la Monarchie de Juillet.* 3rd ed., 7 vols. Paris, 1884–1892.

——— *Les Libéraux et la liberté sous la Restauration.* 2nd ed. Paris, 1888.

——— *Le Parti libéral sous la Restauration.* Paris, 1876.

Trannoy, André. *Le Romantisme politique de Montalembert avant 1843.* Paris, 1942.

Vernon, René. *L'Abrogation de la Loi Falloux.* Paris, 1904. Clear and brief presentation of all stages leading up to Loi Falloux, the period of its enforcement, and then its abrogation.

Veuillot, Eugene. *Louis Veuillot.* 4 vols. Paris, 1899–1913.

Vial, Francisque. *Trois siècles d'histoire de l'enseignement se-*

condaire. Paris, 1938. Well known, but quite inaccurate in too many details on church schools.

Viansson-Ponté, L. *Les Jésuites à Metz*. Strasbourg, 1889.

Weill, Georges. *Histoire du catholicisme libéral en France, 1828–1908*. Paris, 1910. Complete for its times, with good bibliography and notes.

———— *Histoire de l'idée laïque en France au XIXᵉ siècle*. Paris, 1925. Again, a very helpful bibliography.

———— *Histoire de l'enseignement secondaire en France: 1802–1920*. Paris, 1921. Relatively brief but very informative.

Zalenski, Stanislas, S.J. *Les Jésuites de la Russie blanche*. Paris, 1888.

INDEX

HARVARD HISTORICAL STUDIES